当代外国语言文学研究文库

目的与策略

——庞德翻译研究

张曦 著

上海交通大學出版社

内 容 提 要

本书旨在促进翻译的多元化研究，从社会文化角度进行文学翻译研究、寻找评判诗歌翻译的多元化标准。本书从目的论角度对庞德的译作进行深入研究和探讨。本书拓宽了翻译研究的范围，从简单的文本分析欣赏转向多元化视角分析，将译者思想、社会文化环境和翻译策略融合起来进行全面研究。在目的论原则的参照下，翻译的诸多要素，如译者的作用、接受者的角色以及源语文本的地位在新的理论视角中出现了新的意义。同时，本书融合了共时性与历时性的研究视角，所谓共时性研究，即研究庞德翻译思想、翻译风格以及社会文化环境，从而更完善地了解其翻译的目的；所谓历时性研究，即进行细致深入的文本对比与分析研究，揭示出庞德翻译目的对其翻译策略的决定性作用。

图书在版编目(CIP)数据

目的与策略：庞德翻译研究/张曦著．—上海：上海交通大学出版社，2013

(当代语言学文库)

ISBN 978-7-313-09515-2

Ⅰ．目…　Ⅱ．张…　Ⅲ．翻译理论—研究
Ⅳ．H059

中国版本图书馆 CIP 数据核字(2013)第 042882 号

目 的 与 策 略

——庞德翻译研究

张　曦　著

上海交通大学出版社出版发行

(上海市番禺路 951 号　邮政编码 200030)

电话：64071208　出版人：韩建民

常熟市梅李印刷有限公司 印刷　全国新华书店经销

开本：787mm×960mm 1/16　印张：12.75　字数：259 千字

2013 年 3 月第 1 版　2013 年 3 月第 1 次印刷

ISBN 978-7-313-09515-2/H　定价：34.00 元

前 言

本书从目的论角度对庞德的译作进行深入研究和探讨。庞德是20世纪英美文坛极具影响力的人物之一，既是意象派诗歌的创始人，也是开创美国现代主义诗歌的诗人和翻译家。庞德的翻译跨越时空，涵盖古英语诗歌、中国古诗、日本俳句，以及法国、意大利和古希腊诗歌，此外还包括《大学》、《论语》、《中庸》等中国古代哲学著作。庞德的翻译特色鲜明，以"创造性翻译"或"改写性翻译"著称。长期以来，翻译学界研究焦点集中在庞德译诗的文学成就以及对其"误译"的质疑上，而对庞德大量译作全面系统的分析较为缺乏。

近几十年来，翻译研究视角不断变化，翻译的多元文化研究视角成为主流，目的论正是百花争艳的众多翻译理论中的一朵奇葩，功能派学者赖斯、弗米尔、诺德等提出和发展了目的论，把翻译行为所要达到的特殊目的作为翻译批评模式，提出决定翻译方法和策略的是译文的预期目的，而不是源语文本的功能，提出原文和译文的关系由译文的预期功能所决定，读者的反应是翻译质量的重要决定因素。目的论给我们提供了研究翻译的新的视角。本书从目的论理视角出发，运用历史研究、汉英对比研究等领域的成果与方法，对庞德在翻译选材和翻译策略上的主体性、翻译策略的文化环境和意义等作了全面的探索与研究；运用共时的方法，了解庞德所处时代的具体社会文化环境，全面解读庞德的翻译思想，试图将一个完整、真实的译者庞德呈现于读者面前，从而能够更好地理解庞德的翻译目的和他为了实现翻译目的的苦心造诣，也为翻译批评研究提供了建设性的理论视角与启示。

本书拓宽了翻译研究的范围，从简单的文本分析欣赏转向多元化视角分析，将译者思想、社会文化环境和翻译策略融合起来进行全面研究。在目的论原则的参照下，翻译的诸多要素，如译者的作用、接受者的角色以及源语文本的地位在新的理论视角中出现了新的意义。同时，本书融合了共时性与历时性的研究视角，所谓共时性研究，即研究庞德翻译思想、翻译风格以及社会文化环境，从而更完善地了解其翻译的目的；所谓历时性研究，即进行细致深入的文本对比与分析研究，揭示出庞德翻译目的对其翻译策略的决定性作用。本书旨在促进翻译的多元化研究，从社会文化角度进行文学翻译研究、寻找评判诗歌翻译的多元化标准，同时为庞德研究做出应有的贡献。

编 者

前言

目　录

Chapter 1 Ezra Pound and Skopos Theory

1.1 Ezra Pound: Life and Works

Ezra Pound (1885-1972) is the combination of poet, translator, editor, librettist and critic in one. His erudition and experimentation opens a new page in the history of poetry. He is a pioneer to usher in the modernist aesthetics in poetry with his advancing of Imagism and later Vorticism. He is the controversial translator of many classic works ranging from Anglo-Saxon, Italian, French works to Greek and Chinese classics. His innovation has created a new poetic style concentrating not on rigid meter but on emotion itself without the restriction of form. He is also a generous advancer of major contemporaries as W. B. Yeats, Robert Frost, William Carlos Williams, Marianne Moore, H. D., James Joyce, Ernest Hemingway, and especially T. S. Eliot.

Pound was born in Hailey, Idaho, in 1885. After two years of college at the University of Pennsylvania, he earned a degree from Hamilton College in 1905. When he was appointed as "Foreign correspondent" for Harriet Monroe's Chicago-based *Poetry*, he began his life as an expatriate in Venice, London, Paris and Rapallo. London was also the place where he became the literary executor of the scholar Ernest Fenellosa and developed a growing interest in Japanese and Chinese poetry. In 1924, he moved to Italy where he became involved in Fascist politics, delivering a series of anti-American and antisemitic radio broadcasts supporting fascist Mussolini. That led to his arrest, trial and imprisonment in the United States in 1945. In 1946, he was acquitted, but declared mentally ill and committed to St. Elizabeths Hospital in Washington, D. C. His confinement bred the production of *The Pisan Cantos*, which won the prestigious Bollingen Prize as the jury of the Bollingen-Library of Congress Award decided to overlook his political career in the interest of recognizing his poetic achievements. After continual appeals from writers, he won his release from the hospital in 1958 and returned to Italy where he died, a semi-recluse, in 1972.

Pound's major contributions to poetry stemmed from his promulgation of Imagism, a movement in poetry which derived its technique from classical

Chinese and Japanese poetry — stressing clarity, precision, and economy of language, and foregoing traditional rhyme and meter. As one of the establishers of Imagism, Pound set up new standards in poetry writing and evaluation. He asserted that the image itself was the pillar of poetry, which would unleash tremendous energy and evoke strong emotions in readers. His doctrine of establishing images in the poetry paved the way for the development of modernist poetry, as "his insistence on allowing images to stand by themselves as objective realities without abstract meaning was bound to lead to the poetry now called modernist". (Carpenter, 1988: 198) When the poets wrote through detached images without any comment instead of using simile, metaphor, or symbolism, the images themselves became the poetry and the reader was left to do all the interpretations. It was an illuminating doctrine that contributed significantly to the development of modernism in the 20th century.

When Imagism declined in the charge of Amy Lowell, which Pound snickered as Amyism, Pound, amazed by a new trend in modern art, swerved to Vortism. The word "vortex" has appeared once in his poetry and several times in his letters since 1908, either as a term for the artist's mental process —"Energy depends on one's ability to make a vortex, genius meme". (Carpenter, 1988: 246)— or as a way of describing the intense cultural life of London. In 1914, Pound defined Vorticism in the first issue of *Blast* magazine: "The vortex is the point of maximum energy. It represents, in mechanics, the greatest efficiency. The vorticist relies... on the primary pigment of his art, nothing else. Every conception, every emotion presents itself to the vivid consciousness in some primary form. It is the picture that means a hundred poems, the music that means a hundred pictures, the most highly energized statement, the statement that has not yet SPENT itself in expression, but which is the most capable of expressing THE TURBINE." (Carpenter, 1988: 246) The image, as he perceives, is "a radiant node or cluster; it is what I can, and must perforce, call a Vortex, from which and through which, and into which ideas are constantly rushing". (Pound, 2005: 289) To Pound, immense energy should be released in an instant of time in poetry just as what is created in the vortex.

Throughout his literary career, Pound is the versatile writer of poetry, of translations, of critical essays. Firstly, Pound is a prolific poet that boasts a large output of poetry. His poetry covers widely in form and theme including *The Cantos* 1-117 (1970), *Personae* (1909), *A Lume Spento* (1908), *A Quinzaine for this Yule* (1908), *Exultations* (1909), *Canzoni* (1911), *Ripostes* (1912), *Lustra* (1916), *Hugh Selwyn Mauberley* (1920). In his poetry there are both the worship of beauty and the reform of culture. In *Personae*, his first London volume published in 1908, Pound put on masks in his translation and in the imitation of his favorite medieval poems like *The Seafarer* and Villon's *Testament* and other revered poets of his like Yeats and Browning. In 1912, he had Ripostes published, which marked the transition from the early romantic style to the modern style. With his establishment of Imagisme from 1912, a movement towards the modernization of poetry, Pound focused more on the economic language and the precise image and the restrained emotions in poetry. In 1914, Pound abandoned imagism and declared himself a "Vorticist". The "Vortex" in poetry was the swirl of creative energy within the artist and the intense emotions were to be evoked in the readers. His collection of poems *Lustra* published in 1916 was a reflection of his tenets, with the Greek lyrics, the Roman satires and the Japanese haiku as the models of the poems. The most classical one was the poem *In a Station of the Metro*, with its vivid association of the illuminating faces in the dark metro crowd to the "petals on a wet, black bough". Reinforcement of the Imagist aesthetics emerged in 1915 when he published his translations of ancient Chinese poetry *Cathay*, which were more creative interpretations and adaptations than literal transferences. It was hailed by the critics and the general readers with its unique beauty in images and its restrained yet intense emotions. *Homage to Sextus Propertius* came out in 1919, marking his transition to more impersonal expression in poetry. The grandest of his poetic achievements was his massive epic *The Cantos*, a grand poem "including history" (Pound, 1960: 46) and combining history with cultural identity. A culture across the Atlantic between Europe and America was created through parallel themes of individuality, rebellion and between the old and the new stands China in *Cantos* LII-LXI and the climax about the poetic self in *The Pisan Cantos*. The poem was a historical and cultural encyclopedia with allusions and references ranging from the classical world of Greece, the European Renaissance of Italy, the Tang dynasty of China, the American War of Independence, and Europe before and during the Second World War, and with languages covering Greek, Latin, French, Chinese, German, Provencal and English. Pound should never be underestimated in his accomplishment in poetry, having "repeatedly achieved the rarest standards of poetic excellence and invention" with "his imaginative writing" "so frequently touched with greatness that only Yeats and Eliot seem of a clearly superior order of magnitude among contemporaries". (Alexander, 1979:18)

Pound is also an insightful critic in literature. His literary essays range from the enlightening ones in culture to the trailblazing ones about poetry development, including the *The Spirit of Romance* (1910), *Gaudier-Brzeska: A Memoir* (1916), *Pavannes and Divisions* (1918), *Instigations* (1918), *ABC of Reading* (1934), *Make It New* (1934), *Jefferson and/or Mussolini* (1935), *Polite Essays* (1937), *Guide to Kulture* (1938), collected and selected by T. S. Eliot into *Literary Essays of Ezra Pound* (1968) and by William Cookson in *Selected Prose*: 1900-1965 (1973). In his critical essays, Pound advances his modern poetics, reveals his motivations behind the creation and translation and his insight of the artists' responsibilities and more. In *I Gather the Limbs of Osiris*, he first proposes the notion of "luminous details" in poetry and points the way to the Imagist poetics. He despises the hackneyed poetic practice and calls for the modernity in themes and in approaches. In the article *Virtu*, he defines as the essential personality of the artist the ability to present intense emotions in accurate images and expressions. In the famous essay *A Retrospect*, Pound declares his tenets of the Imagistme movement, asserting the three major principles as direct treatment, economy of words, and the sequence of musical phrases, and warning against some malpractice in poetry. He also makes a distinction between three kinds of poetry: Melopoeia (poetry in music), Phanopoeia (poetry of the visual image), and Logopoeia ("the dance of the intellect among words"). (Pound, 1968: 5) As a learned scholar, Pound is discriminating about the merits of classic literature, classifying Homer, Dante, Chaucer and Shakespeare as great writers who "constructed some sort of world into which we may plunge ourselves and find a life not glaringly incomplete". (Pound, 1973: 30) The most perceptive and illuminating articles are about his motives behind large volumes of his translations, the merits of the original works and his deliberate appropriation to present certain qualities in the original, which shed light on his translation process and on the interwoven link between the purpose of translation and the ultimate version of translation. Pound is "a poet with a distinct personality", "a rebel against all conventions except sanity" who "writes with fresh beauty and vigour" "revolting against the crepuscular spirit in modern poetry". (Homberger, 1972: 46) With the profusion of his works and his rebellion against the conventions, he enjoys reputation of being uniquely original in his lifetime and beyond. Carl Sandburg claims that "If I were driven to name one individual who, in the English language, by means of his own examples of creative art in poetry, has done most of living men to incite new impulses in poetry, the chances are I would name Ezra Pound". (Homberger, 1972: 112)

Apart from the achievements mentioned, Pound is also a profuse translator with translations spanning a long history and covering various civilizations. His translations roam from east to west, from the ancient to the medieval times, from Anglo-Saxon poetry and Greek drama to Chinese poetry and Japanese Noh, including *Sonnets and Ballate of Guido Gavalcanti* (1912), *Cathay* (1915), *Certain Noble Plays of Japan* (1916), *Divine Comedy* (1934), *Odyssey* (1934), *Homage to Sextus Propertius* (1934), *Confucius: The Unwobbling Pivot, The Great Digest & The Analects* (1947), *The Classic Anthology Defined by Confucius* (1954), *Sophokles, Women of Trachis, A Version by Ezra Pound* (1956), *Le Testament de Villon*(1926).

Between 1908 and 1910, Pound made first experiments of interpretative translation in the Provencal of Arnaut Daniel, Bernart de Ventadorn, Bertran de Bofrn, Arnaut de Mareuil, Peire Vidal, and others. His innovative translation stepped into the stage of his poetic career and became a primary part of his poetic originality. Arnaut Daniel was the inventor of the sestina and the music master of the troubadours which represented the high point of lyric poetry and reached the height of its popularity in Europe in the 12th century. Bernart de Ventadorn was regarded as the greatest composer of melodies and the master of the canso (love song) and the sirventes (political song). Pound drew the essence of poetic music from the translation of their verses.

In 1911, Pound published the Anglo-Saxon poem *The Seafarer*, which was much disputed in his creative approach, the omission of the final section of the Christian preach of monks and the mistranslation of many words to preserve the original rhyme. Pound intended the translation to recover the original flavor of the Anglo-Saxon poem, yet it was a translation that aroused mixed response. The criticism pointed to the inaccuracy of the version, with misunderstandings of words and elimination of Christianity references. The acclaim went to Pound's fascinating music with his deliberate employment of alliteration and assonance to revive the Anglo-Saxon musical effect. Pound was faithful to the original rhythm and tone instead of words, seeking to "render not the words of the original but the sensibility or thing identified". (纳代尔, 2008:34)

Later Pound resorted to the translation of cazone of the 12th century Italian poet Cavalcanti to reinforce his poetics of precision of poetic language. Pound adopted a similar creative approach in his translation of Cavalcanti's works so as to restore the tradition of linguistic precision and poetic musicality of the original. Pound hoped to "revivify" (Pound, 1968: 224) these classics through his creative translation. He responded to the criticism of "the atrocities" of his translation, saying that "all that can be said in excuse is that they are, I hope, for the most part intentional, and committed with the aim of driving the reader's perception further into the original than it would without them have penetrated". (Pound, 1968:172)

Then Pound's interest shifted to the Japanese Noh play and he was most impressed by the presentation of a single image of life. Translations from Japanese Noh plays first appeared in abbreviated form during 1914-15 in *Poetry*, *Quarterly Review*, and *Drama*, and later published with more translations as *"Noh" or Accomplishement: A Study of the Classical Stage of Japan by Ernest Fenollosa and Ezra Pound* (1916). Pound was fascinated by the concision and suggestiveness of Japanese haiku forms and especially, "unity of image". He then incorporated it into his imagist poetics to build an image as "a single, elaborated metaphor of life". (Pound, 1968:87)

After his translation of Noh plays, Pound had contact with Ernest Fenollosa's notes of Chinese poetry, in which he believed he had found "a new Greece in China" (Pound, 1968:215) and from which he was further inspired to develop his new Imagistic principles. In 1915, Pound's publication of *Cathay* including his translations of 19 Chinese poems based on Fenollosa's notes was a sweeping success, acclaimed as great poetry by many critics and earning him recognitions as "the inventor of Chinese poetry for our time". (Alexander, 1979:100) Ford Madox Hueffer claimed the poems in *Cathay* to be "things of a supreme beauty". (Homberger, 1972:108) Michael Alexander, in his book *The Poetic Achievement of Ezra Pound*, extolled *Cathay* as assuming "so interesting and unique a position in the history of English translations of Chinese poetry". (Alexander, 1979: 99) He claimed some of the critical reactions to the translations were "frigid" and the appearance of *Cathay* was "miraculous" as "combinations of skillful genius with happy casualty" and Pound's close approach to the original author was perhaps from "a kind of clairvoyance". (Alexander, 1979:100) In his translations, Pound revived the images of the original poetry and reinforced the emotional quality and the aesthetic sensibility through his interpretative approaches.

Pound's fascination with Chinese culture and philosophy led him towards the further translation of Chinese ethic works, especially that of Confucius. Pound encountered the English translation of Confucius as early as 1907. Fascinated by the concept of harmony and order throughout the book, he took it as the medicine to address the social malaises after the devastating world war. He believed that only through Confucian ideas of order and sincerity and harmony could the social and ideological chaos end in the western world. He published his first translation of *Da Xue* (*Ta Hio*: *The Great Learning of Confucius*) in 1928 based on Guillanume Pauthier's French version. In 1937 Pound obtained a Chinese-English edition of *Four Books* comprising *Da Xue*, *Zhong Yong*, *Lun Yu*, and *Mengzi* translated by the renowned sinologist James Legge, which became the major source of Pound's translation of Confucius. His translation of *Lun Yu* came out in 1937 titled *Confucius*: *Digest of the Analects*. His two English translations of *Da Xue* and *Zhong Yong* were published in 1947 as *The Great Digest and The Unwobbling Pivot*. By 1951, Pound has obtained an even older Chinese text of Confucian works and based on it came his translation in 1954 as *Translation of the Chinese Shih Ching*: *The Classic Anthology Defined by Confucius*. Pound's version was uniquely different from his predecessors' through his ideogrammic method, of dissembling the notions into individual components and analyzing the new composite meaning. His perspective shed new light in the key notions of Confucianism, and the ideogrammic method became a major vehicle of poetry writing in *The Cantos*. Early in the summer of 1923, Pound wrote a poem dedicated to Confucius ending with three memorable lines that represented Pound's almost lifelong commitment to Confucianism:

"The blossoms of the apricot
blow from the east to the west,
And I have tried to keep them from falling"

(*The Cantos*, XIII/60) (Lan, 2005:3)

Later ancient Greek dramas by Sophocles appealed to Pound and his book of *Translations from Sophocles*: *Women of Trachis* was first published in 1954 in *Hudson Review*, and reprinted as *Sophokles*: *Women of Trachis*: *A version by Ezra Pound* in 1956. It was the result of his growing appreciation of Greek tragedy, and of Sophocles in particular since he found in the drama an economy of expression that bore similarity to Noh drama he was previously interested in. In his translation, Pound made omission or condensation of what he considered to be rhetorical and inconducive to the drama. And in his interest with "the poetic part of a drama"(纳代尔, 2001:214), he simply omitted the prose part of the drama. Another peculiar feature of Pound's drama translation was his adoption of colloquial language, and sometimes even modern American slang in the dialogues, which read more an actual speech of the modern human speaker than the pretentious and pompous ancient Greek play. What Pound tried to do, again, was the restoration of the lost tradition and of the vital values in the ancient, which could only be vivified again through creative translation.

Pound's translations were not renowned for its accuracy but sometimes criticized for their inaccuracy. His translation of the Anglo-Saxon poem *The Seafarer* was accused of being inaccurate with abundant mistranslations when Pound intentionally omitted the references to a transcendent God and other religious sentiments and even eliminated the last nine lines that preached Christian values and morals. His version was no longer a faithful representation of the original but reflective of his secular views and of his emphatic purposes in his intention to build a secular hero fighting and enduring with courage in face of physical harshness and spiritual solitude and torture. Pound also resorted to creative interpretation to approximate the sound-effects and alliterative stress patterns of the original so that throughout the long poem, the readers' attention was inevitably veered in the direction of the certain qualities of the original. Pound conceived of *The Seafarer* not as a source-text of translation but as a poem to be recreated with equivalent effects and matching strength, which was sometimes "loose and inventive", but "inventive within the limits of what he took to be faithful, philological translation". (纳代尔, 2001:223) Pound revived the unique rhyme of alliteration and assonance and a impersonal depiction of *The Seafarer* against the barbarian elements in his free play of translation. "His intention was simply to recover what he perceived to be the real, original Anglo-Saxon poem". (纳代尔, 2001:206) To Pound, translation was to "revive the original through their effects" (Pound, 1968: 93) so that the readers could perceive the original poem to its depths through the translation. Also, his inventive translation was seen in his translation of Chinese poetry, which was then accused by some as inaccurate in certain lines. But Pound was deliberate in many of his mistranslations for the propaganda of his imagist principles, abandoning the rigid verse form and reviving the qualities he perceives as intrinsic to express intense emotions. His aim with his translation was to free himself from the pompous sentimentalism in the previous age and overthrow the Victorian "pretentious and decorate verse" (Pound, 1968:216) and to promote his imagist tenets. Moreover, in his translation of Confucius, Pound's intuitive approach of ideogrammic method generated some semantic errors yet still conformed to his purpose of building the precise vivid images and reaching deep down into the origin of meaning, and also to his purpose of restoring order in the chaotic society. Then, in his translation of Greek tragedy, Pound converted the archaic language to the modern colloquial language. Sophocles' tragedy became alive in the modern circumstances when the characters spoke in the live language of the day, even in slang. It was Pound's invention in translation, which was in accordance to his purpose of bringing the ancient alive just as the Pound scholar

Ming Xie evaluated in his book: "his passionate desire to make past and foreign literature accessible and vital again, accounted in large part for his creative translations". (纳代尔, 2001: 205) Pound is "essentially an appropriative translator" (纳代尔, 2001:207) and his translation was closer to an adaptation, converting the ancient original to the contemporary language rather than blindly following the source text into a literal translation.

However, Pound's creative translations were in accordance with his Skopos. One of the major purposes in Pound's translations was to revivify the history and restore the tradition. For example, in his *Homage to Sextus Propertius* in 1919, he made some deliberate conversions to achieve certain ironic effects which he believed was an indispensable part of Propertius. He defended himself: "there was never any question of translation, let alone literal translation. My job was to bring a dead man to life, to present a living figure". (Pound, 1968, 148-149) Also, Pound used translations as the effective means to promote his modern poetics. In Cavalcanti's poetry, he noted the precise language and the musical beauty which he decided to promote through his translation: "He (Cavalcanti) keeps the sound sharp and light in the throat by the rhymes inside the long line. ... The melodic structure is properly indicated — and for the first time — by my disposition of the Italian text, but even that firm indication of the rhyme and the articulation of the strophe does not stress all the properties of Guido's triumph in sheer musicality". (Pound, 1968:170-172) Pound, as a response to the criticism of some of his inventive translations, pointed out his purpose as the guide of his translation: "I have not given an English 'equivalent' for the Donna mi Prega; at the utmost I have provided the reader, unfamiliar with old Italian, an instrument that may assist him in gauging some of the qualities of the original". (Pound, 1968:172) In *Cathay*, Pound built up delicate and precise imagery to express intense emotions. In *Ta Hio*, Pound "discovered its value to the modern world". (Pound, 1973:89) When "the whole Occident is bathed daily in mental sewage" (Pound, 1973:90) and "the life of Occidental mind fell apart into progressively stupider and still more stupid segregations" (Pound, 1973:91), *Ta Hio* offered the cure, as Pound proclaimed in his essay *Immediate Need of Confucius*: "hence the Western need of Confucius, and specifically of the *Ta Hio*, and more specifically of the first chapter of the *Ta Hio*; which you may treat as a *mantram*, or as a *mantram* reinforced, a *mantram* elaborated so that the meditation may gradually be concentrated into contemplation." (Pound, 1973: 91) In his translations, Pound was more interested in "the implication of the word" (Pound, 1971: 271) and what was "inherent in the original text".

(Pound, 1968:235) Pound's primary aims in translation, as he put it, were to revive "real speech in the English version" and to achieve "fidelity to the original" in both "meaning" and "atmosphere". (Pound, 1971:273) Pound considered it unnecessary to keep "verbal literality for phrases which sing and run naturally in the original" (Pound, 1971: 273), but more importantly, to revive the "atmosphere" that encompasses the original work. Therefore, through his inventive approaches, Pound often succeeded in penetrating through the surface of the original and grasping the essential integrity and letting the translation shining with the equivalent intrinsic qualities and its own inner strength, which was often able to substitute the original in the modern circumstances. Pound's purpose was a major determinant in his creative translation just as he defended himself from the accusation of the problematic translation: "As to the atrocities of my translation, all that can be said in excuse is that they are, I hope, for the most part intentional, and committed with the aim of driving the reader's perception further into the original than it would without them have penetrated". (Pound, 1968:172) The Pound scholar Ming Xie gave a justifiable evaluation of Pound's translations: "Pound's translations stimulated and strengthened his poetic innovations, which in turn guided and promoted his translations. Pound's poetics is essentially a poetics of translation and he has largely redefined the nature and ideal of poetic translation for the twentieth century". (纳代尔, 2001: 204)

1.2 Skopos Theory

Translation study is a complex area not confined in the mere analysis of translated texts. There are many elements that intervene in the operation of translation and the translator scholar Theo Hermans notes at least four: "the source text (and its determinants), the target text (and its determinants), the translator as a subjectivity, and the translator as historicity" and the translator is in his term, "an historicized subjectivity or subjectified historicity". (赫曼斯, 2007:95-96) In the past two or three decades, there has emerged in the translation study "the turn into the social: the increasing awareness that translation is not an abstract equivalence game, divorced from real people's actions in a social context, but a richly social process" (鲁宾逊, 2006: 25) involving entities in multiple sections of society. Typical of the newer social approaches is "a refusal to normalize translation, an insistence on describing the processes by which translations come to be commissioned, made, and disseminated with complete indifference to the question of which translations are better or worse than others". (鲁宾逊, 2006:29) Among the social approaches of translation study, the Skopos theory is one of the most prominent theories emerging in the 1970s and then making increasing impact. The theory represented by Katharina Reiss, Hans J. Vermeer, Justa Holz-Manttari, Christiane Nord has witnessed four major stages of development: Reiss's and Vermeer's Skopotheorie, Manttari's Action Theory and Nord's Text Analysis and Function plus Fidelity Rules, among which the skopotheorie is the most influential core theory.

In the 1950s and 1960s, Linguistics was the dominant discipline, conceiving of language as a code of language universals that could fall in the sphere of strictly scientific investigation. Meanwhile, structuralist linguistics stressed that language, like any object in the natural world, could be studied scientifically through the analysis of the linguistic elements and so could translation as a linguistic operation. Translation was less an art than a science and many definitions of translation highlighted the linguistic aspect, regarding translation as a code-switching operation: Catford defined translation as "the replacement of textual material in one language (SL) by equivalent material in another language (TL)". (Catford, 1965: 20) Nida defined translation as consisting in "reproducing in the receptor language the closest natural equivalent of the source-language message". (Nida & Taber, 1969:12) The source text was emphasized as the fundamental information that should be preserved. Equivalence-based linguistic approaches focused on the source text, stressing that the source-language content, form, style and function must be preserved as far as possible and depreciating any target text not equivalent to the corresponding source text as the nontranslation.

The more pragmatic approach emerged at the beginning of the 1970s with the shift from the word or phrase to the text as a unit of translation towards the functional approach. In the early 1970s, Reiss, the creator of the Skopos theory in translation, approached translation from the perspective of the language function, dividing the language into representational, expressive, and appellative functions and basing her "relevant text typology for the translation process" (Gentzler, 2004:70) on the function of the language in the text. The texts were classified with their different purposes, inhaltsbetonte texts (emphasizing content or information), formbetonte texts (emphasizing the form of the language), and appellbetonte texts (emphasizing appeal to the reader). (Gentzler, 2004: 70) In 1971, Reiss advanced the embryonic Skopos theory, attaching the purpose of translation actions as the yardstick in translation evaluation. Since 1978, Vermeer, Reiss' student, established Skopos as a general principle in translation, pointing out that "the top-ranking rule for any translation is thus the 'Skopos rule'" meaning "that a translational action is determined by its Skopos" or in other words, "the end justifies the means" (Nord, 2001: 29) and the translator should adopt the most appropriate translation strategies to achieve the Skopos in the target text. In the late 1970s and early 1980s, Reiss and Vermeer posited the Skopos theory, which stressed the interactive pragmatic features in translation, arguing that the form of target text was primarily determined by its function, that is, the Skopos to be achieved in the target context. In 1984, Reiss and Hans J. Vermeer published the influential book which established Skopos as a general principle in translation, which then became the foundation for the functionalist approach to translation. Reiss and Vermeer summarized the doctrine into two major principles: interaction being determined by Skopos and Skopos varying among receivers. According to his Skopostheorie (the theory that applies the notion of Skopos to translation), "the prime principle determining any translation process is the purpose (Skopos) of the overall translational action". (Nord, 2001:27) The Skopos rule means to "translate/interpret/speak/write in a way that enables your text/translation to function in the situation in which it is used and with the people who want to use it and precisely in the way they want it to function". (Nord, 2001:29) "Each text is produced for a given purpose and should serve this purpose" (Nord, 2001: 29) and "genuine reasons for actions can always be formulated in terms of aims or statements of goals". (Nord, 2001:27) That is to say, the translator should be able to justify their choice of a particular Skopos in a given translational situation. The source text is not the given facts to be transferred from the translator to the target readers, but an offer of information which the translator should decode by selecting those features that conforms the most closely to the target context. Therefore, translation is viewed as what conveys the new and the original instead of simply offering the same information through different coding by the translator. The success of the translation is determined by two factors: whether the target readers are able to interpret the translation in a coherent way within their contexts, and whether the translation in its form or meaning evokes protest of any kind. The receiver's response is a major determiner in the quality of translation because the Skopos can be described as a "variable of the receiver" which means that "the receiver, or rather the addressee, is the main factor determining the target-text Skopos". (Nord, 2001: 29) The Skopos theory presents two most important changes in the translation theory over its predecessors, the superiority of the target text to the source text and the inclusion of cultural factors as well as linguistic factors in translation study. Translation, in the eyes of functionalists, becomes the purposeful action performed by the translator with specific goals for the texts. Thus, it is often the translators' choice, either to be faithful to the literal text of the source text through word-to-word translation or to the spirit of the original text through his intentional addition, deletion or adaptation as to be fit for the cultural conditions and for the needs of the readers. In this way, translation is more like interpretation or writing or adaptation in certain circumstances as Vermeer has used "translate/interpret/speak/write" as one concept. Based on the previous relevant theories, Justa Holz-Manttari, a German functionalist scholar, made further development on the Skopos theory by using the term "message transmitters" as the appropriate terms for the intercultural communication, and considering translators as the responsible partners in communication events. She also advanced the translational action theory, defining translation as a complex action to achieve the special purpose, and considering the function of the translation as the core product specification of necessary translation qualities. In the 1990s, Nord advanced "Function plus Fidelity Rules" as further expansion of the theory, stressing the relation between the source text and the target text, whose quality and quantity are determined by the Skopos of the translation. On the basis of the Skopos theory, Nord suggests that the translation is to bear relationship with the corresponding source text because a translation is an offer of information about a preceding offer of information. She postulates the further principle as the fidelity rule. Together with function rule, the fidelity rule is "intended to solve the eternal dilemmas of free vs faithful translation, dynamic vs formal equivalence, good interpreters vs slavish translators, and so on. It means that the Skopos of a particular translation task may require a 'free' or a 'faithful' translation, or anything between these two extremes, depending on the purpose for which the translation is needed". (Nord, 2001: 29) If the translator has created a coherent text as a unified whole, if the creation is consistent with the original Skopos, it is judged faithful and accepted as a good translation, which show that the translator has made the justifiable choice. What the translator should do is detect the elements in the source text contributive to achieving the communication purpose and reconstruct those elements in the target culture.

Specifically, each of the promoters of the Skopos theory has enlightening contributions and at the same time limitations. Katherina Reiss, the creator of the Skopos theory and the most prominent representative, postulated that translations should be equivalent to the cognitive meaning, linguistic form and communicative functions of the source text and argued for the necessity of translation brief permitting the different functions of the source text and the target text for the translators to consider the functional features of the translations. In her classic *Translation Criticism: Potentials and Limitations*, Reiss put forward a comprehensive and objective system of translation evaluation, aware of the inadequacy of the criteria of normal translation criticism and the necessity to discover the motives which prompted the translator to change either the form or the content of the original as well as their implications for the version in the target language. The breakthroughs in Reiss' translation theory include primarily the shift from the linguistic elements to the text. Reiss attaches importance to the type of text represented, which has significant implications for a valid translation, and then the consideration of "the characteristics of each type of text, its linguistic elements, and the non-linguistic factors affecting the linguistic form of the original". (Reiss, 2004: 168) Also, Reiss emphasizes the importance to construct an objective system of translation evaluation, arguing that "the parallel emphasis on the positive quality of a translation, or its consistency with 'the overall spirit of the book', should not be determined on the basis of a subjective impression" and "judgment must be based on strict and objective criteria". (杨建华, 2009: 342) Such emphasis on objectivity in translation criteria is more scientific and operation-friendly than the previous abstract concepts of fidelity and equivalence. Reiss points out the criteria of intent for translation evaluation, arguing that "one of the most important principles for translators in complete fidelity to the intent of the original author. Only by comparing with the source language can it be discovered whether this fidelity has been achieved, how well the intent of the author has been understood, how it has been interpreted, and how successfully it has been expressed in the target language". (杨建华, 2009: 342) She mentions if the translation intended for a special function that "has to do with the subject matter, the purpose of the translation may be something other than that of the original" and "if it has to do with persons, the translation must be addressed to a different readership than the original". (杨建华, 2009: 342) Reiss, conscious of the limitations of subjectivity in translation evaluation, sensitively realizes the extralinguistic factors that affect translation, especially that of intent and then advances the standard of evaluating the original and the target text in the functional category, which is a remarkable advance in translation theory with its comprehensiveness and openness and dynamism.

Vermeer makes further specification of the Skopos theory, trying to distinguish between the purpose of the writer of the original text and that of the receiver of the information to interpret the translation by using the related words aim, purpose, intention and function apart from the term Skopos:"'Aim' is the final result an agent intends to achieve by means of an action... 'Purpose' is a provisional stage in the process of attaining an aim. ... 'Function' refers to the intended meaning of the text from the receiver's point of view. ...'Intention' is an aim-oriented plan of action on the part of both the sender and the receiver, pointing toward an appropriate way of producing or understanding the text" (Nord, 2001: 28) Vermeer abandons the conventional linguistic approach of translation, pointing out the futility of linguistics in translation study "First, because translating is not merely and not even primarily a linguistic process. Secondly, because linguistics has not yet formulated the right questions to tackle our problems". (Nord, 2001: 12) She forsakes the idea of translation as the simple transference of linguistic elements and advances translation as a communicational action, the intentional action to achieve the certain purpose in certain circumstances: "Any form of translational action, including therefore translation itself, may be conceived as an action, as the name implies. Any action has an aim, a purpose". (Nord, 2001: 12) And the action is modified in the certain situation as situations are embedded in cultures and determined by the verbalized and non-verbalized elements in that particular culture systems. (Nord, 2001:11) Thus, the translation action, as other actions, is determined also by the addressee, the intended receiver or audience of the target text with their culture-specific world-knowledge, their expectations and their communicative need and the action will lead to a new situation or event and possibly to a new object in the target culture. Vermeer's perspective is fresh and authentically reflective of the real translation process, which enhances our perception of the essential nature of translation. Vermeer also points out that the Skopos determines the translational strategy, which is a revolutionary liberation from the conventional manacles of linguistic equivalence. She distinguishes between three possible kinds of purpose in the field of translation: the general purpose aimed at by the translator in the translation process, the communicative purpose aimed at by the target text in the target situation, and the purpose aimed at by a particular translation strategy or procedure. Translators can, according to the Skopos of translation, choose the most appropriate strategies among the various possible ones. Such a viewpoint might shed light on the superiority of literal translation or liberal translation, domestication or foreignization in certain situations and therefore end the ceaseless dispute. In the framework of theory Skopostheorie, one of the most important factors determining the purpose of a translation is the addressee. Vermeer reflects on the status of the source text and points out the limitation of conceiving the source text as inviolable. The status of the source text becomes much lower in Skopostheorie than in equivalence-based theories. Vermeer regards the source text as an "offer of information" that is partly or wholly turned into an "offer of information" for the target audience. The response of the receiver becomes much more important and is the major determinant of the target-text Skopos. Just as the sheer source-oriented theory causes blind spots in the study of certain translations, the sheer target-oriented theory might not be entirely adequate for all the translations. And Vermeer, realizing such inadequacy, posits in his article that "What the Skopos states is that one must translate, consciously and consistently, in accordance with some principle respecting the target text. The theory does not state what the principle is: this must be decided separately in each specific case". (Nord, 2001:29)

Justa Holze-Manttari is a German scholar, professional translator and the trainer of translation in Finland. She advances the theory of translation action that conceives translation as an interaction between people motivated by the Skopos and oriented towards the ultimate result. She rejects the term "text" and replaces it with "message" as she considers the text as only the vehicle of transmitting message. She replaces "translator" with the new term "message transmitter" so that it includes the transference of other media such as pictures, sounds, and body movements combined with the texts. She substitutes the term "translational action" for "translation" so that the focus is not on the conventional expectation of the final result of the translation but on the process itself, in which the purpose and the motivation of the translator, the expectation by the customer might all play certain roles. She argues that "translational action is the process of producing a message transmitter of a certain kind, designed to be employed in superordinate action systems in order to coordinate actional and communicative cooperation". (Nord, 2001: 13) Mantarri believes that the translational action is determined by its function and purpose so that the result should also be judged from such functional factors. In the theory, the status of the translator is enhanced while that of the source-text is delegated, which runs counter to the previous translation theories which simplify the translation as a mechanic linguistic transference. The translator, instead of being the servant of the two masters of the source text and the target text, should be the expert in intercultural communication, "a cross-cultural professional, not as a secondary, mechanical scribe". (Gentzler, 2004:71) Her theory attaches greater importance to the role of the translator and endows the translator with more flexibility yet more responsibility. What is unsatisfactory is that she neglects the source-text to a marginal role.

Christiane Nord, a student of Reiss', is also a distinguished scholar in functional approach of translation. She is the integration of translator, teacher and translational scholar, having published over 80 articles and many books on functional approach, including *Translating as a Purposeful Activity: Functionalist Approaches Explained* (1991), *Scopos, Loyalty and Translational Conventions* (1991), *A Functional Typology of Translations* (1997), *Translation as a Text-Production Activity* (1999), *Function and Loyalty in Bible Translation* (2002), *Manipulation and Loyalty in Functional Translation* (2002), etc. Nord posits that "translating means producing a functional text in a linguaculture T (target text) that is needed for specific communicative purposes by processing the information given in a previous text produced in a different linguaculture S (source text)". (卞建华, 2008:120) It means that translation is not the photocopy of the source text but the selective treatment of the source of the information in the source text and the re-creation in the target culture with functions. The selection of the information in the source language is determined by the translator in the light of the expectation in the target text. Nord makes constant efforts to incorporate the conventional equivalence-based translation theory and the radical functionalist approach of translation. She inherited from Reiss and Vermeer by focusing on the extra-linguistic factors in the translation equations and on translation as a form of action, a communicative interaction. What is most innovative in Nord's theory is the term of "initiator" of the translation process, "the person, group or institution that starts off the translation process and determines its course by defining the purpose for which the target text is needed". (Nord, 2001:20) These goals or aims may be very different from the source-text author, the target-text receiver, and the translator. Thus, the role of the translator is to fit his action for the purpose of the translation. When the target text is intended to achieve a purpose or function other than that of the original or when the target text addresses an audience different from the intended readership of the original, it is the responsibility of the translator to achieve the required Skopos. To compromise the conventional and the radical, Nord posited her theory of

Function plus Loyalty Rule. She praised the advantages of skopotheorie as it can account for different strategies in different translation situations, and coincides with a change of paradigm of language as individuals involved social, cultural-bound occurrence under certain spatiotemporal conditions with certain communicative intentions and functions. It is pragmatic as it accounts for the needs and expectations of the addressees or prospective receivers of the target text and even making the target receiver the most important yardstick of translational decisions. It is culture-oriented as it gives consideration to the culture-specific forms of verbal and nonverbal behaviour involved in translation. (Nord, 2001:123) Apart from the praises, Nord notices the disadvantages. The idea of Skopostheorie, as she paraphrases, is that "the translation purpose justifies the translation procedures", "the end justifies the means", which might be controversial with its emphasis on the subordination of fidelity to the Skopos rule when the translation purpose is not in line with the communicative intentions of the original author. Nord tries to justify the merits of Skopotheorie with her supplementation of the term "Loyalty" as the responsibility of translators to their partners in translational interaction. Loyalty not only commits the translator to the source side but also to the target side. It is a useful supplement to the conventional stress on fidelity or faithfulness because it is an interpersonal category referring to a social relationship between people. (Nord, 2001:125) Loyalty refers to the interpersonal relationship between the translator, the source-text sender, the target-text addressees and the initiator and the loyalty rule takes account of the interests of the three parties involved: initiators, target receivers, and original authors. (Nord, 2001:126) The loyalty principle works when the translators, as a responsible and trustworthy partner, make changes or adaptations of certain translation units needed to make the translation work in the target culture so that the target-text purpose should be compatible with their intentions. In her theory, translators gain the prestige with greater responsibility as they are the mediator between the three partners when conflicts of interests arise among their intentions. Nord is a comprehensive integrator of the functionalist theories and her perceptions, together with those of other functionalists, have far-reaching influence in translation studies.

The Skopos theory provides a new perspective in the evaluation of translation, which used to fall into the dispute by the yardstick of faithfulness. In the literary translation, especially poetry translation, literal faithfulness falls short as the sole criterion, for poetry is the comprehensive composite of image, meaning and music. Pound, though criticized as unfaithful in some of his translations, creates some of the classical pieces of English poetry through his translation practice. From the perspective of the Skopos theory, many of his strategies are justified in the service of his aims in poetics or in politics. The Skopos approach delegates more power to the translators who are capable of making rational deliberate decisions in their action for the cross-cultural communication purpose and also endows more flexibility to the target text which is justified in certain circumstances as far as the intended communication is achieved. Prior to the functionalist approach, the focus of the translation theory is on the accuracy of the translation, which falls short in the study of certain literary translations. The functionalist translation theory, by relating the translation activity to the motivations behind the action, casts new light on some controversial translations. Gentzler, in his book, gives a justifiable evaluation: "The emergence of a functionalist translation theory marks an important moment in the evolution of translation theory by breaking the two-thousand-year-old chain of theory revolving around the faithful vs. free axis". (Gentzler, 2004:71)

Chapter 2 Skopos of Imagism

"Translations are not normally produced for their own sake, but for a purpose". (阿尔瓦雷斯 & 比达尔, 2007:40) Pound makes translations for clear purposes, among which establishing Imagism and promoting imagist poetics stand as the most prominent one. Imagism is a movement of poetry in the early 20th-century that favors precision of imagery and clarity of language as a revolt against the sentimentality and discursiveness typical of much Romantic and Victorian poetry in the early 20th century. It is also the starting point of modernism. Before Imagism, Longfellow and Tennyson were considered the paragons of poetry, and their sometimes moralising tone in the writings was valued by the public. By contrast, Imagism called for a return to the more classical values, such as directness of presentation and economy of language, as well as a willingness to experiment with non-traditional verse forms. The imagist poets attempted to isolate a single image to reveal its essence, focusing on the "thing" as "thing" itself. Imagism originated from T. E. Hulme's two short poems, *Autumn and A City Sunset* that were published in January 1909 by the Poets' Club in London. Ezra Pound was introduced to the group in April 1909 and found that their ideas were close to his own. In particular, Pound's studies of Romantic literature had led him to an admiration of the condensed, direct expression that he detected in the writings of Arnaut Daniel, Dante, and Guido Cavalcanti. These criteria of directness, clarity and lack of rhetoric were the defining qualities of Imagist poetry. Soon Pound took it upon himself to be the spokesman of Imagism and began to publish on the movement. In 1913, *Poetry* presented Flint's avant-garde article *Imagism*, declaring the fundamental principles of imagism: "1. Direct treatment of the 'thing' whether subjective or objective. 2. To use absolutely no word that does not contribute to the presentation. 3. As regarding rhythm: to compose in the sequence of the musical phrase, not in sequence of a metronome". (Pound, 1968:3)

In the later article *A Few Don'ts*, Pound reiterated the importance of no redundant adjectives and no abstract words in poetry. And Pound gave his clear definition of image as "that which presents an intellectual and emotional complex in an instant of time" and "It is the presentation of such a 'complex' instantaneously which gives that sense of sudden liberation; that sense of freedom from time limits and space limits; that sense of sudden growth, which we experience in the presence of the greatest works of art. It is better to present one Image in a lifetime than to produce voluminous works". (Pound, 1968:4) Taken together, the two texts by Flint and Pound comprised the Imagist programme for a return to what they saw as the best poetic practice of the past. All in all, their principles aimed to the condensation of poetic images and the dryness of poetic language, presenting objects as they were as a departure from the exaggeration of emotions in Romantism and as a creation of a new genre of cold, real and dry style of modernism.

After the American Imagist Amy Lowell intervened and took charge, which led Pound later to sardonically dub this phase of Imagism Amygism, the imagism came to an end and Pound swerved to Vorticism for innovation of poetry. Despite the movement's short life, Imagism had far-reaching impact on the course of modernist poetry in English, influencing a number of poetry circles and movements such as the objectivist poets in the 1930s, the Beat generation, the Black Mountain poets in the 1950s.

2.1 Luminous Detail — Emotional Equation

Pound, tired of the Victorian extravagance in poetic language, was devoted to developing a new style in poetry. He made tentative efforts through his translations. His publication of the first piece of translation, *The Seafarer*, was denounced by some readers who knew about Anglo-Saxon as inaccurate. Yet Pound made the explanation of his intentional new approach used in his translation — *Luminous Detail*. He advanced the method in his essay *I Gather the Limbs of Osiris* as a principle method in Imagist poetry writing: "When I bring into play what my late pastors and masters would term, in classic sweetness, my 'unmitigated gall', and by virtue of it venture to speak of a 'New Method in Scholarship', I do not imagine that I am speaking of a method by me discovered. I mean, merely, a method not of common practice, a method not yet clearly or consciously formulated, a method which has been intermittently used by all good scholars since the beginning of scholarship, the method of Luminous Detail". (Pound, 1973:21) He then asserted: "The artist seeks out the luminous detail and presents it. He does not comment". (Pound, 1973:21) Pound, in face of the ornamental sentimentality of Romantist poetry, felt the urgency to reform the conventional languishment with something more active and energetic and hence the luminous detail, through which Pound advocated the accurate presentation of details, words and images and the later Ideogrammic Method of juxtaposing concrete instances to express an intense emotion in abstraction.

Through the method of luminous detail, Pound asserted the importance of concrete depiction of details and at the same time the emotional force through such details. To Pound, luminous detail is the universal "emotional equation" in poetry. With a passion for science, Pound often used scientific terms to clarify his poetics. He believed in the significance of details to the illumination of life force and in the concreteness of the details as he gave an analogy of the experience in a gallery in which "A few days in a good gallery are more illuminating than years would be if spent in reading a description of these pictures". (Pound, 1973:23)

Apart from the focus on the detail of life instead of vague general sentiment, Pound also emphasized the importance of the luminous quality of the detail. He compared the Arts with the histories, arguing that the artist should seek the luminous detail and presents it without any comment to establish his work as the permanent basis of psychology and metaphysics just as historians present only the significant ideas to illuminate and scholars would err in "presenting all detail as if of equal import". (Pound, 1973:90) Pound also made an analogy between the method and electricity, arguing the importance of luminous details which "governed knowledge" just as the switchboard of electric circuit. If the details refer to the wisdoms and treasures of past centuries, Pound made a meticulous selection of them to be enlightening to the contemporary society. If the details refer to the concrete imagery or particulars in poetry, Pound gathered them in the hope of presenting the emotional force that intensified poetic experience, to illuminate the general readers. Pound, in his translation of Arnaut Daniel's poetry, stated how he tried to achieve the same beauty in his translation through the method of luminous detail: "In the translations... I give that beauty — reproduced, that is, as nearly as I can reproduce it in English — for what it is worth. What I must now do — as the scholar — in pursuance of my announced 'method' is to justify my use of Arnaut's work as a strategic position, as 'luminous detail'". (Pound, 1973:26)

2.1.1 Detail — Concrete Imagery

Pound's Imagism was a direct revolt against the previous Romantism in literary and artistic works which emphasized intuition, imagination, and feeling as an authentic source of aesthetic experience and which embraced the exotic, the unfamiliar, and the distant as the power to envision and to escape from reality. It was the excessive sentimentality and pompous style of Romantism in the early 19th century that Pound was determined to overthrow with his new principles of concreteness and precision. He said in his essay *I Gather the Limbs of Osiris*: "... the method of Luminous Detail, a method most vigorously hostile to the prevailing mode of today — that is, the method of multitudinous detail, and to the method of yesterday, the method of sentiment and generalization. The latter is too inexact and the former too cumbersome to be of much use to the normal man wishing to live mentally active". (Pound, 1973:21) He was opposed to the abstract generalization that is too vague to express the mental state of the poet and his resolution was to build concreteness in language through concrete imagery.

Pound attached great importance to concrete imagery in poetry. The primary principle for Imagism revised by Pound was "Direct treatment of the 'thing' whether subjective or objective". (Pound, 1968:3) That is, whether the imagery concerns the real objects in nature or the genuine sentiment of the humans, the poet should present them with clarity and precision without abstract ideas or descriptions. Pound always argued against abstraction of ideas in the art of poetry. In his *A Few Don'ts*, he warned against the practice of abstraction:"Go in fear of abstractions." "Don't use such an expression as 'dim lands of peace'. It dulls the image. It mixes an abstraction with the concrete. It comes from the writer's not realizing that the natural object is always the adequate symbol". (Pound, 1968: 5) Such image as "the adequate symbol" is Pound's lifetime pursuit in his artistic works. For him, "It is better to present one Image in a lifetime than to produce voluminous works". (Pound, 1968: 5) The concrete imagery in the poetry is to Pound what differs from prose and thus should be the major focus of poetry. To him, Poetry is not "a counter language" but "visual and concrete", expressing "a language of intuition" which will hand over sensations with energy consisting in the novelty of its figurability to "continuously see a physical thing" against jaded abstractions while verse is "a pedestrian taking you over the ground, prose — a train which delivers you at a destination". (Bell, 1981: 96) Pound stressed such concreteness of imagery to achieve objectivity he constantly pursued as opposed to the sentimentality of Romantism. The typical example of Pound's proposition of concrete imagery is his short poem of *Liu Che*. He shortened Giles' long translation of the original poem into three lines titled *Fan-Piece, for her Imperial Lord*:

O fan of white silk
clear as frost on the grass-blade,

You also are laid aside.

Here, "clear as frost on the grass-blade" is an example of Pound's idea that "the natural object is always the *adequate* symbol". Without any comment on the blamelessness of the girl, the simple presentation of the clearness of the white silk is adequate enough for the effect. The selection of the concrete images frost and grass-blade is sufficient enough to elicit the abstract associations of being fresh, delicate, minute, pristine, lowly, common, natural, short-lived. The array of properties is transferred both to the silk fan and to the discarded imperial concubine. Without any abstract terms in the simple three-line poem, the tension is created through juxtaposition of precise images and the melancholy is elicited in readers and the beauty of the poem appeals directly to the reader's sensibility.

Chinese poetry, in its simple presentation of imagery, fascinated and inspired Pound in his pursuit of poetic innovation. In his translation of Chinese poetry *Cathay*, concrete images were common practice to present the profundity of nature and of human emotions. In his later works of *The Cantos*, Pound, with the ambition of composing an epic, presented history through concrete details of facts. The impressive richness imparted by these particular cantos was due to their comprehensive dealing with proper things such as Napoleon, money, Mr. J. Q. Adams, etc. whereas much contemporary poetry explored or sought to explore quandaries in the main abstract, Pound achieved his purpose of concrete imagery through his poetic and translational practices. That's why Yeats came to the comment that "Ezra is the best critic of the two. He helps me to get back to the definite and concrete". (Carpenter, 1988:192)

The prominent feature of luminous detail is the accuracy of images. Under the influence of modern science, Pound took a more scientific view towards art when he found the similarity between bad art in inaccuracy and bad science in false reports: "Bad art is inaccurate art. It is art that makes false reports. If a scientist falsifies a report either deliberately or through negligence we consider him as either a criminal or a bad scientist according to the enormity of his offence". (Pound, 1968: 43) With that comparison, Pound came to the conclusion that "By good art I mean art that bears true witness, I mean the art that is most precise". (Pound, 1968:43) The language could be accurate only when the images in the poetry are concrete and the utterance direct and simple. Pound said: "The only way to escape from rhetoric and frilled paper decoration is through beauty... I mean by that that one must call a spade a spade in form so exactly adjusted, in a metric in itself so seductive, that the statement will not bore the auditor... We must have a simplicity and directness of utterance".

(Pound, 1968: 163) In the pursuit of ultimate beauty, Pound is in constant support of accuracy of images in his Imagism.

The accuracy of images, firstly, consists in the employment of the concrete reality instead of the abstract idea. The imagists shun the mystical idea and depict earthly reality and the everyday objects. Pound's forerunner in Imagism T. E. Hulme denounces other worldliness as a "drug", exhorting the poet to renounce "infinity" and turn to "the contemplation of finite things". (Painter, 2006:128) Pound, with his enthusiasm for medicine and science as models for poetry, renounces Symbolists preference for the mythical and the unearthly and embraced the concrete images as an efficient means of immortal art of poetry. Pound's forceful emphasis on earthliness is represented in his first tenet of Imagism as "the direct treatment of the thing," which is a stark opposite to the romanticized or symbolic treatment favored by nineteenth-century poets, that is, the vagueness and abstraction of poetic language. He writes: "It mixes an abstraction with the concrete. It comes from the writer's not realizing that the natural object is always the adequate symbol". (Pound, 1968:4) Natural object, to Pound, is the adequate source of poetic source and there is no necessity to resort to the deliberate decoration of it or the conscious intensification of emotions. Earthly reality and the everyday object is what Pound employs in the Imagist poetry and natural object is comprehensive enough to present the poetic feeling. The image is mainly natural object. The Americans have the tradition of indulging in nature as the source of aesthetic experience and Pound followed the convention of nature depiction and advanced the pictorial analogy, resorting to the revival of natural objects for the presentation of spiritual facts. Pound's interest in Japanese Noh and Chinese poetry stemmed from the conformity of the abundance of concrete natural images in them to his tenets of Imagism. Chinese poetry has the tradition of taking refuge into the nature for spiritual comfort. The cities with wealth and power and the corrupting influences, in Chinese tradition, compose the world of "red dust", a name for the world with earthly cares and troubles, but the mountains and the lakes offer a realm of serenity, the freedom from care. Different from the western poets who look upon nature as the marvelous craftwork of the Supreme Being, the Chinese poets take nature as it is with every object, every man as one element of the nature as a whole. Man is no longer the creator of nature but simply another element. Such objectivity intrigues and inspires Pound, who gives prominence to such objective treatment in his translation of Chinese poetry. In his translation *The River-Merchant's Wife: A Letter*, the young lady is in solitary sorrow in the longing of her husband's return at the sight of the butterflies in pair in the garden: The paired butterflies are already yellow with August/Over the grass in the West garden;/ They hurt me. I grow older. In the poem Song of the Bowmen of Shu, the growing of fern shoots is an indication of the long lapse of time: "Here we are, picking the first fern-shoots/And saying: When shall we get back to our country? /.../We grub the soft fern-shoot,/When anyone says "Return," the others are full of sorrow. /.../We grub the old fern-stalks. /We say: will we be let to go back in October?" In the poem *The Beautiful Toilet*, the verdant grass on the riverbank and willows in the yard is set as a contrast to the sorrowful solitude of the young lady and her miserable fate. In the poem *Lament of the Frontier Guard*, the desolate landscape is depicted to reflect the abject life of the frontier soldiers: "By the North Gate, the wind blows full of sand,/Lonely from the beginning of time until now! /Trees fall, the grass goes yellow with autumn. /I climb the towers and towers/to watch out the barbarous land:/ Desolate castle, the sky, the wide desert. /There is no wall left to this village."

Pound's eagerness to set the concrete image as the luminous detail is manifest in many of his translations. Take an example from Pound's translation of *Book of Songs*:

The original text: 江有沱,之子归,不我过。不我过,其啸也歌。

Ezra Pound: As the T'o flows back to Kiang,
First she pouted, then she flouted,
Then, at last, she sang. (Pound, 2003:764)

The original poetry conveys the resentment of an abandoned wife. Her lover is accused with the lady's echoing lines of "not remembering the past" and she stated firmly about his regret for his desertion of her. The last line of the last stanza, "sob like song", shows the shift from misery to joy and thus reflects the strong will of the lady. Pound is unique in his translation by creating three vivid actions of the lady, "pouting", "flouting" and "singing". The first action "pouting" reveals her dissatisfaction with the man, "flouting" her sneering of him which shows she has become superior to him and to the situation, and the last action "singing" reflects the joy of the lady after her transcendence of the misery. Pound's translation is not tantamount in words to the original conveyance of emotions but depicts a vivid image of a lady growing from the abandoned misery to the transcended joy. It is creative yet reflects Pound's purpose of building concrete images in poetry. Another example also comes from *Book of Songs*:

The original text: 二子乘舟,泛泛其逝。愿言思子,不瑕有害?

Ezra Pound: The boat floats past the sky's edge, lank sail a-flap;
and a dark thought inside me: how had they hap? (Pound, 2003:776)

The poem is a song of departure. The original first line depicts the scenes nearby when the two young men said goodbye to the relatives and boarded the boat. In the second line, the shot is pulled far in which the boat becomes a solitary small leaf floating away in the vast river. The picture is integrated with the reluctance and the worry of those who see the young off and look far into the distance. Where the original states simply the boarding of the two young men, and the sprinkling of waves, the disappearance of the boat, Pound's translation focuses more on the visuality of the poetry and the scene is vividly presented to the reader with his creative depiction of images: "The boat floats past the sky's edge, lank sail a-flap". "Lank sail a-flap" is an additional image created by Pound in his translation as a depiction of violent wind, which implies the surging waves as a metaphor of the risks and dangers in the journey of life. The misgivings among the seers-off conveyed in the last two lines of the original are just naturally instilled without direct statement.

The following example is also from Pound's translation from *Book of Songs* together with the versions from other translators:

Ezra Pound: When we set out, the willows were drooping with spring,
We come back in the snow.

James Legge: At first, when we set out,
The willows were fresh and green;
Now, when we shall be returning,
The snow will be falling clouds.

Xu Yuanchong: When I left here,
Willow shed tear.
I came back now,
Snow bends the bough.

Wang Rongpei: At first, when we started on our track,
The willows green were growing.
And now, when we think of the journey back,
'Tis raining fast and snowing.

William Jennings: When I set out so long ago,
Fresh and green was the willow.
When now homeward I go,
There is a heavy snow.

Hu Pinqing: Long ago when we set off,
Thick, thick were the willow shades.
Now that we start for home,
Heavy, heavy are the rain and snow.

Where other translators tend to use abstract adjectives to depict the verdant willows at their departure time, "fresh" by Legge and Jennings, "thick" by Hu, and the abstract metaphor of "shed tear" by Xu, Pound builds a vivid image of "drooping" willows to reflect their life and vigour. The scene in contrast at their arrival time is also depicted in the abstract by some translators, "heavy" used by Jennings and Hu, "fast" by Wang, the abstract metaphor of "falling clouds" by Legge, Pound resorts to the omission to retain the simple image of "snow" as a stark contrast to the previous image. The approach in translation is often the reflection of Pound's purpose of building vivid concrete images as against generalization and abstraction.

Apart from the depiction of the objective detail, Pound focuses on the "luminous" elements in the earthly objects and the everyday phenomena that turn the simple and trivial into the representative and extraordinary from fresh perspectives. Different from his predecessors, Pound looks upon the earthly objects not as a vehicle of the mystical idea, but as a form of beauty in themselves. For him, the rose once again has become beautiful in itself, in its petals, scent, and color, and not in its imagined resemblances to mythical love. He tries to look upon the familiar from a new perspective, as a more ordinary object, stripped of the idealized or metaphysical associations that the predecessors often employ. Pound advocates the fresh perspective to look upon the ordinary object rather than slip into the conventional resort to the mystical. The fresh perspective lies in the practice of seeing the world anew. The natural objects are depicted microscopically and they are no longer the association of the mythical but the expression of the emotions of the poet at the moment within the poet's grasp. According to the imagist principles, the natural object should be scrutinized to give the precise depiction. Pound always stresses the importance of precision of images:

"The touchstone of an art is its precision". (Pound, 1968:48)

"Bad art is inaccurate art. It is art that makes false reports". (Pound, 1968:43)

"By good art I mean art that bears true witness, I mean the art that is most precise. You can be wholly precise in representing a vagueness". (Pound, 1968:44)

For Pound, the precise image is the efficient means to replace the vagueness in the previous century. The natural objects are under meticulous observation to liberate the poetic sense. In Pound's famous poem *In a Station of the Metro*: "The apparition of these faces in the crowd/Petals on a wet, black bough." there is no superfluous use of abstract adjectives, but two concrete ones "wet" and "black" to focalize the ugliness of the bough as a background to foreground the beauty of petals and the jubilation at the sight of them. The focalizing of the two particular elements of the bough conjures up the picture of the dreary world after the rain emitting decadence in the wet air as a reflection of the dark corner of the city, the metro line, where the crowd move in mechanical indifference. Against the backdrop, the colorful petals bring vigor and liveliness to the gloomy picture, just as the beautiful faces suddenly awaken the numb spirit to life. Such microscopic attention to the object magnifies the tiniest details and steers the poem away from the generalized world towards greater concreteness. It is the devotion to the minute specific details for the concreteness. Pound once made a comparison between the artist and the teacher of science: "Any teacher of biology would tell you that knowledge can not be transmitted by general statement without knowledge of particulars. By this method of presentation and juxtaposition leave a moderately ignorant teacher can transmit most of what he knows without filling the student's mind with a great mass of prejudice and error". (Pound, 1968:60) And therefore, for an artist, it is necessary to present the particulars to reveal the whole, to reintroduce the everyday into poetry, to make the object and the process of observing alive.

The accuracy of images, secondly, lies in the precise language in poetry. The flowery ornamental language is discarded in Pound's new trend as he believes in the accurate and clear language to be an efficient means in communication. Pound, in the term "concrete", not only refers to the earthliness of images, but also to the concrete language and rejection of Symbolist abstraction. Pound, in particular, denounces abstraction and generalization as a sign of poor technique. "Language is made out of concrete things. General expressions in non-concrete terms are a laziness; they are talk, not art". (Pound, 1971: 49) Pound describes "good writers" as "those who keep the language efficient. That is to say, keep it accurate, keep it clear... Language is the main means of communication". (Pound, 1960: 32) His emphasis on concreteness revolutionizes the poetic language that reflects the western way of thinking, the habit of abstraction in particular. Pound always opposes abstraction in language as he argues in his *A Few Don'ts*: "Don't use such an expression as 'dim lands of peace'. It dulls the image. It mixes an abstraction with the concrete. It comes from the writer's not realizing that the natural object is always the adequate symbol". (Pound 1968: 5) Pound's interest in Chinese poetry and Chinese language is inspired by its concreteness, believing that when the westerns are apt to define by abstract concept such as "red, color, vibration, mode of being, etc.", Chinese tend to put together concrete objects such as "cherry" for "red", "flamingo" for "iron dust". (Xie, 1999: 22) Pound's poetry and translations are evident representations of his tenet of concreteness in language. Pound loathes the excessive use of adjectives to depict the objective. He warns the artists to "use no superfluous word, no adjective which does not reveal something". (Pound, 1968: 4) He is constantly opposed the use of ornamental adjectives of abstraction to depict the natural world. In his letter to Harriet Monroe, he stresses the objectivity of language in reiteration:

> "Objectivity and again objectivity, and expression: no hindside-beforeness, no straddled adjectives, no Tennysonianness of speech; nothing — nothing that you couldn't in some circumstance, in the stress of some emotion, actually say. Every literaryism, every book word, fritters away a scrap of the reader's patience, a scrap of his sense of your sincerity". (Pound, 1971: 49)

His practice is a convincing proof to his tenet. Take Tao Yuanming's *The Unmoving Cloud* as an example.

Table 1

	霭霭停云,蒙蒙时雨。	八表同昏,平路伊阻。
Ezra Pound	The clouds have gathered, and gathered, and the rain falls and falls,	The eight ply of the heavens are all folded into one darkness, And the wide, flat road stretches out.
Burton Watson	Heavy and dull, the motionless clouds, the seasonal rains drenching down;	all eight directions a single darkness, all the level roads cut off.
Fang Zhong	Thick and dusty, the lingering clouds, Misty and drizzling, the season's rain;	In all directions, the haze unbroken, The level roads are blocked from access.
Wang Rongpei	The clouds are pending dense and high While spring rain drizzles from the sky.	So dim and somber is the day That no one rides along the way.

Table 2

	霭霭停云，蒙蒙时雨。	八表同昏，平陆成江。
Ezra Pound	Rain, rain, and the clouds have gathered,	The eight ply of the heavens are darkness, The flat land is turned into river.
Burton Watson	Motionless clouds dull and heavy, these drenching seasonal rains;	all eight directions a single darkness, all the flat land turned to rivers.
Fang Zhong	The lingering clouds, thick and dusky, The season's rain, misty and drizzling;	In all directions, the haze unbroken. The level roads, with waters swelling.
Wang Rongpei	The clouds are pending dense and high While spring rain drizzles from the sky.	So dim and somber is the day That floods are running on the way.

Table 1 and table 2 are the different translations of the repeated stanzas in Tao Yuanming's poem *The Unmoving Cloud*. A look at the different translations will shed light on Pound's distaste for empty adjectives as opposed to others. Where Pound uses none of adjectives but the repetition of verbs to revive the original reduplication of characters: "The clouds have gathered, and gathered, and the rain falls and falls," the other translators resorts to various adjectives to depict the scene, Burton Watson with "heavy and dull", Fang Zhong with "thick and dusky", "misty and drizzling" and Wang Rongpei with "dense and high", all of which are abstraction incapable of creating a vivid imaginary picture. Pound, however, with no adjectives to amplify the subjective feelings, reduced the words into the mere depiction of the objective, the gathering of the clouds and the falling of the rain, the endless motion emphasized in his repeated verbs. The only adjectives Pound uses is to depict the road, which he translates as "wide, flat" where other uses "level". Again, his words are simple without excessive decoration yet cinematic enough to arouse an imaginary picture. His translation is in accordance with his preach: "The only adjective that is worth using is the adjective that is essential to the sense of the passage, not the decorative frill adjective". (Pound, 1971:49)

2.1.2 Luminous — Emotional Force

Apart from the concrete details, Pound stresses the "luminous" quality of the detail. The detail is luminous only when the objective is depicted not for the sake of their existence, but the revealing of the complex emotions felt at that moment. The detail is illuminating and enlightening which "governs knowledge as the switchboard of electric circuit". (Pound, 1973: 24) Thus the selection of the detail should be meticulous in that it is the source to release latent energy. Pound compares the similar experience in art and science in his essay. He mentioned that the various engines in the engineering laboratory are the same to the laymen, but they gather the latent energy of Nature and "the latent energy is made dynamic or revealed to the engineer in control, and placed at his disposal". (Pound, 1973: 25) Similarly, for an artist, he should perceive the sources of latent energy, "latent forces, or things present but unnoticed, or things perhaps taken for granted but never examined". (Pound, 1973: 25) Pound once talked about his experience in writing his famous poem *In a Station of the Metro*: "Three years ago in Paris I got out of a 'metro' train at La Concorde, and saw suddenly a beautiful face, and then another and another, and then a beautiful child's face, and then another beautiful woman, and I tried all that day to find words for what this had meant to me, ...". (Pound, 1974: 86-7) Pound seized this intuitive impact on him and tried to restore the similar impact in his poem. He selected the image of "petals on a wet, black bough" that would represent exactly what he felt at the sight of such beautiful faces in the gloomy crowd. It is the accurate and clear denotation of a world outside the poetic self yet to the immediate access of all separate selves. Pound's definition of the image as "that which presents an intellectual and emotional complex in an instant of time" (Pound, 1968: 4) is an evident proof of his idea, which he further expanded as follows: "It is the presentation of such a 'complex' instantaneously which gives that sense of sudden liberation; that sense of freedom from time limits and space limits that sense of sudden growth, which we experience in the presence of the greatest works of art". (Pound, 1968: 4) The image is composed of language "charged with meaning to the utmost possible degree". (Pound, 1968: 23) It is the reservoir of energy from intense emotions that touch "the nature of man, of individuals". (Pound, 1968: 47) It is not only the external detail but the intersection of the textures with the person who walks through them.

In his translations, Pound intentionally highlights certain qualities that are "luminous" to enlighten the readers. Poetry, if intended to be touching and inspiring, should possess the power to evoke emotions. Pound, in his definition of image as "that which presents an intellectual and emotional complex in an instant of time", presents the importance of such emotional force, as image is more than the natural objects in its superficial or literal sense, but an integrated combination of intense emotions and poetic experience that would be elicited through the presentation. Image, to Pound, is not the ultimate goal but its power "which gives that sense of sudden liberation; that sense of freedom from time limits and space limits; that sense of sudden growth, which we experience in the presence of the greatest works of art". (Pound, 1968:4) In the luminous detail, the concrete detail presented in the form of image is luminous in that it is enlightening because the poet, when depicting the image, "was thinking of inner, instinctive motives, of the aroused and focused desires and hates that are the natural springs of action". (Moody, 2007:228) The inspirations in the poet are presented in the skillful way so that the readers will be inspired in the same way because imagism presents a technique "for the precise, scientific, expression of that process of the life force in and through the individual mind". (Moody, 2007:228)

Thus, Pound's imagery is apt to have the intensity of emotions with its freedom from the excessive depiction of the subjective. He distinguished between prose and poetry and concluded that poetry should be "departing in no way from speech save by a heightened intensity (i. e. simplicity)". (Pound, 1968:48) The poet should, in the most compact language, inspires the intense emotions. Pound practices what he preaches in his translation. Through luminous details, the poet should strive to create the intense feelings through the powerful image which is capable of arousing the readers' sympathy through their interpretation. Luminous details were "'interpreting' details that in embryonic form, predicated knowledge of an entire range of cultural values, resuming a complete social, historical or aesthetic complex in order to instigate 'intelligence of a period'". (Bell, 1981: 44) The luminous effect comes from the readers' interpretative power through the inspiring image, which is possible when the artist presents and juxtaposes images without any comment. Pound made an analogy in electricity to demonstrate the way to function by the luminous details: "Let us imagine them charged with a force like electricity, or, rather, radiating a force from their apexes — some radiating, some sucking in. We must have a greater variety of activity than with electricity — not merely positive and negative; but let us say +, −, x, −, +a, −a, xa, −a, etc. Some of these kinds of force neutralise each other, some augment; but the only way any two cones can be got to act without waste is for them to be so placed that their apexes and a line of surface meet exactly. When this conjunction occurs let us say their force is not added one's to the other's, but multiply the one's by the other's; thus three or four words in exact juxtaposition are capable of radiating this energy at a very high potentiality". (Pound, 1973:34)

Pound's translation is an explicit exemplification of such poetic ideas. Take Pound's poem *Liu Ch'e* translated from an ancient Chinese poem as an example listed below along with Giles' version.

Ezra Pound: The rustling of the silk is discontinued,
Dust drifts over the court-yard,
There is no sound of foot-fall, and the leaves
Scurry into heaps and lie still,
And she the rejoicer of the heart is beneath them:
A wet leaf that clings to the threshold.

Herbert Giles: The sound of rustling silk is stilled,
With dust the marble courtyard filled;
No footfalls echo on the floor,
Fallen leaves in heaps block up the door...
For she, my pride, my lovely one, is lost,
And I am left, in hopeless anguish tossed.

Pound's conversion of the last line into a vivid image of "A wet leaf that clings to the threshold" is widely acclaimed as classic which has been imitated then by many other poets. No such image occurs in the original or in Gile's version of abstract emotion as "hopeless anguish" but Pound ingeniously creates the image which to him is the emotional equivalent he felt at the moment as the token of the gone woman. The simple adjective "wet" presents us with the dull, lifeless leaves scattered by rain in the bitter cold weather. It creates in the reader the emotional impact of "bleakness". (Wilson, 2005:138) The relative clause that stresses the activity of the leave's "clinging to the threshold" almost personifies the leaf hanging on hopelessly. It is the image that reflects "the thing inward and subjective", that acts as a perfect equation of the emotion of the emperor, the grief, the despair in the gloom of his wife's loss. Gile's direct statement lacks emotional charge and leaves no space for the readers to imagine in empathy. Pound, however, by highlighting the desolate elements in the leaf, the coldness, the lifeless despair, translates the emotional devastation of the emperor across to the reader. Pound is also careful in his choice of verbs. The "discontinuing" of the "rustling" of silk, the "drifting" of the dust, the "scurrying" of the leaves into heaps, the "clinging" of the wet leaf to the threshold, every of the verbs is contributive to the establishment of a vivid image. The verbs form the sharp contrast, from the vigorous dynamic world into the still bleakness. Where Giles uses static verbs like "stilled", "filled", "block", Pound adopts dynamic ones, depicting mobile pictures with dust "drifting" around instead of just "filling" the courtyard, the leaves "scurrying" about instead of merely "blocking" the door. Such mobile images are reflective of the internal turbulence in the melancholy reminiscence of his bereaved wife and contrasting the stillness in the following lines, the leaves then "lie still" and a wet leaf "clings" so that the bleakness is emphatically felt by the readers in sympathy with the poet. Every word Pound uses is intended to illuminate the detail to reflect, to inspire, to carry forward the emotion. Every word is charged with meaning, with his intentions for them to be luminous. He said: "Great literature is implied language charged with meaning to the utmost possible degree". (Pound, 1968: 23) It is the language as simple as possible, the exact word striped of all associations and comment yet conveys to the readers the poetic experience as intense as is felt by the poet himself at the moment.

2.2 Permanent Metaphor

Permanent metaphor is another important component of Imagism which Pound aims to establish as a guideline for the poetic practice and to achieve by assimilating traditions from other cultures through his translation. It is a metaphor "concentrating imagery by understatement, by keeping words to a minimum", (Pratt, 2007: 10) a metaphor evoking subjective interpretations within the readers' imagination instead of presenting the emotions directly. Permanent metaphor is the typical method Imagists use, focusing on the direct verbal description of an object to form a mental image. "The Imagists did not suggest; they evoked immediately". (Pratt, 2007: 21) Permanent metaphor is unique in that it is a union of the subjective and the objective, a fusion of reality in words that evoke emotions immediately. Taupin is precise in his evaluation of its effect: "the pleasure of their poetry is not the satisfaction of discovering little by little, but of seizing at a single blow, in the fullest vitality, the image, a fusion of reality in words". (Pratt, 2007: 22)

In his translation of Chinese poetry, Pound highlights the function of permanent metaphor through his creative translational methods. In his eyes, Chinese poetry is the perfect carrier of permanent metaphor, with its characteristics of suggestiveness in presenting emotions and revealing beauty through natural images without moralizing. Chinese poetry scholar Wai-lim Yip defines the characteristics of Chinese poetry as follows: "1. The suppression of linking-agencies allows the images to form a kind of ambiguity or pluri-signification, 2. And allows the reader to exercise his imagination to establish relationships among the images, 3. The use of self-contained images heighten the poem's overtones/nuances". (Yip, 2008: 128) That is to say, Chinese poetry highlights the presentation of images as implicit metaphor intended to intensify the poetic emotions. This unique, powerful means of presenting poetic experience amazes Pound and after receiving Fenollosa's notes on Chinese poetry, Pound devotes himself to the translation in the full exploration of such metaphor. On the release of his translation *Cathay*, critics showered Pound with praises on the effectiveness of his new technique: "Mr. Pound's little volume is like a door in a wall, opening suddenly upon fields of an extreme beauty, and upon a landscape made real by the intensity of human emotions", "Beauty is a very valuable thing, perhaps it is the most valuable thing in life; but the power to express emotion so that it shall communicate itself intact and exactly is almost more valuable. Of both of these qualities Mr. Pound's book is very full". (Homberger, 1972: 108)

2.2.1 Union of Subject and Object

Pound's permanent metaphor, like traditional metaphors, builds a bridge of correlation between the tenor and the vehicle, the subjective and the objective in its case. The effect of permanent metaphor depends on the correlation between subject and object or even the integration of them. On one hand, subjective emotions should be realities to be objectively recorded in images. On the other, permanent metaphor takes effect when the objective could be interpreted to inspire and represent the subjective emotions: "In a poem of this sort one is trying to record the precise instant when a thing outward and objective transforms itself, or darts into a thing inward and subjective". (Pound, 1968: 89) In this way, an image is no longer a mere objective record of the thing outward but the presentation of the real inward and subjective state. The objective images and the subjective emotions are merged into one through readers' interpretation in Pound's permanent metaphor. In his definition of the image as "that which presents an intellectual and emotional complex in an instant of time", (Pound, 1968: 4) Pound makes explicit his idea of the image not as merely a reflection or depiction of the objective world, but, more importantly, as the means to express intellectual ideas and emotional force and it is the union of subject and object which gives' that sense of sudden liberation... that sense of sudden growth, which we experience in the presence of the greatest works of art". (Pound,

1968:4) To achieve such union, Pound coins a new term "absolute metaphor" or "permanent metaphor" to demonstrate the interaction of actually perceived objects and of the poetry and the readers. "in ... poem(s) of this sort, one is trying to record the precise instant when a thing outward and objective transforms itself into a thing inward subjective". (Lewis, 2007:4) His words reveal that permanent metaphor is the transformation of a thing already in the mind and adds new meaning through its being more intensely felt and more deeply understood. And 'The real' for Pound was not the thing in its outward and objective form but the subjective condition as objectified in the Image. (Moody, 2007:226) The objective world is intertwined with the subjective. The permanent metaphor is a mental experience of blending the natural objects and emotions and intensifying the subjectivity. The Imagists attempt to preserve emotional expressiveness through tangible imagery, creating "an equilibrium and, at times, a creative tension between interiority and exteriority, subject and object". (Painter, 2006:152)

Firstly, Pound insists that the subjective poetic experience should be presented through objective imagery. Pound's Imagist principle of "direct treatment of the thing whether subjective or objective" is the register. In many of Pound's poems and translations, such substitution of the objective imagery for subjective emotions is common. In his poem *Gentildonna* (1916) :"She passed and left no quiver in the veins, who now/Moving among the trees, and clinging/ in the air she severed./Fanning the grass she walked on then, endures:/*Grey olive leaves beneath a rain-cold sky.*" the image in the final line is the precise substitute for the emotions the previous lines evokes and the colon-contraction makes the balance between the objective and the subjective which, in an instant, conjures up the relationship between them and intense emotions are inspired in the readers. Such emphasis on the physical objects to present psychic experience was a prominent feature of Pound's poetry and his poetic translations. The following example comes from Pound's translation of Chinese classic *Book of Songs* titled *Guan Ju*. (关关雎鸠,在河之洲。窈窕淑女,君子好逑。参差荇菜,左右流之。窈窕淑女,寤寐求之。求之不得,寤寐思服。悠哉悠哉,辗转反侧。参差荇菜,左右采之。窈窕淑女,琴瑟友之。参差荇菜,左右芼之。窈窕淑女,钟鼓乐之。) In the translation, Pound impressively uses creative translational approach to highlight the harmony between man and nature, between the psychic experience and the physical image. First of all, he uniquely translates the onomatopoeia "Guan Guan", the call of the fishing hawk, to the two monosyllabic words "Hid! Hid!", which also implicitly generates the association of shyness and modesty of the fair lady. Pound also reinforces the deep and concealed nature of the lady image to echo the onomatopoeia image: "Clear as the stream her modesty;/As neath dark boughs her secrecy", "High reed caught in ts'ai grass/so deep her secrecy". In addition, Pound's treatment of the line about "the long and short weed" is a testament to his purpose of building explicit natural image for the reflection of psychological experience. There list seven different versions of the line below:

James Legge(1871):	Here long, there short, is the duckweed
James Legge(1876):	See how the duckweed's stalks, or short or long
William Jennings:	Waterlilies, long or short ones, —
Clement F. R. Allen:	They sent me to gather the cresses, which lie And sway on the stream, as it glances by
Arthur Waley:	In patches grows the water mallow
Ezra Pound:	reed against reed/tall on slight
Xu Yuanchong:	Of cresses here and there

In the original line, the first two words means "long and short" literally and Legge and Jennings give the literal meaning in their translations. Also, in ancient Chinese, the word "Cen Ci" also takes the meaning of "multiple grace". The weed presents the verdant fragrance of spring and hence the vigorous fair maiden. Allen's version "sway on the stream" is the reflection of that meaning. Waley's and Xu's translations stress the quantity of the plant without implication of length or grace. Pound's version is an obvious creative one. The image of "reed against reed/tall on slight" "as the stream moves left and right" depicts a picture of the shadowy reed on the surface of the water so that there is the "dark and clear/dark and clear" hue that shows the serene beauty of the water and therefore of the lady sought by the gentleman. Pound, through the creation of natural image, reveals the subjective sense, the mystery, the retiring coyness. The call of the fish-hawk "Hid! Hid!" echoes the depiction of the "dark and clear" lady in all her secrecy and modesty. Pound's amplification reflects his Skopos of the integration of the natural and the psychic, as his additional two lines "Clear as the stream her modesty;/As neath dark boughs her secrecy" well integrates the subjective abstract features of the lady with the objective image, and the two words used, "clear" and "dark", form a coherent echo to the previous depiction of the lady —"dark and clear". Thus, through the conversion from the abstract to the concrete, from the subjective to the objective, Pound, in multiple aspects, reveals his Skopos of imagism in his creative translation.

Secondly, the union of subject and object is achieved through the treatment of emotions as universal. The emotions conveyed in his translations of the exotic and the ancient works could be universally felt as the historical entity in the universe. In the permanent metaphor, Pound resorts to such universality of human emotions as the bridge between the past and the present in spite of the sharp difference in traditions and cultures over time and space. "We are nevertheless one humanity, compounded of one mud and of one another...". (Pound, 1973:33) He is in constant efforts to reveal the universal to touch the readers, to inspire them to interpret. In his foreword of the collection of his prose, Pound talks about the advantage of removal of the pronoun "I" at the sentence beginning to be replaced by the common pronoun "we" or "one" because "The substitution of 'I' by a comprehensive claim in which 'we' or 'one' is used to indicate a general law may be a pretentious attempt to expand a merely personal view into a universal law". (Pound, 1973: Foreword) In accordance, Pound, in his career, tries to find something universal across time and space in his poetry. Chinese poetry is on the whole humanistic, rendering emotions of the ordinary, of the everyday life in simple diction. Burton Watson, in the foreword of his translation of Chinese poetry, notes the unique poetic tradition in China: "... the Chinese poetic tradition is on the whole unusually humanistic and commonsensical in tone, seldom touching on the supernatural or indulging in extravagant flights of fancy or rhetoric. For this reason, even works that are many centuries removed from us in time come across with a freshness and immediacy that is often quite miraculous. The Chinese poetic world is one that is remarkably easy to enter because it concentrates to such a large degree on concerns that are common to men and women of whatever place or time". (Watson, 1984: 3) Pound translates some Chinese poetry in Fenollosa's notes and compiles the poetry collection *Cathay*, which strikes the sympathy among readers and wins widespread acclaim. Pound is successful because he finds the common nature between the native and the foreign, the archaic and the modern, which can be considered as objective as the stones that will exist unchanged throughout the ages. The beauty of *Cathay* lies less in the strangeness of old China but the familiarity it evokes in readers. The emotions of exile and homesickness, of friendship and convivial joys and pleasures, of war, of contemplation, are all projected as familiar as what might be felt natively in *Cathay*. The emotions and feelings expressed in his translations are strikingly familiar to the modern readers even in a different culture. The selected war poems struck people with similar experience during or after World War I and aroused sympathy in them. When Pound sent his friend in the battlefield his translations of a couple of war poems, Gaudier felt the situation and feelings in them so familiar that he exclaimed that "They depict our situation in a wonderful way". Pound, in his meticulous selection of themes and adoption of free verse as colloquial speech, shortens the distance between the ancient and the modern, the foreign and the native, and "expands a merely personal view into a universal law". (Pound, 1973: Foreword) The beauty of the poetry collection does not come from the exotic strangeness of old China, but from the striking common emotion it projects on the contemporary readers. Michael Alexander commented that "the beauty of *Cathay* is not merely exotic, alien or sensuous — it comes from a recognition of human emotion". (Alexander, 1979: 101) Similar praises poured upon Pound: "Mr. Pound's little volume is like a door in a wall, opening suddenly upon fields of an extreme beauty, and upon a landscape made real by the intensity of human emotions. We are accustomed to think of the Chinese as arbitrary or uniform in sentiment, but these poems reveal them as being just ourselves". (Homberger, 1972: 108) "His translations from the Chinese are vivid in feeling and keen in sympathy. One realizes the closeness of the Chinese soul as a next-door human neighbor, fellow-traveler on an old, old planet, after reading *Cathay*". (Homberger, 1972: 114)

2.2.2 Interpretation of Taciturn Emotion

Permanent metaphor is known as "interpretative metaphor" as opposed to ornamental metaphor. It presents images austerely rather than embellish emotions ornamentally and thus creates the experience of intense emotions through the interpretation of readers in the empty space unfilled in the poetry. Pound advances the necessity of the new form of metaphor in his footnotes to Fenollosa's essay that "The poet, in dealing with his own time, must also see to it that language does not petrify on his hands. He must prepare for new advances along the lines of true metaphor, that is interpretative metaphor, or images, as diametrically opposed to untrue, or ornamental, metaphor". (Pratt, 2007: 124)

Firstly, equation of taciturn emotion in permanent metaphor is achieved though the absence of comment. In his essay *The Spirit of Romance*, Pound asserts the necessity of the artist's detachment: "the artist seeks out the luminous detail and presents it. He does not comment". (Pound, 1968: 4) It is in conformity with his previous credo of imagism as "Don't be viewy". (Pound, 1968: 6) Pound, in his contact and translation of Chinese poetry, discerns the characteristics of graphic presentation and the absence of moralizing which echoes and reinforces his Imagist credo: "It is because certain Chinese poets have been content to set forth their matter without moralizing and without comment that one labors to make a translation". (Pound, 1968:135) The approach means the non-interference with the flow of nature and the mere record of the objective reality to indicate and inspire the subjective consciousness. Pound advocates austere use of objective languages because "The image is itself the speech. The image is the word beyond formulated language". (Lewis, 2007: 13) Chinese poetry, under the influence of Taoism upholding the harmony between man and nature, and the integration into self-contained universe, presents nature without human interference or the imposition of morals on it. Fenollosa observes that in his essay: "Chinese poetry... speaks at once with the vividness of painting, and with the mobility of sounds. It is, in some sense, more objective than either, more dramatic. In reading Chinese we do not seem to be juggling mental counters, but to be watching things work out their fate". (Yip, 2008:187) The absence of comment has long been the tradition in Chinese poetry. The great Chinese sage Confucius once happily told his student that he wanted to comment on nothing. The student was puzzled and asked how they could record if there was no comment. Confucius said: "Does the universe comment? Yet seasons come and go and all creatures live in vigorously. Does the universe comment?" It is an interesting anecdote. Yet it tells the fact that sense is sometimes beyond words as words are finite while sense is infinite and unpredictable. The seemingly thorough depiction of senses leaves no space to savor, to ponder over the inexpressible. Beauty of artistic works, in many cases, consists in the absence of comment. That is why Keats says in his poem: "Heard melodies are sweet; but those unheard are sweeter." The famous aesthetician Zhu Guangqian concluded that "thoughts and emotions are better expressed in reservation than in effusion without qualification and it is better to leave something for the readers to interpret than to convey everything in mind because the aesthetic feelings and impressions are more intense in reservation in the admirers' minds". (朱光潜, 2005:8)

Pound, an acute perceiver of beauty in life and in poetry, has perceived the value of reserved implication in the expression of beauty in poetry. Unlike prose that stresses on entire demonstration and effusion for its effect, poetry relies more on implicit aloofness for its appeal. Pound bases his innovation on the work of previous works and drew the essence from contemporary artists, among whom Flaubert's Le Mot Juste influences on him with "the exact word stripped of all associations and comment" (Lierbregts, 2004: 82) and T. S. Hulme with his building the image as a means to "enable us to experience without abstract discursiveness the freshness of the world and to appreciate its ever-changing newness". (Lierbregts, 2004:82) The direct presentation and precise depiction of the image without any comment is, to Pound, the most effectual means to make the readers see the deeper truth and beauty in the universe behind prosaic reality. The following example is his translation *Liu Ch'e*. A comparison of the different versions will reveal Pound's preference of permanent metaphor in conveying emotional force. The following are respectively the translations by Ezra Pound, Herbert Giles and Amy Lowell:

Ezra Pound: The rustling of the silk is discontinued,
Dust drifts over the court-yard,
There is no sound of foot-fall, and the leaves
Scurry into heaps and lie still,
And she the rejoicer of the heart is beneath them:
A wet leaf that clings to the threshold.

Herbert Giles: The sound of rustling silk is stilled,
With dust the marble courtyard filled;
No footfalls echo on the floor,
Fallen leaves in heaps block up the door...
For she, my pride, my lovely one, is lost,
And I am left, in hopeless anguish tossed.

Amy Lowell: There is no rustle of silken sleeves,
Dust gatheres in the Jade Courtyard.
The empty houses are cold, still, without sound.
The leaves fall and lie upon the bars of doorway after doorway.
I long for the Most Beautiful One; How can I attain my desire?
Pain bursts my heart. There is no peace.

Pound builds, in his last line, an almost entirely autonomous image apparently detached from the main strophe of the poem yet evoking the emotion that is closely related. In where Giles and Lowell translated as the direct statement of abstract emotion, Pound substitutes the vague naming with the concrete image ("A wet leaf that clings to the threshold"). Giles gives in his final line the direct and clear terms of the emperor's feeling: "And I am left, in hopeless anguish tossed". Lowell's closure is even more abstract and flat with simple assertion of obvious emotion. Pound, as always, does not state the emotion directly but seeks to inspire, through permanent metaphor, such interpretations in the readers. The image presents us with the dreary and lifeless scene with the fallen leaf battened down by rain from an evergreen tree. The leaf is fallen in the soaking rain and then stuck to a doorstep. It is a pathetic sight that evokes sympathy, the leaf at the end of its life yet unwilling to leave. The bitter coldness of rain, the loneliness of an isolated leaf, the hopelessness of its clinging all create the bleakness that well represents the emotion of the protagonist and of the readers' emotional experience. In the original Chinese poem, *Liu Ch'e*, the Chinese emperor of the second century BC, states the lingering memory of his bereaved wife, lamenting the unheard rustling of his wife's dress and the sound of her footsteps, the neglect around the place of his once cherished wife. Thus, in Pound's translation, the image is an attempt to find "an equation for the thing inward and subjective", (Wilson, 2005: 141) "an equation for the bleakness of the poet in the aftergloom of beauty's loss". (Wilson, 2005:138) Many scholars make positive evaluation of Pound's treatment of the subjective as the objective image in this poem. Peter Wilson criticizes Giles' version that "lacks any emotional charge because it makes no attempt to find an equation for the feeling whereby readers can imagine their way into or empathize with the feeling itself" and then praises Pound's as "Pound 'translates' the feeling by providing a concrete image of the motional devastation felt by the emperor, carrying it across to the reader". (Wilson, 2005: 141) Ming Xie evaluates Lowell's version as "flat" and then praises Pound's version as "the more pungently oblique suggestiveness" with feeling "implied obliquely and instantly". (Xie, 1999:80) Kenner acclaims the translation as the image conforms to Imagist canons with "the mind's creative leap fetching some token of the gone woman into the poem's system". (Kenner, 1972: 197) The image is so effective that later quoted in many of other literary works in the western world. Lowell, for example, writes in her poem *Pictures of the Floating World* (1919): "And I walk, bent, unseeing, /Waiting to catch the first faint scuffle/Of withered leaves."

In the absence of comment, Pound stresses detachment instead of active engagement. Pound is amazed by the aesthetics of Chinese poetry. Chinese poetry has its roots deep in the tradition of Taoist aesthetics. In Taoism, the real world, "quite without human supervision and explanation, is totally alive, self-generating, self-conditioning, self-transforming and self-complete". (Yip, 2008: 157) As humans and things are integrated as one in the universe, humans, to represent the primal state of the world, should know their place in the world, and their relations with things in it. Humans, being among the million creatures in the universe, are not in a dominant position and have no prerogative to command cosmic arrangement. Therefore, humans should not impose their viewpoints upon things but view things as things view things because things exist in their distinctive forms with their beauty and truth and develop with their own activities and rhythms long before humans name them. Thus Lao Zi said, "to view the Universe through the Universe", (Yip, 2008:54) and Zhuang Zi said, "to hide the Universe in the Universe", (Yip, 2008:54) that is, to discover the inner life of every being instead of impose views upon them. The only way to view the world in its comprehensive state is to merge the subjective and the objective, the phenomena and the consciousness into one, without domination and subordination. In this way, the human subjectivity is retreated from the scene but in detachment, we perceive and present the inter-penetration and inter-illumination of humans and things. For poets, active responsiveness and vigilant attention are necessary to depict the surrounding world, yet should be kept in detachment that will help produce the ultimate artistic effect. The following example is from the translations of Li Bai's poem *The Jewel Stairs Grievance*.

Ezra Pound: The jeweled steps are already quite white with dew,
It is so late that the dew soaks my gauze stockings.
And I let down the crystal curtain,
And watch the moon through the clear autumn.

Witter Bynner: Her jade-white staircase is cold with dew;
Her silk soles are wet, she lingered there so long...
Behind her closed casement, why is she still waiting,
Watching through its crystal pane the glow of the autumn moon?

In Pound's *The Jewel Stairs' Grievance*, he portrays the natural scene of jeweled steps, the soaked gauze stockings, the human activities of descending the curtain and watching the moon in hard and cold precision without any trace of sentimentality. Bynner, in contrast, uses the adverbs of degree "so long" (she lingered there so long) that betrays his compassion for the lady lonely in futile waiting and the interrogative that directly expresses his concern (why is she still waiting,/Watching through its crystal pane the glow of the autumn moon?) Pound is concerned about the precise image while Bynner cares about the sentiment. Where Pound puts as "The jeweled steps are already quite white with dew" to form the vivid image of the white steps sparkling in the moonlight with late-night dew, Bynner depicts the coldness of the staircase which conveys his sympathy (Her jade-white staircase is cold with dew). Where Pound states simply as "it is late" for the indication of the time, Bynner emphasizes his sympathy for the abandoned lady by the statement of "she lingered there so long...", what is unstated implying his concern for the miserable fate of the protagonist. From the comparison, Pound's intention for detachment is evident in his translation.

Also, the absence of comment creates empty space for the readers to interpret the possible relationships and expand and reinforce the aesthetic experience by working on readers' imagination. The example is also from Pound's translation *The Jewel Stairs Grievance*. Apart from his translation of the original verse, Pound also adds a short note of what he interprets from the poem: "Note: Jewel stairs, therefore a palace. /Grievance, therefore there is something to complain of. /Gauze stockings, therefore a court lady, not a servant who complains. /Clear autumn, therefore he has no excuse on account of weather, also she has come early, for the dew has not merely whitened the stairs, but has soaked her stockings." The original poem is the accumulation of objective images of the "white" "jeweled steps" "gauze stockings", "crystal curtain", "clear autumn" without an obvious tint of the lady's mood. Yet the scene, as the readers will feel, is an interpretive vehicle for the situation the note describes. The mood of the court lady is embedded deep in the objective scene and it feels real in the readers as the "inward and subjective" is well "set beneath" the "outward and objective" even without direct statement.

Another example comes from Pound's translation of a poem in *Book of Songs*:

The original text: 击鼓其镗，踊跃用兵。土国城漕，我独南行。
从孙子仲，平陈与宋。不我以归，忧心有忡。
爰居爰处？爰丧其马？于以求之？于林之下。
死生契阔，与子成说。执子之手，与子偕老。
于嗟阔兮，不我活兮。于嗟洵兮，不我信兮。
（《诗经·击鼓》）

Ezra Pound: Bang, the drum. We jump and drill,
home folks are working on Ts'ao Wall still
or hauling farm loads in Ts'ao
but we're on the roads, south, on the roads.

Under Tsy Chung.
Sung and Ch'en come.
We've rolled 'em flat but
We'll never get home.

To stay together till death and end
for far, for near, hand, oath, accord:

Never alive
will we keep that word. (Pound, 2003:769)

The poem conveys the sorrow of a soldier to be on the battlefield for too long to fulfill his promise to his newly-wed wife. The beating of the drum at the beginning brings the reader immediately to the battlefield. Pound, instead of depicting the action, starts his poem with a powerful onomatopoeia "bang", which captures the attention to the beginning of a war. The original poem, after the narration of the long war in the first two stanzas, shifts to the description of the subjective consciousness. Pound cut the whole third stanza of the subjective comment after the statement of being unable to go home. The poet then thought of the marriage oath of not parting until death and could not control his sorrow. Pound, in his translation, juxtapose three nouns "hand", "oath", "accord" without any connectives, which creates visuality like shots in montage flashing before the poet and the reader, which inspires strong emotions yet without any direct comment. In the last stanza, the poet could not help his sorrowful sighing when he shifts his thoughts to the cruel reality, where the long departure makes the reunion too far to reach and the promise unfulfillable. Pound, in his translation shortens all the emotional expressions in four lines into a simple inverted line "Never alive will we keep that word". In the translation, Pound presents only the hard facts in hard language yet inspires as overwhelming the grief as the original.

Secondly, liberation of space between the tenor and the vehicle is another effective means for the interpretation of taciturn emotions. The open space allows the readers to view from different angles so as to attain various shades of aesthetic experience. Unlike the thorough statement of feelings or even overflowing of sentimentalism in Victorian poetry, Pound's poetics stresses the vacant space for aesthetic admiration. Chinese poetry, concise and compact, is a prominent carrier of taciturn emotions. "Brevity is indeed the soul of a Chinese poem" (Xie, 1999:9) and what is valued is more what it suggests than what it actually says. In the the four-line epigram, what is unsaid is sometimes more than what has been said. With the abruptness of sense groups, it carries the sense much farther and when it stops, the sense lingers because what is suggested leads the readers to carry on their train of thought. "it is only the words which stop, the sense goes on" (Xie, 1999:9) The liberation of space in Chinese poetry allows multiple interpretations through the placement of an object in relation to another and the transformation of a fact to an idea, from the concrete to the abstract so that a much intense experience is created with the active participation and empathy from the readers. The free-floating activity in its flexible syntactic structures enables objects and events to "maintain their multiple spatial and temporal extensions", and enables the readers to move back and forth in the poetic experience by "providing a gap between objects, events, or frames of meaning, an emptiness, a subversive space". (Yip, 2008:162) The liberation of space enables the middle-ground stance of the readers to interpret the various possible shades so as to expand the aesthetic experience. With the liberation of space, the readers, neither in the foreground nor the background, remain in "the middle ground between engaging and disengaging" (Yip, 2008: 165) and can move freely and "approach them from various vantage points to achieve different shades of the same aesthetic moment". (Yip, 2008: 165) The readers are the witness of objects and events in their natural acting-out, and at the same time, they are the participants in the powerful emotions aroused at the scene. The building of possible relationships among the images inspires the readers' imagination and enriches their poetic experiences. The relationship is not established through the explicit connectors that mark the tenor and the vehicle, the objective and the subjective. Yip notices the unique mode of representation in the poetics of the Chinese which is possible by the peculiarity of the Chinese language. He categorizes the major relationships of units in a line of Chinese verse:"国破山河在,城春草木深", saying that the line is composed of two units in a paratactic relation that inspires the imagination to compare and contrast and elicits the unique poetic experience... "the two phases of perception, like two cones of light, cut into one another simultaneously. Any attempt to reconnect them even syntactically will destroy the simultaneity and fall back on the logic of succession". (Yip, 1969:18) Pound applies the feature into his translations. He does not link the tenor and the vehicle with obvious marks of connection. Instead, he resorts to colon and semi-colon to create empty space between the tenor and the vehicle. For example, in his famous poem *In a Station of the Metro*: "The apparition of these faces in the crowd:/Petals on a wet, black bough", the tenor, the image of faces of the crowd in the metro station and the vehicle, "petals on a wet, black bough" is connected with a colon, rather than the explicit marker of "like". It is a striking example of permanent metaphor, originally separated into five sense groups to indicate the five phases of perception, presented in linguistic incontinuity with its verbless juxtaposition of two noun phrases. The grammatical incompleteness is for the presentation of momentary qualities of perception. The simple juxtaposition of the images forms the chord between the two images and builds the equation for the intellectual and emotional experience. From then on, Pound even develops a style of his own in which each of the poems ends with a line of noun phrases syntactically detached from what has gone before, yet relates to it by the punctuation marks colon or semi-colon. In this way, Pound capitalizes on the suggestive power of image juxtaposition to evoke the intended emotion and create the ethereal poetic experience. The union of two separate images forms a chord between the two or more objective images to suggest the subjective. The coexistence of images in spatial relationships forges an atmosphere that will move and evoke the readers. The absence of the connector to indicate the relationship between images enables the readers to see them simultaneously and though syntactically uncommitted, the resemblance is easily interpreted and the ambiguity expands the possible relationships. The simultaneous presence of two objects, like the juxtaposition of two separate shots, resembles (in Eisenstein's words) "not so much a simple sum of one shot plus another shot — as it does a creation. It resembles a creation — rather than a sum of its parts — from the circumstance that in every such juxtaposition the result is qualitatively distinguishable from each component element viewed separately". (Yip, 1997: 15) In Pound's translations, there is the liberation of space embodied in the paratactic structure such as "The phoenix are gone, the river flows on alone" or even the more innovative one in the poem *Lament of the Frontier Guard*: "Desolate castle, the sky, the wide desert." and in the poem *South-fold in Cold Country*: "Surprised. Desert turmoil. Sea sun." Later in his *Cantos*, Pound even uses the technique as the central one as follows.

Rain; empty river, a voyage
...
Autumn moon; hills rise above lakes
...
Broad water; geese line out with the autumn (*Cantos*, XLIX/38)

Prayer; hands uplifted
Solitude: a person, a Nurse (*Cantos*, LIV/101)

Moon, cloud, tower, a patch of the batteistero
all of whiteness (*Cantos*, LXXIX/62)

The following is an example of Pound's translation of Li Bai's poem *The City of Choan* for the interpretation from the readers as the key role of the poetic sense.

The original text: 凤凰台上凤凰游，凤去台空江自流。

吴宫花草埋幽径，晋代衣冠成古丘。
三山半落青天外，一水中分白鹭洲。
总为浮云能蔽日，长安不见使人愁。

Ezra Pound: The phoenix are at play on their terrace.
The phoenix are gone, the river flows on alone.
Flowers and grass
Cover over the dark path
where lay the dynastic house of the Go.
The bright cloths and bright caps of Shin
Are now the base of old hills.

The Three Mountains fall through the far heaven,
The isle of White Heron
splits the two streams apart.
Now the high clouds cover the sun
And I can not see Choan afar
And I am sad.

Xu Yuanchong: On Phoenix Terrace once phoenixes came to sing;
The birds are gone but still roll on the river's waves.
The ruined palace's buried under weeds in spring;
The ancient sages in caps and gowns all lie in graves.
The three-peaked mountain is half lost in azure sky;
The two-forked stream by Egret Isle is kept apart.
As floating clouds can veil the bright sun from the eye,
Imperial Court now out of view saddens my heart.

Li Bai is a renowned poet in China and this poem is one of his masterpieces. He was degraded from the court because of the conspiracy of some corrupt officials and he departed from the capital Chang'an (Choan in Pound's version). The first two lines see the repetition of "phoenix" thrice to give the light rhythm to the poem. Phoenix is a symbol of prosperity in China, the advent of which prophesizes the rise of the dynasty and therefore the disappearance of it in the poem symbolizes the vanishing of the prosperity of the previous dynasties. What is left is the ceaseless running of the Changjiang River, which in comparison is the only eternity in the universe. The readers will interpret from the changing images of the phoenix terrace the decline of dynasties, the disappearance of prosperity, the only eternity in the natural world. The third and fourth lines are the further development of the lament on the vicissitudes of the world, of the history. The country of Wu in Three Empire Period (220AD-280AD) and the following East Jin both established their capitals in this city. The poet described how the magnificent palaces in Wu had gone barren and the high-rank official in the East Jin Dynasty had been buried in the graves. The desolate tombs of the great aroused the readers' sighing on the vanity of all the competitions and factions of mankind. The fifth and sixth lines divert the readers' attention from the mourning on the vanity in history to the ceaseless vigor of the natural world, from the history to the reality. The mountain is indistinct in the distance, half hidden and half visible while the river is divided into two by the island in the middle. The two lines depict the splendor of the natural world in perfect symmetry, which contains a force eternal and infinite in stark contrast to the frequent rise and fall of empires and of man's destiny. The last two lines is the poet's sighing on his own fate and melancholy mood in deposition. The sun being covered by floating clouds serves as a metaphor of the darkness of injustice in court because of the schemes of evil forces in court. The poet's distress is not directly stated but well conveyed through the metaphor and arouses the readers' sympathy and compassion. Pound, in his translation, makes efforts to restore the suggested taciturn emotion of the original, permanent metaphor in Pound's term. The cutting of the third line and the fourth line into halves is an indication of such efforts: "Flowers and grass/cover over the dark path where lay the dynastic house of the Go. /The bright cloths and bright caps of Shin/Are now the base of old hills." In this version, the reality and the history, the desolation and the prosperity are separated in clear-cut lines, exerting strong visual impact with images in sharp contrast, the brightness of flowers and grass and the darkness of path at present and the brightness of palace in the past, the brightness of cloths and caps in the past and the darkness of old hills at present. What's more, Pound's separation of poetic lines in the last line is another effort to stress the metaphoric image to instill emotions in the readers. Where Xu connects the metaphor and the tenet with a vague connective "as" (As floating clouds can veil the bright sun from the eye,/Imperial Court now out of view saddens my heart.), Pound uses two repetitive connective "and" to link the objective image of clouds covering the sun to the reality of the invisibility of the capital in the far distance and then to the mood of the poet (Now the high clouds cover the sun/And I can not see Choan afar/And I am sad.). The paratactic structures adopted by Pound effectively render the readers' linking of the objective and the subjective, which also reflects his belief in the power of permanent metaphor.

2.3 Ideogrammic Method — Sculptural Beauty in Language

2.3.1 Origin of Ideogrammic Poetry

The ideogrammic principle, first advanced by the scholar of Chinese and Japanese language Ernest Francisco Fenollosa, refers to the image as the external object, which, through the mediation of the image, acts upon the human mind. Pound's idea of ideogram and ideogrammic poetry could be traced back to about 1916, after he had acquired the Fenollosa manuscripts. The ideogrammic method also stemmed from Bugson's and Hulme's philosophical perspective towards language and the whole notion of the ideogram took shape with Pound's experimentation with Vorticist principles in poetry. It is, in Pound's words, out of the awareness of "the word of literary art which presents, defines, suggests the visual image; the word which must rise afresh in each work of art and come down with renewed light", (Pound, 1971: 321) which, with the clusters of concrete materials, give the powerful precision through their implied relations.

Ernest Fenollosa was an American professor of philosophy at Tokyo Imperial University, an important educator during the modernization of the Meiji Era and an enthusiastic orientalist who did much to preserve traditional Japanese art. His book *The Chinese Written Character as a Medium for Poetry* impressed Pound, who published it with approving footnotes. Fenollosa argued that as the ideograms were pictures of thing, the Chinese script was by its very nature more concrete and poetic than alphabetic writing: reading the character for sunset, the Chinese actually saw the descending sun tangled in a tree's branches. Pound learned from Fenollosa's essay about the pictorial nature of Chinese language, believing Fenollosa's word that Chinese ideograms were "based upon a vivid shorthand picture of the operations of nature", (Pratt, 2007: 124) that Chinese was closer than English to things in that it was pictographic, made up of visual images rather than phonetic transcriptions of sounds. Chinese ideogramic characters presented a capability to demonstrate the objects directly and a possibility to blend different parts to achieve a new effect, such as spring(春) being the sun hiding behind the growing tree and man(男) being the combination of the images of fields and strength. The Chinese characters presented different images without resorting to their logical relationship, the effect of new sense stemming only from the juxtaposition of images. Pound believed in Fenollosa's view of the ideogram, the role of latent visual etymology in the Chinese script.

Fenollosa helped crystallize certain ideas in Pound's propaganda for modern poetry.

Montage is also a contributor to Pound's idea of ideogrammic method. As a landmark in the development of cinematic theories, montage was explored by Sergei Eisenstein with the evolution of the film from one long take to the assembly of different lenses. Eisenstein developed "The Film Sense" with fast editing and juxtaposition, that is, showing two irrelevant objects or images through their combination yet through it creating a new meaning. Eisenstein's montage theories are based on the belief that montage will inspire through the "collision" between different shots in an illustration of the idea of thesis and antithesis, the discontinuity in graphic qualities and temporal senses. As to the effect of montage, Eisenstein's view is most widely accepted that "montage is an idea that arises from the collision of independent shots" wherein "each sequential element is perceived not *next* to the other, but on *top* of the other" (http://en.wikipedia.org/wiki/Soviet_montage_theory). For example, in tonal montage, a sleeping baby would convey calmness and relaxation. The images could synthesize the effect on the audience for an even more abstract and complicated effect. In Eisenstein's film *Strike*, a shot of striking workers being attacked cut with a shot of a bull being slaughtered created a film metaphor carrying the suggestion that the workers were being treated like cattle, a suggestion that did not exist in individual shots but would arise in juxtaposition. Influenced by the montage theory, Pound came to the belief that from the juxtaposition of concrete images, just as of shots in a film, poetry would achieve the similar effect of newly-created sense or emotion much more profound yet abstract. The Pound scholar Zhu Chaowei detected the similarities between Montage Method and Pound's Imagism. (祝朝伟, 2005:172) Montage had the function of selection, rejection, assembly and generalization, of gripping the attention of the audience and inspiring their associations, of creating an unique spatial and temporal cinematic realm, of forming different rhythms and of organizing and synthesizing different elements. Similarly, imagism had the function of selection and rejection. The juxtaposition of images would form new platforms of presentation, thus drawing the attention and stimulating the imagination. It would also achieve the synchronicity of images, thus creating a new time and space in poetry.

Also, the ideogrammic method bears relation with the development of Vorticism. In the years from 1910 to 1914, in line with the social changes of the times, there emerged in Britain radically new ideas and practices in the visual arts. Pound first used the word "vortex" on 19 December 1913 in a letter to the poet friend William Carlos Williams. The idea of the vortex and its use as a label for the artistic movement were first explicitly discussed in a definite meaning in the original issue of the journal *Blast*. By 1914 Vorticism reached its climax and became a recognized movement of modernism in the early decades of the 20th century. Just as the philosopher Bergson advanced the theory that time was a dynamic, continuous process in which things would develop and create through impulse and would move and change ceaselessly in the dynamic world, the Vorticists defined the nature of their trend as dynamism, aggression and energy. The Vorticists sought the center of the hurricane, the quiet eye of the storm, from which point they could concentrate on the chaos raging around them, and control it. They focused all their energies in this point: "At the heart of the whirlpool is a great silent place where all the energy is concentrated. And there, at the point of concentration, is the Vorticist. The vortex is the point of maximum energy". (Edwards, 2000:17) To follow the idea, the Vorticists were in sharp opposition to sentimentalism and romanticism. When the age of the modern world was defined by the industrial process where machines, railways, steamships take the central stage, the Vorticists took it as the main subject with the cold sharp form like that of machines. The Vorticists favored the idea of purity and clarity of thought, hardness and power of language or form. The detachment of the artists from reality represented the chief characteristic of the modern world: dehumanization. Hulme noted that in his essay: "There is... a desire among modern artists to avoid those lines and surfaces which look pleasing and organic, and to use lines which are clean, clear-cut and mechanical. You will find artists expressing admiration for engineer's drawings, where the lines are clean, the curves all geometrical, and the colour, laid on to show the shape of a cylinder for example, gradated absolutely mechanically". (Edwards, 2000:20) Pound's tenets to create poetry austere, direct, free from emotional slither were the reflection of the trend. His principles for Imagism included the direct treatment of the poetic subject, the rejection of the superfluous words and the adoption of a natural musical rhythm. The clear-cut form was to project the image that evokes the emotion, which, to Pound, was interchangeable with energy. "The image is more than an idea. It is a vortex or cluster of fused ideas and is endowed within energy". (Pound, 1973:344) The vortex, then, is to him, the point of maximum energy captured at the moment instead of being the mere external pictorialization. The Vorticist art was defined as being not existent in time but was held in space. There was, in the Vorticist works, the assemblage of separate elements to convey the intense energy of emotion. The loosening ties between elements and the juxtaposition of contingent material was also manifest in Pound's major poem *The Cantos* as an effort to capture the constant dynamics of the universe in the various phenomena of nature, and various cultures and historical fragments.

2.3.2 Ideogram as Reflection of Nature

Nature has long been the prominent poetic theme. Emerson asserts that "Nature offers all her creatures to him as a picture-language" in *The Poet* (Xie, 1999:26) and then proposes three important doctrines to form a "natural and thus spiritual language" : "1. Words are signs of natural facts. 2. Particular natural facts are symbols of particular spiritual facts. 3. Nature is the symbol of spirit". (Xie, 1999: 26) Nature, in the eyes of poets, becomes the concrete equivalent of spiritual enlightenment and therefore forms the major source and "the powerful reservoir of energy in poetry". (Xie, 1999:27) Fenollosa, whose views on concrete language have great influence on Pound, insists on Nature as the roots of language that transfers energy and force. Language is not the abstract product of human mind, but the reflection of the natural world and it is only through the discovery of nature that language is able to convey significant sense and powerful energy. Fenollosa attaches importance to the concreteness in language in accordance with natural processes and structures: "In a poet's hands, this is not simply an imaginary structuring of nature by an arbitrary language but a rediscovery of nature through the natural roots still buried in language. Language can structure the world as well as it does because the world once structured language". (Xie, 1999: 27) Therefore, the rediscovery of nature is indispensable for the vigor of language, which Pound adopts as one of the components of his ideogrammic method.

Firstly, nature is tangible concreteness instead of abstract concept. Chinese characters, in the form of ideograms, are the epitomes of natural concreteness. Fenollosa summarizes three characteristics of the Chinese character. The first is its pictorialness: "Chinese notations are something much more than arbitrary symbols" "based upon a vivid shorthand picture of the operations of nature." He cites an example of 人见马 and concludes that in Chinese, "the group of words holds something of the quality of a continuous moving picture" and "Chinese writing was bound not to linguistic rules but to natural ones". (Park, 2008:34) The second characteristic of the Chinese character lies in its metaphoricity. The formation of the Chinese character is the reflection of the signification from the concrete "thing" to the abstract "thingness", that is, "the use of material images to suggest immaterial relations." The third characteristic is the etymological stability of Chinese characters. The constant visibility of the etymology of Chinese characters defies many of the semantic changes in the course of history. All meanings it has acquired, as Fenollosa notes, "centre about the graphic symbol". (Lan, 2005: 30) In *ABC of Reading*, Pound applies Fenollosa's insight to his philosophy of ideogrammic composition. In the eyes of Pound, European language is apt to be abstract by systematizing and classifying things into various sets of linguistic codes while Chinese language, rooted in the laws of nature, tends to reveal natural principles of things even in the making of an abstract concept. One example Pound offers is a Chinese definition of red by juxtaposing "Rose/Cherry/Iron dust/Flamingo." For Pound, the abstract definition is prosaic, whereas the concrete representation is poetic. (Pound, 1960:18-22) Chinese poetry is a reflection of ideogrammic nature of Chinese language. Pound perceives the prominent feature when he classifies the Chinese poetry into phanopoeia, that is, "a casting of images upon the visual imagination". (Pound, 1968:25) He says: "Chinese attained the known maxim of Phanopoeia, due perhaps to the nature of their written ideograph". (Pound, 1968:26) In Chinese poetry, the emotion is presented through the demonstration of details in nature, which is in stark contrast with the abstraction in western conceptualization: "the Western concept of being... turns us away from the appeal of the concreteness of objects and events in Phenomenon rather than bringing us into immediate contact with them". (Yip, 1997:6) In Pound's view, phanopoeia can be translated almost entirely without loss or distortion. (Pound, 1968:25) In his translation, his stress of concreteness of language is seen in the faithful revival of the original natural images. For example, in *The River-Merchant's Wife: A Letter*, the wife's sorrow of being left alone is reflected in her sight of the paired butterflies in the garden: "The paired butterflies are already yellow with August/Over the grass in the West garden;" In *The City of Choan*, the poet's sad reflection of the vicissitudes of life is reflected in the change of scenes in history: "Flowers and grass/Cover over the dark path/where lay the dynastic house of the Go. /The bright cloths and bright caps of Shin/Are now the base of old hills." In *Leave-taking near Shoku*, the predetermination of man's rise and fall in destiny is shown in the wax and wane of the natural beings and Pound expresses the hope for the force of life to find its own way out through his additional images of bursting tree trigs and freshets: "Sweet trees are on the paved way of the Shin, /Their trunks burst through the paving, /And freshets are bursting their ice/in the midst of Shoku, a proud city."

Secondly, in the ideogrammic method, nature is seen as dynamic rather than static. The actions constitute natural processes that contribute to the dynamism of the universe. Fenollosa discerns in his essay the prominence of dynamism in Chinese in that Chinese commands an enormous number of verbs and at the same time, the nouns, from its etymogological components, display the verbal processes. He says: "A true noun, an isolated thing, does not exist in nature. Things are only the terminal points, or rather the meeting points, of actions, cross-sections cut through actions, snap-shots. Neither can a pure verb, an abstract motion, be possible in nature. The eye sees noun and verb as one: things in motion, motion in things, and so the Chinese conception tends to represent them". (Fenollosa, 1936:14) And Fenollosa believes that the "verbal poetry" is a remarkable advantage of Chinese poetry: "One superiority of verbal poetry as an art rests in its getting back to the fundamental reality of time. Chinese poetry... speaks at once with the vividness of painting, and with the mobility of sounds". (Fenollosa, 1936: 13) Pound, under the influence of Fenollosa with regard to Chinese language, advocates the demonstration of nature as a dynamic process, with the simultaneous display of phenomena to reveal the successive operations of nature. The belief in the possible mobile force in the nouns, in nature itself reinforces Pound's poetics of imagism, with the plain display of natural images, and the simple combination of them to revive the dynamic process in nature. Take an example from Pound's translation of a departure poem by Li Bai along with other versions:

The original text: 孤帆远影碧空尽
Pound: His lone sail blots the far sky
Witter Bynner: Your sail, a single shadow, becomes one with the blue sky,
Hope: That shadow there is his lonely sail.
Now there's nothing left of it.
All the blue is empty now.
Xu Yuanchong: His lessening sail is lost in the boundless blue sky,
Sun Dayu: A solitary sail's distant speck
Vanisheth in the clear blue:
Qiu Xiaolong: Against a single sail
fading into the blue, distant skies...
Tang Yihe: The distant figure of a solitary sail
Gradually vanished on the edge of blue sky.
Wang Shouyi: how far away the lone sail

fading into the clear blue sky

In Pound's version, three static shots are juxtaposed to create the dynamic process of the friend's departure: a lone sail, a distant shadow and the far sky. The last character in Chinese is a dynamic word in the static picture to depict the disappearance of the sailboat from the sight. It is a gradual process unfolded in three independent shots, the farther and farther away of the boat until it merges into the blue sky in the far distance. The three pictures are isolated yet continuous, all the dynamism reflected in the stationary depiction. A look at the verbs various translators employ is an evident proof to their translational principles or motives. Where the other translators uses verbs as "fade" (Qiu and Wang), "vanish" (Sun and Tang), "becomes one" (Bynner) to indicate the dynamic motion of the sailboat, Pound creates a static picture with his original verb "blot" which well depicts the distance the boat goes with all its conciseness. It is a far cry from the sentimental subjective expression such as "Now there's nothing left of it. /All the blue is empty now" by Hope. Xu, in his translation of "His lessening sail is lost in the boundless blue sky" also uses the dynamic participle "lessening" to depict the gradual process. Pound's translation, "His lone sail blots the far sky", is a motionless picture yet well-expressive of all the motion the sailboat has undertaken. It is an image that inspires the emotions and the ideas in an instant. In the evaluation of Pound's poetic achievements, Michael Alexander mentions this particular treatment and points out the motivation behind it: "He stresses the moving and leaping faculty of the language. The breaking up of the line into smaller units and their graphic arrangement... must be understood, not only as musical bars but as separate gestures of an actor in a play emphasized by the spotlight". (Alexander, 1979: 100)

Thirdly, in the ideogrammic method, nature is conceived of as an organic whole that involves the harmony of man and nature into one. Man is not the dominant force in the universe but an indispensable part of it interwoven with other beings in nature and nature itself is a substantial reflector of human emotions. "Underlying the classical Chinese aesthetic is the primary idea of noninterference with Nature's flow". (Yip, 1997: preface) Romantist poetry, by contrast, features the subjectivity where the ego governs and unifies poetic experience. Many lyric poems are private emotional responses spoken from the heart by a first-person narrator where the poet reveals feelings about himself, his true state of mind. The translation of Chinese poetry into English not only requires the transference of language itself, but, more importantly, the conversion from one aesthetic value to the other. Pound, in his translation, often treats images of natural beings and of human beings as an integral whole, interwoven to represent each other. Take an example from Pound's translation of *Book of Songs*:

The original text: 鹑之奔奔，鹊之彊彊。人之无良，我以为兄！
鹊之彊彊，鹑之奔奔。人之无良，我以为君！（《诗经·鹑之奔奔》）

Ezra Pound: Quails and pies
show enmities,
but a man with no savoury quality
is my own brother apparently.

Pies and quails
tear each other's entrails
and there's a fair lady would do no less:
Let me present out Marchioness. (Pound, 2003:778)

In Chinese *Book of Songs*, there is the tradition of starting the poetry with natural scenes which then lead to the expression of emotions or of intellect. The integration of the natural and the intellectual is sometimes vague and detached but presents the beauty of poetic sense. Pound, in his belief that the natural world is the full expression of the universal law, will reinforce the relationship between the objective image and the subjective emotions on such occasions. In this poetry, the flocking of quails and pies leads to the contrastive persecution of relatives in the human world. Pound, in the perception of the weak linkage, reinforces the force of the natural image by creating the images of hostility between quails and pies: they "tear each other's entrails". Pound's translation is more like adaptation, yet it reflects his purpose of discovering natural force.

2.3.3 Ideogram in Pictorial Etymology

The ideogammic method concerns the rediscovered semantic connotations of the words through pictorial etymology and of the poetic aesthetics through assemblages of images. In Fenollosa's *The Chinese Character as a Medium for Poetry*, which Pound approves with a footnote and promotes to be published, Fenollosa contends that "(Chinese notation) is based upon a vivid shorthand picture of the operations of nature". (Fenollosa, 1936:12) Thus, the Chinese ideogram, according to Fenollosa and Pound, is not only the carrier of sound and sense, but "the picture of a thing." Enlightened by the essay, Pound is impressed by the visuality of Chinese poetry, which he tries to revive through the ideogrammic method. The disconnected juxtaposition of characters in Chinese language enables the reader to infer the relations in between and characters, with their pictorial nature, present images united only through the readers' interpretations. Pound, in his translation, devotes himself to restore such visual quality and the semantic complexity to be conveyed regardless of the superficial simplicity. In his essay *How To Read*, Pound categorizes poetry into three kinds, including "Melopoeia", poetry with prominent musical property, "Phanopoeia", poetry stressing the building of images, and "Logopoeia", "the dance of the intellect among words". (Pound, 1968:25) Pound notes the pictorial quality in Chinese language that may put it into Phanopoeia and believes in the translatability of Phanopoeia:"Phanopoeia can, on the other hand, be translated almost, or wholly, intact. When it is good enough, it is practically impossible for the translator to destroy it save by very crass bungling, and the neglect of perfectly well-known and formulative rules". (Xie, 1999:20) In his translation of Chinese poetry, Pound frequently ignores the phonetic aspect of Chinese characters but emphasizes their primitive pictorial element, although the common knowledge of Chinese language is that combinations of Chinese ideographs frequently contribute only a phonetic value. The ideogramic method is embodied in Pound's simple assemblages of images in *Cathay* and *The Cantos* and then in the disintegration of pictorial etymology in the translations of Confucian works, in which he started making new poetic images by analyzing the components of some of the Chinese characters.

As to the ideogrammic method, Pound posits two major techniques:"super-positioning to create Images (by joining 'ideas' in interpretive symbolic relation); and super-repositioning to create ideograms that are not Images (by joining 'ideas'— referred to in the context of the ideogram as 'particulars'— in non-symbolic relations"). (Lewis, 2007:106) The super-positioning "convey the ideas they convey" and "keeps the ideas separate and distinct" in the form of interpretive metaphor and the super-repositioning "conveys the unspeakable and unpresentable" through the simple connection of things without symbolic implication. (Lewis, 2007:25)

The super-positioning method is first mentioned by Pound in the examination of a Japanese hokku:"The footsteps of the cat upon the snow:/(are like) plum-blossoms." Pound comments that "The 'one image poem' is a form of super-position, that is to say, it is one idea set on top of another". (Yip, 1969:23) This simultaneous presence of two objects resembling each other is to reveal complex human emotions, the conscious experience of artistic beauty by suggestive images. In his translation, Pound tends to employ the suggestive power to imply the relationship of the objective and the subjective instead of direct comment or the sentimental exclamation.

The super-repositioning technique is the presentation of fragmented details. It is represented in the parallel lines in Chinese poetry:"枯藤老树昏鸦,古道西风瘦马"(withered vine, old tree, dusk raven; ancient road, west wind, lean horse) with images coexisting pictorially rather than semantically, or "星垂平野阔,月涌大江流"(Stars dangle: flat plain broadens. /Moon surges: big river flows.), or the parallel lines "国破山河在,城春草木深"(Empire is broken: mountains and rivers remain. Spring in city: grass and trees grow thick.) The relations between detailed images might be cause and effect, concussion or contrast or any other possible ones, yet the linkless connection enables the two perception phases to present themselves simultaneously like two cones of light on the stage, with multiple interpretations and inspirations in the audience. Pound the translator is devoted to preserving the original paratactic structure and the independence of two coexisting visual events makes it possible for one to "interdefine" the other. (Yip, 1997:20) Thus, in the translation, Pound applies the ideogrammic method, using "broken phrases, fragmentary quotations, and sentences left in suspense". (Makin, 2006:71)

Parallelism of construction abound in Pound's translation of Chinese poetry as one of the Imagist poets John Could Fletcher claimed: "What had happened was that I had somehow, as a poet, guessed at the way the Orientals had constructed their poems. The parallelism of construction, casting back and forth from the observer to thing observed, is surely manifest: and the self-same quality is omnipresent in Ezra Pound's *Cathay*". (Xie, 1999: 7) Take the example in Pound's translation for Chinese poetic line "凤去台空江自流". When three separate shots are involved in a simple line of poem (phoenix gone (shot 1), terrace empty(shot 2), river flows on alone(shot 3)), it is a typical example of super-repositioning, with the solitary melancholy and vanity against the vicissitudes of life tapped by the simple collage of three shots of natural things.

Ezra Pound: The phoenix are gone, the river flows on alone.

Xu Yuanchong: The birds are gone but still roll on the river's waves.

Sun Dayu: They flew off, leaving the empty terrace to overlook
The well-nigh boundless River flowing by itself away.

Tang Yihe: When phoenixes had flown away, the Yangtze River
flew as usual, but became empty the terrace.

Where other translators tend to add transitional elements between the different visual events, Pound leaves them as they are without any connectors to revive its original effect of open interpretations. The similar approach could be seen in Pound's translation for "木落秋草黄，登高望戎虏": "Trees fall, the grass goes yellow with autumn. /I climb the towers and towers/to watch out the barbarous land". There is mistranslation in the line when the original refers to the falling of leaves and Pound put it as the falling of trees. Yet what is prominent is still the absence of connectors between the various activities of the plants and between them and those of humans. Also, in the translation of the two lines in Lu Zhaolin's depiction of the prosperity of royal life, details are displayed in an array to indicate the luxurious life of the court officers, which Pound, though making out of them complete sentences, create unconventional mode of expressions as "Dark oxen, white horses,/drag on the seven coaches with outriders" and "Night birds, and night women,/Spread out their sounds through the gardens". Pound's intention, explicit as it is, is the demonstration of phenomena in coexistence to give prominence and independence to the images themselves.

Pound goes even further in *The Cantos*, where he presents the ideogrammic method as "the best approach to a definition to the ideogrammic method" (Makin, 2006: 66) *Canto* XLIX: *For the Seven Lakes* is Pound's translation of Chinese poetry on Chinese paintings:

For the seven lakes, and by no man these verses:
Rain; empty river; a voyage,
Fire from frozen cloud, heavy rain in the twilight
Under the cabin roof was one lantern.
The reeds are heavy; bent;
And the bamboos speak as if weeping.

Autumn moon; hills rise about lakes
Against sunset
Evening is like a curtain of cloud,
A blurr above ripples; and through it
Sharp long spikes of the cinnamon,
A cold tune amid reeds.
Behind hill the monk's bell
Borne on the wind.
Sail passed here in April; may return in October

Boat fades in silver; slowly;
Sun blaze alone on the river.

Where wine flag catches the sunset
Sparse chimneys smoke in the cross light

Comes then snow scur on the river
And a world is covered with jade
Small boat floats like a lanthorn,
The flowing water closts as with cold. And at San Yin
They are a people of leisure.

Wild geese swoop to the sandbar,
Clouds gather about the hole of the window
Broad water; geese line out with the autumn
Rooks clatter over the fishermen's lanthorns,

A light moves on the north sky;
Where the young boys prod stones for shrimp.
In seventeen hundred came Tsing to these hill lakes.
A light moves on the South sky line.

State by creating rishes shd. thereby get into debt?
This is infamy; this is Geryon.
This canal goes still to TenShi
Though the old king built it for pleasure

KEI MEN RAN KEI
KIU MAN MAN KEI
JITSU GETSU KO KWA
TAN FUKU TAN KEI

Sun up; work
Sundown; to rest
Dig well and drink of the water
Dig field; eat of the grain
Imperial power is? And to us what is it?

The fourth; the dimension of stillness.
And the power over wild beasts.

(*Canto* XLIX: *For the Seven Lakes*)

In *Canto* XLIX, juxtapositions of noun phrases are remarkably common, which are connected only through semicolons or commas. Without the conventional connectors of prepositions and connectives, they are like etymons of Chinese characters, which, through combination without explanation, present complex meaning upon readers' mind with flexible possibilities of their relations. For example, "Rain; empty river; a voyage" is a conventionally ungrammatical construction, which normally should go as "With rain over empty river, (I'm) on a voyage", "Sun up; work/Sundown; to rest" as "when sun is up, (I) work and when sun is down, (I) rest", "The reeds are heavy; bent;" as "as the reeds are heavy, they bent", "Dig field; eat of the grain" as "after (I) dig field, (I) can eat the grain." Pound's a-syntactic structure is a subversion of the conventional syntax in English, with the fragmentary noun phrases as "Fire from frozen cloud, heavy rain in the twilight", the non-subject clause as "Dig field; eat of the grain", the unfinished clause as in "Imperial power is? And to us what is it?". The most prominent feature in such structures is the absence of connectors between fragments, leaving them in a paratactical relation, which, according to Wai-lim Yip, inspires the imagination to compare and contrast that elicits the unique poetic experience. "... the two phases of perception, like two cones of light, cut into one another simultaneously. Any attempt to reconnect them even syntactically will destroy the simultaneity and fall back on the logic of succession". (Yip, 1969: 18)

Pound even resorts to ideogrammic method in *The Cantos* with the blocks of facts without apparent logical relations displayed on the same plane. The implicit parallelism between two blocks in *The Cantos*, paradoxically, reinforces the isolation of each block and creates subtle and profound implications in the imaginative interpretation of readers just as Pound pursues, "by this parallel both become more transparent". (Makin, 2006: 71) In his essay, Pound asserts the function and the advantage of the ideogrammic method: "That being the point of the writing. That being the reason for presenting first one facet and then another — I mean to say the purpose of the writing is to reveal the subject. The ideogrammic method consists of presenting one facet and then another until at some point one gets off the dead and desensitized surface of the reader's mind, onto a part that will register". (Pound, 1973: 51) The facts are treated in *The*

Cantos as ideograms, the cluster of Odysseus, Divus, Pound, Homer, Aeneas, Virgil all being the ideograms that reveal the historical lessons and enlighten higher knowledge by their assemblage and all the proper things and cultural moments such as Napoleon, money, Mr. J. Q. Adams also being ideograms juxtaposed to present the history and to inspire the meditation. Pound, with the method, establishes an actuality aiming to educate the reader in the present world by highlighting these past states of mind in juxtaposition. Pound believes the ideograms, that is, "a phalanx of particulars", which, brought together, will cause the reader "suddenly to see or reveal the whole subject from a new angle". (Homberger, 1972:298)

2.3.4 Etymological Translation

Pound, enlightened by Fenollosa's assertion that Chinese character "is based upon a vivid shorthand picture of the operations of nature" (Fenollosa, 1936:21) with the capacity to imply the abstract "immaterial relations" through concrete etymological formation, resorts in his translations to a more analytical variation of ideogrammic method, etymological method, that is, the disintegration of Chinese characters to represent the original visual signification. Pound discerns Chinese language as "grounded in the etymological visibility of the ideogram". (Lan, 2005:31) The unique sign system in Chinese assumes its authenticity and beauty through the pictorial nature of ideograms which have become, in Pound's words, "a treasury of enduring wisdom and an arsenal of living thoughts". (Lan, 2005:31)

Thus, the ideogrammic method, in a more analytical level, should be capable of establishing a direct relationship with the source of meaning. The unique approach could be discerned in Pound's list of terminology in his translation of Confucius's *Da Xue*: "厶 One readily sees the similarity of this element to the bent heraldic arm of Armstrong and Strongi'tharm. I have never found it in composition save where there is indication of energy, I think we may say, a source of personally directed energy. 彳 The man in two successive positions. Serves as prefix to indicate motion or action. 儿 The running legs indicate rapid motion or at least the capacity for motion". (Pound, 2003:617) The detailed analysis of the visuality of each ideogram shows his fresh perspective to the pictorial nature of Chinese language, which then becomes the foundation of his Confucian translations as he thinks the translations can't express the original to the fullest "without knowing at least the nature of ideogram". (Pound, 1973: 96) Pound makes his experimental translation by relying on the visuality of

Chinese characters for an intuitive grasp of the Confucian works. He makes meticulous observation of the ideograms and explores the semantic from the components of the character. He mentions the process of his Confucian translation: "Having been three times through the whole text and having perforce to look at the ideograms and try to work out the unfamiliar ones from their bases, I should have now a better idea of the whole and the unity of the doctrine, at any rate I believe that I have, and that the constants have been impressed on my eye". (Pound, 1973:99) Pound's unique etymological approach is different from other translators' in its presentation of the integral semantic content in the analysis of how the Chinese character is formed as "For single etymons, as found in the words they help to constitute, are pretty large grab-bags: they can include a lot of senses". (Makin, 2003: 124) Pound adopts the method with the conviction that Chinese characters are composed of etymons as reflections of natural processes. He sees the Chinese character 明 as composed of "The sun and moon, the total light process, the radiation, reception and reflection of light; hence, the intelligence". (Pound, 2003:615) He sees 慎 as "The eye (at the right) looking straight into the heart". (Pound, 2003:616) He sees 信 as "The man here standing by his word". (Pound, 2003: 616) In such interpretation through disintegration, Pound believes that he has reached the semantic depths of the word and given it the most precise definition. He comments on his understanding of the Chinese character 德 as "the action resultant from this straight gaze into the heart", saying that the motivation behind the practice is that "to translate this simply as 'virtue' is on a par with translating rhinoceros, fox and giraffe indifferently by 'quadruped' or 'animal'". (Pound, 2003:616) Despite all the controversy as to whether the method brings about real faithfulness, the Pound scholar Makin believes that the adoption of such method "produces translations that are not merely beautiful and curious, but coherent, at a high level of coherence". (Makin, 2003:124)

Etymological translations abound in Pound's translation of Confucius's works and in his *Cantos* as shown in the following examples:

Example 1: 明

The original text:《康诰》曰:"克明德。"《大甲》曰:"顾諟天之明命。"《帝典》曰:"克明峻德。"皆自明也。

Ezra Pound: It is said in the *K'ang Proclamation*: He showed his intelligence by acting straight from the heart. It is said in the *Great Announcement*: He contemplated the luminous decree of heaven, and found the precise word wherewith to define it. It is said in the *Canon of the Emperor* (Yau): His intelligence shone vital over the hill-crest, he clarified the high-reaching virtue, *id est*, that action which is due to direct knowledge. All these statements proceed from the ideogram of the sun and moon standing together [that is, from the ideogram which expresses the total light process] (Pound, 2003:620)

James Legge: In the *Announcement to Kang*, it is said, "He was able to make his virtue illustrious." In the *Tai Jia* it is said, "He contemplated and studied the illustrious decrees of Heaven." In the *Canon of the Emperor Yao*, it is said, "He was able to make illustrious his lofty virtue." These passages all show how those sovereigns made themselves illustrious. (理雅各, 1992:5)

In the foreword of *Ta Hsio*: *The Great Learning*, Pound defines the character as "The sun and moon, the total light process, the radiation, reception and reflection of light; hence, the intelligence." In this chapter, for the character, Pound uses respectively "intelligence", "luminous", "his intelligence shone", "the sun and moon standing together" while Legge literally translates that into "illustrious".

Example 2: 巍

The original text: 子曰,巍巍乎,舜禹之有天下也而不与焉。

Ezra Pound: He said: lofty as the spirits of the hills and the grain mother, Shun and Yu held the empire, as if not in a mortar with it. (Pound, 2003:691)

The word "lofty" is an adequate choice for translating this Chinese character. Obviously, Pound is not contented with the mere reproduction of the idea "lofty"; he wants to restage the metaphorical process through which, he believes, this idea is engendered. Pound does so by adding the simile, "as the spirits of the hills and the grain mother". The simile depends on manipulating the four ideogrammic components of the character wei 巍 as if they themselves were autonomous ideograms with their own meanings in this instance: shan 山 (mountain), he 禾 (grain), nu 女 (female), and gui 鬼 (ghost or spirit). That is how Pound comes up with the phrase of "as the spirits of the hills and the grain mother".

Example 3: 德

The original text: 大学之道，在明明德，在亲民，在止于至善。

Ezra Pound: The great learning takes root in clarifying the way wherein the intelligence increases through the process of looking straight into one's own heart and acting on the results; it is rooted in watching with affection the way people grow; it is rooted in coming to rest, being at east in perfect equity. (Pound, 2003: 618)

James Legge: What the Great Learning teaches, is — to illustrate illustrious virtue; to renovate the people; and to rest in the highest excellence. (理雅各，1992:3)

The original text:《康诰》曰："克明德。"

Ezra Pound: It is said in the *K'ang Proclamation*: He showed his intelligence by acting straight from the heart. (Pound, 2003: 620)

James Legge: In the *Announcement to Kang*, it is said, "He was able to make his virtue illustrious" (理雅各，1992:5)

Where James Legge translates as "virtue", Pound resorts to complicated disintegration of the character as "the process of looking straight into one's own heart and acting on the results" or "acting straight from the heart". He believes the word "virtue" is too general to cover the complex character, which could only be understood by knowing the meaning of each component. There is listed another example to show the similar approach:

The original text: 古之欲明明德于天下者，先治其国。

Ezra Pound: The men of old wanting to clarify and diffuse throughout the empire that light which comes from looking straight into the heart and then acting, first set up good government in their own states; (Pound, 2003:618)

James Legge: The ancients who wished to illustrate illustrious virtue throughout the empire, first ordered well their own States. (理雅各，1992:3)

Pound intends to combine the components of two characters 明 and 德，日(sun) and 月(moon) and 目(eye) and 心(heart), hence the translation as "that light which comes from looking straight into the heart and then acting".

Example 4: 道

The original text: 物有本末，事有终始，知所先后，则近道矣。

Ezra Pound: Things have roots and branches; affairs have scopes and beginnings. To know what precedes and what follows, is nearly as good as having a head and feet. (Pound, 2003:618)

James Legge: Things have their root and their completion. Affairs have their end and their beginning. To know what is first and what is last will lead near to what is taught in the Great Learning. (理雅各,1992:3)

In his terminology, Pound defines 道 as "Footprints and the foot carrying the head; the head conducting the feet, an orderly movement under lead of the intelligence" (Pound., 2003: 617) He visualizes the character in its two components "head" (首) and "feet" (辶), hence here in the translation as "having a head and feet".

Example 5: 诚

The original text: 物格而后知至,知至而后意诚,意诚而后心正,心正而后身修。

Ezra Pound: When things had been classified in organic categories, knowledge moved toward fulfillment; given the extreme knowable points, the inarticaulate thoughts were defined with precision [the sun's lance coming to rest on the precise spot verbally]. Having attained this precise verbal definition [aliter, this sincerity], they then stabilized their hearts, they disciplined themselves; (Pound, 2003:619)

James Legge: Their knowledge being complete, their thoughts were sincere. Their thoughts being sincere, their hearts were then rectified. Their hearts being rectified, their persons were cultivated. (理雅各,1992:5)

Where Legge uses "sincere" and "sincerity" to interpret the word, Pound translates as "precise verbal definition", "extreme precision" and what should be noted that he justifies his translation with the disintegration of the Chinese character as "the sun's lance coming to rest on the precise spot verbally".

In his Terminology for *Da Xue*, Pound defines 诚 as "sincerity" yet explores further its precise definition as "the sun's lance coming to rest on the precise spot verbally". He also notices that "The right-hand half of this compound means: to perfect, bring to focus". (Pound, 2003:615) In *The Great Digest* and in *The Unwobbling Pivot*, it is a recurring Chinese which Pound translates as "precise verbal definition" which is an example of Pound's insistence on the concern with words. The Chinese tradition has always understood the character to mean sincerity that does not have to be verbal at all. But Pound's reading seems to be conceptually arbitrary in relation to Pound's other deep beliefs: "Cannot your actions, your intentions, be sincere, and cannot you know they are, without verbalizing them?" (Qian, 2003:135) As he proceeds with the translation of *The Unwobbling Pivot*, Pound carries the meaning "sincerity" along in parallel with the meaning "precise verbal definition."

Example 6: 习

The original text: 学而时习之

Ezra Pound: To study with the white wings of time passing/is not that our delight (*Canto* LXXIV)

The original first line of the Confucian *Analects* means: "Having studied something, constantly to practice it, is this not a joy?" Pound renders the sentence in a different way by dismantling the Chinese character of "study" as "study with the white wings of time passing", completely missing Confucius's emphasis on the importance of practice in learning.

Example 7: 峻

The original text:《帝典》曰:"克明峻德。"

Ezra Pound: It is said in the *Canon of the Emperor*: His intelligence shone vital over the hill-crest, he clarified the high-reaching virtue, *id est*, that action which is due to direct knowledge. (Pound, 2003:620)

James Legge: In the *Canon of the Emperor* Yao, it is said, "He was able to make illustrious his lofty virtue" (理雅各,1992:5)

For the character which Legge literally puts as "lofty", Pound comes to the visual image of the character as "shone vital over the hill-crest" with the further explanation as "high-reaching".

Example 8: 静/虑

The original text: 知止而后有定,定而后能静,静而后能安,安而后能虑,虑而后能得。

Ezra Pound: Know the point of rest and then have an orderly mode of procedure; having this orderly procedure one can "grasp the azure," that is, take hold of a clear concept; holding a clear concept one can be at peace [internally], being thus calm one can keep one's head in moments of danger; he who can keep his head in the presence of a tiger is qualified to come to his deed in due hour. (Pound, 2003:618)

James Legge: The point where to rest being unknown, the object of pursuit is then determined; and, that being determined, a calm unperturbedness may be attained. To that calmness there will succeed a tranquil repose. In that repose there may be careful deliberation, and that deliberation will be followed by the attainment of the desired end. (理雅各,1992:3)

Where Legge interprets as "a calm unperturbedness" and "calmness" for 静, Pound disintegrates it as "grasp the azure", that is, the reordering of the two components of the character, 争 as "grasp" and 青 as "azure", which, in turn, leads him to the translation as "take hold of a clear concept". The treatment of 虑 is bewildering to many readers yet still based on Pound's belief in ideogrammic feature of Chinese language. Pound sees the character as composed of two parts: tiger(虎) and heart (心), which leads to his translation of "keep his head in the presence of a tiger".

Example 9: 极

The original text: 是故君子无所不用其极。

Ezra Pound: Hence the man in whom speaks the voice of his forebears cuts no log that he does not make fit to be roof-tree [does nothing that he does not bring to a maximum, that he does not carry through to a finish]. (Pound, 2003:621)

James Legge: Therefore, the superior man in everything uses his utmost endeavours. (理雅各,1992:5)

For the Chinese character which means "extreme" or "the utmost", Legge resorts the direct translation as "utmost endeavours" while Pound, again dismantling the character, put it as "cuts no log that he does not make fit to be roof-tree", which is hard to interpret and he adds the further note for the expression in the bracket.

Pound's unique etymographic approach to Chinese characters is central in his interpretation of Confucius. It is an interpretive strategy he believes to be the most productive instrument for appropriating Confucianism, and the ideal tool to represent the origin of meaning. The translation is unconventional in its unconcern about textual fidelity. It is not aimed to convey what is signified abstractly but to revive the process of how it is signified, which to Pound is an important way to revive the original perception. In a 1941 article Pound gave a specified explanation for the approach to analyze ideograms: "The ideogram represents more than just a word; that is, it should indicate the source, and the bottom of the idea, which has only been scratched". (Lan, 2005:32) From the comment, we could note that Pound's etymographic translation, though shattering the conventional means of translation, conforms to his purpose of restoring the original perception. Critics differ in their comments on Pound's etymological translation. Some are caustic: "Pound's etymosinological translation... cannot be reconciled with the Chinese language." Some, like Terrell, defend Pound from the perspective of intent: "Pound's intent is probably to evoke the intelligence of nature in process. Neither birds nor trees think: they express themselves naturally and the right follows". (Qian, 2003:170) Pound, with the assistance of Legge's translation of Confucian works, is fully capable of interpreting the meaning of the text yet he uses a different approach of character disintegration.

2.4 Absolute Rhythm — Musical Aesthetics in Poetry

Pound, the leader of the new poetry movement, has created the Imagist Decade from 1910 to 1920 and promoted a new poetic style "whose touchstone was the short lyric poem, a brief verbal image, without end rhymes and in the looser rhythm of free verse". (Pratt, 2007: 122) Pound has touched off a revolution in the musical aesthetics in poetry, abandoning the conventional meter and rhyme as the requisites for poetry and adopting "imagery, accuracy of language, and musical rhythm" as the substitutes. (Pratt, 2007:122) Against the Victorian over-reliance on the established system of meter and rhyme which sometimes destroys the emotional coherence in poetry, Pound advances "absolute rhythm", basing the measure not on feet but on "the line itself as a unit of sense, reinforced by a parallelism of syntax, of phrasing or of sound within the lines". (Alexander, 1979:28) Usually within a long line of the verse, there are three or four heavy stresses and each highlights an unit of sense, forming the unique musical quality of poetry in line with notional precision and emotional force.

As for the requisites in absolute rhythm, music is firstly stressed by Pound as an indispensable ingredient in poetry. He defines poetry as "an art of pure sound bound in through an art of arbitrary and conventional symbols" and distinguishes poetry from prose in that beauty of poetry relies on music: "In so far as it (poetry) is an art of pure sound, it is allied with music, painting, sculpture". (Pound, 1973: 33) Music is, in Pound's perception, not the conformity with simple conventions of meter and rhyme, but the possession of musical aesthetics that will "delight the expert". (Pound, 1968:5) In his critical essay, Pound classifies the poetry into three categories, "Melopoeia, wherein the words are charged, over and above their plain meaning, with some musical property, which directs the beating or trend of that meaning", "Phanopoeia" as "a casting of images upon the visual imagination", and "Logopoeia" as "the dance of the intellect among words". (Pound, 1968: 26) Melopoeia is the poetry of music, in which music serves as "the bridge between consciousness and the unthinking sentient or even insentient universe" and tends to "lull or to distract the reader from the exact sense of the language". (Pound, 1968:26) As Pound points out, Melopoeia should be revived in translation of its music quality because it "can be appreciated by a foreigner with a sensitive ear, even though he is ignorant of the language in which the poem is written." Music is practically impossible to transfer from one language to another and Pound also admits that music is only capable of being revived "save perhaps by divine accident, and for half a line at a time". (Pound, 1968:26) Despite the fact, Pound makes fruitful efforts in transferring the musical quality of poetry from other languages into English language through his employment of "absolute rhyme", preserving the music in poetry and protruding the emotional force in it at the same time.

Secondly, absolute rhythm consists of regular rhythm in the poetry in accordance with emotional force. In his article *A Retrospect* that posits the essential components of imagist poetry, Pound advances the concept of "absolute rhythm" for the first time: "I believe in an 'absolute rhythm', a rhythm, that is, in poetry which corresponds exactly to the emotion or shade of emotion to be expressed. A man's rhythm must be interpretative, it will be, therefore, in the end, his own, uncounterfeiting, uncounterfeitable". (Pound, 1968:9) The idea is under the influence of F. S. Flint, who, in 1910, wrote about his ideal music verse, "... but for the larger music verse must be free from all the restraints of a return and a squared-up frame; the poet must forge his rhythm according to the impulse of the creative emotion working through him...". (Homberger, 1972: 65) Pound's expansion of the term demonstrates his emphasis on emotional force rather than the rigid meter as the measurement of musical quality in poetry. The music is not expressed for the sake of music as in meter or rhyme, but in accordance with the actual ebb and flow in the emotional resonance in the readers, in the harmony with human excitement, ecstasy, sorrow, melancholy and other emotions that create the music in the universe. Later, in his prose *As for Imagism*, Pound explicitly reiterates his stance against rigid forms: "one believes that emotion is an organiser of form, not merely of visible forms and colours, but also of audible forms. ... Poetry is a composition or an 'organisation' of words set to 'music'". (Pound, 1973:345)

Pound's absolute rhythm is based on his profound knowledge of traditional system of meter and rhyme, which, according to him, should be adapted to meet the new requirement of the era of modernization and liberation. The difference lies, in Pound's eyes, in the discrimination between rhyme and rhythm, when rhyme requires the rigid rules to govern the choice and usage of words and sometimes becomes the restraint that keeps the poet at bay, and rhythm depends more "upon the manner of sequence and combination". (Pound, 1973:27) Thus Pound develops a rhythm of his own, "a manner of writing in which each word should bear some burden, should make some special contribution to the effect of the whole". (Pound, 1973: 27) It is the music in the poetry that stresses the combination of sound and sense, just as Pound defines in the following statement: "The poem is an organism in which each part functions, gives to sound or to sense something — preferably to sound *and* sense gives something". (Pound, 1973:27) Pound's absolute rhythm is a reaction to the increasing call for realism in literature in the modern world, unable to be represented in most regular metrical schemes but vivid and effective in Pound's seemingly irregular, uncertain, faltering "absolute rhythm".

2.4.1 Preservation of Music — Sequence of Musical Phrase

Music is admittedly an indispensable element of poetry and "poetry is a composition of words set to music". (Pound, 1968: 437) "Poets who are not interested in music are, or become, bad poets". (Pound, 1968: 437) Pound always stresses musical quality in translations as he posits in his *A Retrospect*: "That part of your poetry which strikes upon the imaginative eye of the reader will lose nothing by translation into a foreign tongue; that which appeals to the ear can reach only those who take it in the original". (Pound, 1968: 6) The appeal to the ear becomes a criterion in Pound's translation of poetry. He is in constant pursuit of the most pleasant music to please the ear of the readers.

Pound is an adamant musical poet who attaches primary importance to the beauty of sound in poetry and he stresses this poetics in his translations. In his translation of Italian poems, Pound introduces Calvacanti's canzoni into English for its distinguished musical qualities. He notices that there are three kinds of melopoeia, "poems made to speak, to chant and to sing" and Calvacanti's poetry in general was "all made to be sung". (Pound, 1968: 167) "He (Cavalcanti) keeps the sound sharp and light in the throat by the rhymes inside the long line".

(Pound, 1968:170) The elaborate use of rhyme in the poetry of the Italian poet inspires Pound to perceive the superiority to complement what is absent in the music of English poetry. He thinks that "English two-syllable rhymes are of the wrong timbre and weight" with "extra consonants at the end, as in *flowing* and *going*; or they go squashy". (Pound, 1968:168) Thus, in his translation, there are "the atrocities" that Pound depicts as "intentional" with the aim of "driving the reader's perception further into the original than it would without them have penetrated". (Pound, 1968:172) He writes in his essay about his alteration of the original in his translation for the purpose of keeping certain qualities more prominent: "I have not given an English 'equivalent' for the Donna mi Prega; at the utmost I have provided the reader, unfamiliar with old Italian, an instrument that may assist him in gauging some of the qualities of the original". (Pound, 1968:172) He hopes to borrow the melodic structure, the musical qualities into English poetry through his translation as he states in his essay: "The melodic structure is properly indicated — and for the first time — by my disposition of the Italian text, but even that firm indication of the rhyme and the articulation of the strophe does not stress all the properties of Guido's triumph in sheer musicality". (Pound, 1968:172)

In his translation of the ancient Anglo-Saxon poetry, there are similar atrocities of alteration for the purpose of music. For example, in the first line, Pound renders *wrecan* as "reckon". *Maeg ic be me sylfum sothgied wrecan* means something like "I can tell a true story about myself". *sothgied* is an Old English word associated with traditional and historical feats of war as a boast by the singer about his extraordinary story. The combination of *sothgied* and *sylfum* stress the rhyme through alliteration. Pound's beginning line "May I for my own self song's truth reckon" achieves the closeness to the sound and word order of the original. In other places, there are similar alterations, preserving the sound yet at the cost of the literary sense of the original, such as "berries" for *byrig*(l. 48) which actually means "towns", "stern" for *stearn*(l. 23) which actually means "tern", "moaneth" for *monath*(l. 36) instead of the actual "admonishedth". Pound understands the words perfectly but preferred to render their sound instead of the mere sense of them. He adopts a new approach in translation, subverting the conventional practice of literal conversion of the original text. His practice is manifestly motivated by his aim of translation, to preserve the virtue of the word in the original, and here, the original alliteration and assonance and other means of rhyme that constitute unique music in *The Seafarer*. The Pound scholar Michael Alexander evaluates the translation, noting the aim of Pound as a guide of his translation: "Closeness to the original sound is Pound's aim. . . . He is not rendering the sense of the Anglo-Saxon into standard literary English but rather making the minimum modernization of the Old English to accommodate it modern understanding". (Alexander, 1979: 74) Pound's aim of preserving music in the original poetry is the guide in his translation and he even sacrifices the faithful transference of the semantic contents of certain words for his purpose. Alexander is justified in his evaluation of Pound's translation: "... though the sense of *The Seafarer* bears no consistent relation to the sense of the original, the sound of *The Seafarer* is an authentic new kind of translation". (Alexander, 1979: 75)

Music is "the language when language pauses" (刘象愚, 2002: 34) as music is in natural harmony with our spiritual world, demonstrating its complex dynamism unable to be achieved through language. When Pound feels the rigid rules of meters and rhymes in Victorian poetry hampers the poetic sense and the conventional symmetrical form to preserve music forces the artist to "fill up the remaining vacuums with slush", (Pound, 1968: 7) Pound invents "absolute rhythm" which determines meter by quantity to achieve metric harmony. It allows considerable freedom in form to meet the multiplying information and complicating human consciousness in the modern world yet it preserves the music required in any poetry. The innovation consists in the non-restriction by conventional meters and rhymes through "metre by quantity", (Carpenter, 1988: 174) that is, metrical sequences regulated by the length of time required to pronounce each syllable rather than by fitting the words into a predetermined stress pattern. The resulting poem is widely acclaimed and Yeats says that the poem seemed as if Ezra is "translating at sight from an unknown Greek masterpiece" and creating "the most beautiful poem that has been written in the free form, one of the few in which I find real organic rhythm". (Carpenter, 1988: 174) Pound further establishes a rule concerning rhythm which becomes one of the three cardinal rules of Imagism: "As regarding rhythm: to compose in the sequence of the musical phrase, not in sequence of a metronome". (Pound, 1968: 3) Absolute rhythm injects vigor into English poetry and "introduces a new music into English". (Pratt, 2007: 22)

To preserve music, absolute rhythm, first of all, focuses on musical phrasing instead of end rhyme. Pound "disdains the fetters of regular rhyme" (Homberger, 1972: 54) and seeks his metrical harmonies in a different and unfamiliar way, conjuring largely with assonance and alliteration. With absolute rhythm, each word should have some function in the poetry and "make some special contribution to the effect of the whole". (Pound, 1973:27) In this way, the poem becomes "an organism" in which each part "gives to sound or to sense something — preferably to sound *and* sense gives something". (Pound, 1973: 27) Take Pound's translation *A Poem of Departure* as an example:

Light rain is/on the light dust.
The willows of/the inn-yard
Will be going greener/and greener,
But you, Sir,/had better/take wine/eve your departure,
For you will have/no friends/about you
When you come/to the gates of Go.

The rhythm is created in the alternation of two or three phrases in a line, each of which is composed of two to three words. The first line possesses the strict symmetry of phrases and of metrical emphasis as the spondee in the initial place is echoed by the spondee in the end. The second line is still composed of two spondees with three little words. The alliteration goes throughout the third line, with the doubling of "greener" as a correspondent of the reduplicative in the original and as an echo of the doubling of "light" in the first line. Also, "will" continues the alliteration and assonance with the "willows" in the second line. The fourth line is made up of four phrases of similar length, yet the greater number of phrases lengthens the line to imitate the sighing of friends at departure. In the fifth and sixth line, the assonance continues with "no" and "go" and the alliteration continues with the use of "will" and "when", "gates" and "Go". There is also the continuity in the end rhyme/r/and/n/throughout the poem. The creation of a variety of rhyme and rhythm in the mere six lines yet in line with the emotions of the poet is a manifest testament of Pound's innovation on the music of the poetry. He discovers such possibility of the weight of the smaller rhythmic units in phrases separated within the line and the innovative absolute rhythm is a step forward towards the modernity of poetry by shattering the conventional rigidity of metric forms. He is insightful in the following statement: "Let the candidate fill his mind with the finest cadences he can discover, preferably in a foreign language, so that the meaning of the words may be less likely to divert his attention from the movement". (Pound, 1968:5)

Take another example from Pound's translation of *Book of Songs*.

The original text: 墙有茨，不可扫也。中冓之言，不可道也。所可道也，言之丑也。
墙有茨，不可襄也。中冓之言，不可详也。所可详也，言之长也。
墙有茨，不可束也。中冓之言，不可读也。所可读也，言之辱也。
(《诗经·墙有茨》)

Ezra Pound: The things they do and the things they say
in the harem,
in the harem,
There is no end to the things they say in the harem,
There is no shame in the things they say in the harem,
So pull not the vine away. (Pound, 2003:776)

James Legge: The tribulus grows on the wall,
And cannot be brushed away.
The story of the inner chamber
Cannot be told.
What would have to be told
Would be the vilest of recitals.

The tribulus grows on the wall,
And cannot be removed.
The story of the inner chamber
Cannot be particularly related.
What might be particularly related
Would be a long story.

The tribulus grows on the wall,
And cannot be bound together, (and taken away).
The story of the inner chamber
Cannot be recited.
What might be recited
Would be the most disgraceful of things.

The original text has three repetitive stanzas to imply the futility to cover up the scandals in the harem, which James Legge translates literally and faithfully in his version. For the well-known scandals in the Wei Empire, the poet does not give detailed narration but gives sarcastic implication. The poem is composed of slangs and colloquial words, yet the 12 modal particles at every end of lines slow the pace and add to the music of the poem. Pound's translation, far different from Legge's version, makes bold deletion of the description of rampant vines and leaves only one at the end of the poem: "pull not the vine away" to indicate the necessity of vines to cover the numerous scandals. Pound's remarkable repetition of the phrase "in the harem" for four times is to revive the secrecy of the original poem. Pound's version is composed of sense groups with independent meanings, each standing on its own and with its own musicality. Apart from the repetition of the phrase "in the harem", the iambic phrases "the things they do" and "the things they say" are repeated in parallel to revive the slowdown pace. The sense groups "There is no end" and "There is no shame" strengthen the emotional force with two accents in each of them to emphasize the scandals. Therefore, Pound's free verse still presents strong musicality and takes even better effect in expression with its accordance of rhyme and meaning.

Also, musical coherence throughout poetry is another typical feature of absolute rhythm in contrast to the conventional practice of pausing at the end of each poetic line. Pound, in his essay about "rhythm and rhyme", warns the poets that "Don't chop your stuff into separate iambs. Don't make each line stop dead at the end, and then begin every next line with a heave. Let the beginning of the next line catch the rise of the rhythm wave, unless you want a definite longish pause". (Pound, 1968:6) In this manner, the poem becomes an organic whole, presenting and evoking the emotions in a way similar to the constant stream of consciousness. To Pound, music is to add luster to a poem rather than hamper the flow of meaning and emotions. The coherence in rhythm is achieved, in Pound's translations, through three major means. One is the cutting of a sentence into two or more poetic lines so that the following lines might naturally follow what goes before it. One is the continuity of each line to the next line with the frequent use of the connector "and". Another is the empty space created between some of the lines to indicate its continuity with the preceding line. Take Pound's translation *The Unmoving Cloud* for example:

The original text: 霭霭停云,蒙蒙时雨。八表同昏,平路伊阻。

Ezra Pound: The clouds have gathered, and gathered,
and the rain falls and falls,
The eight ply of the heavens
are all folded into one darkness,
And the wide, flat road stretches out.

Burton Watson: Heavy and dull, the motionless clouds,
the seasonal rains drenching down;
all eight directions a single darkness,
all the level roads cut off.

Fang Zhong: Thick and dusty, the lingering clouds,
Misty and drizzling, the season's rain;
In all directions, the haze unbroken,
The level roads are blocked from access.

Wang Rongpei: The clouds are pending dense and high
While spring rain drizzles from the sky.
So dim and sombre is the day
That no one rides along the way.

As compared to other versions of the poem, Pound's version is uniquely different in its structure. There is the slash of a continuous sentence into two lines (The eight ply of the heavens/are all folded into one darkness), the alternate indention of poetic lines (Line 2 and Line 4), and the connection of sentences with paratactic connector "and" (Line 2 and Line 5). Wang's version also spreads one sentence in two poetic lines, which is different from Pound's means in that his connecting device is the logical connector "while" to indicate contrast and "so... that..." to indicate the relation of cause and effect. Compared to it, Pound's cutting of sentences is more abrupt and creates greater suspense since the noun phrase as the subject of a sentence put in a poetic line (The eight ply of the heaven) will propel the reader's eagerness to move on for the complete sense. Watson and Fang also uses paratactic structures in their translations, with multiple complex noun phrases to depict the variety of elements, the clouds, the rain, the darkness and the roads. The uniqueness of Pound's version consists in the connector "and" to link the informational fragments to build the continuity throughout the poetry, not only between the information groups of the clouds and the rain, the darkness and the road, but also within some poetic lines linking the repetitive verbs to indicate the continuity of the action (The clouds have gathered, and gathered,/and the rain falls and falls). Each translator has his merit in the version, yet Pound's emphasis on musicality of poetry is more prominent, with musical phrases lingering on with pauses in between like the continuous singing recital (The clouds/have gathered,/and gathered,/and the rain/falls and falls,/The eight ply/of the heavens/are all folded/into one darkness,/And the wide,/flat road/stretches out).

2.4.2 Musical Accordance with Emotional Force

Emotional force is an indispensable element in poetry, "an organiser of form, not merely of visible forms and colours, but also of audible forms". (Pound, 1973: 345) In his essay about the distinction of good verse and bad verse, he clearly presents his yardstick as emotional force: bad verse is the verse which "pretends to some emotion which did not assist at its parturition" and which could not make "the words move in rhythm of the creative emotion" while good verse is the precise, the strong, the exact record of "the high voltage of emotions". (Pound, 1973: 346) "Emotion also creates patterns of timbre". (Pound, 1973: 345) Emotional force, therefore, is the fundamental creator of rhythm patterns. Pound asserts that "The rhythm form is false unless it belong to the particular creative emotion or energy which it purports to represent". (Pound, 1973: 345) Emotional force should be stimulated in readers through ingenious techniques. Poets are not the mere receivers of impression, passively recording the natural world or the human consciousness, but the original creators of life force in their artistic works. When "energy, or emotion, expresses itself in form", Pound devises the original "absolute rhythm" as the "primary manifestation" of energy, (Pound, 1973: 346) a rhythm to create music corresponding to the emotional experience by the ingenious arrangement of words. Take an example from Pound's translation *The Beautiful Toilet*.

The original text: 青青河畔草,郁郁园中柳。
盈盈楼上女,皎皎当窗牖。
娥娥红粉妆,纤纤出素手。
昔为倡家女,今为荡子妇,
荡子行不归,空床难独守。

Ezra Pound: Blue, blue is the grass about the river
And the willows have overfilled the close garden.
And within, the mistress, in the midmost of her youth,
White, white of face, hesitates, passing the door.
Slender, she puts forth a slender hand

And she was a courtesan in the old days,
And she has married a sot,
Who now goes drunkenly out
And leaves her too much alone.

The original text of *The Beautiful Toilet* commands delicate beauty with the image of a lady of feminist tenderness and in melancholy sadness. To mark the structural division of description and narration, each of the first four lines of the poem begins with reduplication. Pound adopts ingenious representation of the rhythmic beauty in his translation, beginning with a pairing "Blue, blue" as restored reduplication, and then shifting to the internal rhyme of short i's in the second line: "And the w*i*llows have overf*i*lled the close garden", then to the assonance of short i's in the third line: "And w*i*th*i*n, the m*i*stress, in the m*i*dmost of her youth", and to the same pairing "white, white" as reduplication in the initial position, and then to the gracefully split pairing of "slender" in the sixth line. The original reproduction of the rhythm creates consistent musical effect with the structure of the poem's first lobe "shaped into cohesion" (Kenner, 1972: 194) yet not deviating too much from English rules. In the opening line, three long vowels are used (blue, blue, grass), leaving the readers a sense of heavy and profound sorrow. It presents a picture of a pretty lady in beautiful toilet looking over the blue grass on the riverbank, sighing and missing the departed husband. The use of blue instead of green, despite the connotation of sadness in the semantic aspect, gives a similar sound of sobbing sorrow. The second line follows the first with three words with/u/(willow, overfilled, close), so that the lachrymose sadness is intensified as Edgar Allen Poe once remarked that the most sad phoneme is/u/. Altogether, Pound uses 7 phoneme/u/including willow, overfilled, close, midmost, old, goes, alone, which are absent in Fenollosa's notes. In the third line, the sadness is emphatic in the use of 6 crisp thin vowel/i/(within, mistress, in, midmost. And all in all,/i/is present for 14 times including is, river, willow, overfilled, within, mistress, in, midmost, hesitate, passing, courtesan, in, married, drunkenly), which shows Pound's preference of the phoneme to demonstrate depression. The fourth line ends in each group, with long vowels (passing, door), which indicates the depressed mood of the lady and the hesitation in the dilemma of staying in solitude or leaving in uncertain future. In the fifth line, the stretching out of the hand is made much heavier by the addition of the long vowel in "forth". The last line (And leaves her too much alone) uses 3 long vowels in leaves, too and alone, ends with/u/, echoing the sorrow in the first line. In addition, the repetition of/s/in the first stanza (grass, close, mistress, midmost, youth, face, hesitates, passing, slender, puts, forth, slender) and the recurred/z/in the second (was, courtesan, days, has, goes, leaves) are also means to achieve the emotional force in the poem. Take another example from Pound's translation of *Book of Songs*.

The original text: 采采芣苡,薄言采之。采采芣苡,薄言有之。
采采芣苡,薄言掇之。采采芣苡,薄言捋之。
采采芣苡,薄言袺之。采采芣苡,薄言襭之。

(《诗经·周南·芣苡》)

Ezra Pound: Pluck, pluck, pluck, the thick plantain;
Pluck, pick, pluck, then pluck again.
Oh pick, pluck the thick plantain,
Here be seeds for sturdy men.
Pluck the leaf and fill the lap,
Skirts were made to hide the lap. (Pound, 2003:758-9)

The poem depicts the joy of the working women in picking plantain. In the repetitive singing, it revives the labor scene with vigor and passion and joy. The poem, without portraying the women in labor, conveys the joy of labor with the music through the repetition of stanzas. Pound's translation adopts 10 verbs that relates to the activity of picking, among which "pluck" is repeated 8 times, "pick" 2 times. Two verbs with similar meaning are used alternately and every line of picking presents minor differences. In the first line, "pluck" is used three times to indicate the strength and energy at the beginning of labor and three short single-syllable words are separated with commas are to indicate the tense pace. In the second line, "pick" is used among three "pluck" to indicate the variety of labor and thus the joy of labor since it is not the monotonous boring mechanic repetition. In the third line, Pound alternate "pick" and "pluck" to slow down the pace of labor as it has been going on for some time and blunted the energy of the workers. The last "pluck" is used to indicate a slower pace with the joy of harvest added. Pound ingeniously employs the repetitive words in variety, to revive the musical pace of the original as a reflection of the merriness of labor. That is, Pound achieves the harmonious accordance of rhythm and meaning in his translations.

Chapter 3 Skopos of Modernist Poetry

Pound, noting the declining trend in poetry and its inadequacy to represent the remarkable changes in his contemporary world, dedicated himself to finding the new style and form in poetry. The modern world was under dramatic physical and spiritual changes and brought about new terms to the language such as "Wireless, Automobile, Chippendale, Figures out of Çschylus", "terms which convey to us definite meanings, which they would not convey to creatures of our own faculty but of an earlier time, or different in customs and in culture". (Pound, 1973: 23) Some linguistic terms were dying out when the industrial revolution created a world of iron and steel totally unknown to those of an earlier time. Pound perceived the remarkable changes and concluded: "We are... modern". (Pound, 1973:21) New environment, new circumstances called for the production of new literature. Pound preached for innovations in poetry, in literature, and even in language as a whole. He regarded the task as the responsibility of artists: "As for myself, I have tried to clear up a certain messy place in the history of literature". (Pound, 1973:23) The key to the innovation was the "accuracy of sentiment" against the previous trend of over-sentimentalism and over-decoration in literature, the sentiment which he believed would "make more accurate the sentiment of the growth of literature as a whole, and of the Art of poetry". (Pound, 1973:23) Pound's purpose of being modern is demonstrated in various aspects in his translations, including the depersonalization of objective reality with concision in language, depsychologization of objective reality with restraint of emotions, defiance of authorial presence by presenting multiple and invisible voices and emphasis on individual consciousness through the abandonment of religion.

3.1 Modernism and Modernist Poetry

The 19th century to the early 20th century witnessed immense advances in science and technology, in psychology and philosophy, in art and in other sectors of life. The invention of the internal combustion engine and the subsequent industrialization led to the decline of human activities in society. The relativity theory in physics radically changed people's views of time, of existence, and of the universe. Equally influential in this wave of modernity were the theories of Sigmund Freud, who argued that human mind had a fundamental structure, and that subjective experience was based on the interplay of the parts of the mind. According to Freud's ideas, humans were no longer merely the receptacles of absolute reality, which should actually be subjective perception in the conscious mind based on basic human drives and instincts. Subsequently, Ernst Mach developed a widely accepted philosophy of science, referred to as positivism, arguing that the relations of objects in nature were not guaranteed but only known through mental perception. Such philosophical and psychological breakthroughs represented a departure from the past, against the previous conviction that external reality was absolute existence impressing itself on humans. Charles Darwin's *Origin of Species* astonished the world with its concept of humans as deriving from and developing from animals, yet convincingly planted that on the public mind, which justifies human impulses against social norms as the essential nature of animals. Friedrich Nietzsche came to the stage asserting that the will to power was more important than facts or things, again emphasizing the subjective force in humans. Similarly, the writings of Henri Bergson championed the vital "life force" over static conceptions of reality. All these writers supported, or, in the case of Freud, attempted to explain, irrational thought processes through the lens of rationality.

Artistic works, as the reflection of society, also presented the new trend of modernism as radical departure from previous practices, which embraced discontinuity, rejecting steady development but approved revolutionary disruption and recast the artist as a revolutionary force to overthrow the traditional forms and traditional social arrangements. Poetry in the early 20th century followed the general trend of revolutionizing the traditional mode. With the appearance of the Imagists pioneered by Ezra Pound, poetry became modern in reaction to the gauche and pompous excesses of Victorian poetry, discarding traditional formalism and ornate diction. The beginning of the 20th century marked a revolutionary stage in the history of English poetry, with the emergence of experimental, avant-garde modernist poetry as a far cry from conventional poetry.

The major feature of modernist poetry was the revolt against tradition. The modernist poets tore down the conventional modes of unproblematic poetic self and of conventional poetic techniques, discovering new perspectives and making technical innovations to perceive the objective world and the objective self. Firstly, modernist poetry exposed the social evils in the industrial civilization.

The beginning of the 20th century saw the collapse of values with the cruelty of war and the decline of social morals. The advanced civilization and accumulation of material wealth didn't foster happiness but suppressed individuality and produced isolation and loneliness and hostility of individuals. The poets, doubting the traditional reasoning principles and the humanistic ideals, reflected on the evils of society and proposed the desertion of civilization and the departure from the tradition of idealism of classical Romanticism. Secondly, modernist poetry focused on the inner truth. Modernist poets realized the futility of the previous direct sentimentalism to reveal the universal truth of mind, and also the uncertainty of individual mind to capture the outside world in an era of spiritual wandering. Therefore, many modernists posited the immediacy to decentralize self in the dislocation of the authorial presence. T. S. Eliot preached: "Poetry is not a turning loose of emotion, but an escape from emotion; it is not the expression of personality, but an escape from personality". (Beasley, 2007: 2) The escape was represented in the focus on the literal instead of the metaphorical or symbolic meanings of words. Modernists recommended the use of objective symbols literally to suggest the subjective truth and inner feelings. Thirdly, modernist poets were enthusiastic in the experimentation of poetic language. Modernist poets, discovering the clarity of modern everyday speech against the restriction by conventional rhymes, experimented with poetic language to revolutionize traditional poetry. Walt Whitman's long lines in free verse, Oscar Wilde's prose poetry, Emily Dickinson's compression sparked the innovation of modernist poetic language and the appearance of the Imagists marked the first emergence of distinctly modernist poetic in the language. Apart from the adoption of precise and concise free verse, modernist poets focused on sonic effects through rhythm instead of conventional meter and rhyme. They also employed fresh syntactic techniques, such as collage, the disconnected parallelism to achieve modern effects. T. S. Eliot's epic *The Waste Land* (1922) was considered a landmark masterpiece of modernism with broken, fragmented and seemingly unrelated slices of imagery assembled to form a disjunctive anti-narrative, which thrust the readers into bewilderment at the only sight of a heap of broken images yet induced profound poetic experience and perception from such dislocation and fragmentation. Pound, as the pioneer of modernist poetry, attempted multiple means in his works and in his translations, to make breakthroughs in the poetic theme and form and effect so as to effect modernity against previous trends.

Modernist poetry derived from the previous trend of symbolism and aestheticism and from the prominent figures of Charles Pierre Baudelaire in France, Edgar Ellen Poe in America, and many others. Baudelaire's first and most famous volume of poems, *Les Fleurs du Mal* (*The Flowers of Evil*) switched its principal themes to the corruption of the city and the evil in human nature, swerving from the traditional themes love and sentimentalism. Also notable was his use of concrete imagery to evoke feelings of nostalgia and to reveal the delicate inner world. Edgar Ellen Poe advocated pure art, believing that the sole purpose of poetry was to evoke sense of beauty and that meaning in literature should be an undercurrent just beneath the surface.

Symbolism was art movement of the late 19th century as an anti-idealistic movement attempting to capture reality in the particularity, and to elevate the humble and the ordinary over the ideal. In the 1880s, the French poets published manifesto of symbolism, calling for the pursuit of supreme truth in the inner world, and the embodiment of abstract concepts in concrete forms. They believed absolute truths that art should aim to capture could only find access in indirect methods, through the highly metaphorical and suggestive technique that endowed particular images or objects with symbolic meaning. The symbol was an object animate or inanimate that stands for or points to a reality beyond itself: the cross symbolic of suffering; sunrise, of new beginnings; winter, of aging, decay, and death; spring, of energy, birth, and hope; summer, of childhood, fun, and laughter; autumn, of maturity, wisdom, and fulfillment; a dove representing peace; the rose, purity; the lion, strength and courage; the tiger, of great energy and creativity and so on. Stephane Mallarmé, the most popular figure of the Symbolist movement, tore down the previous structures and revealed complex emotions by presenting concrete objects. Symbolist poetry soon spread across Europe and America and their symbols evolved from the individual and private to the universal and from emotional ones to intellectual and philosophical ones. William Butler Yeats, also an eminent symbolist, practiced allusive imagery and symbolic structures, assembling physical symbols to suggest the significant and abstract thoughts of immaterial, timeless qualities. Like Mallarmé and Yeats, symbolist poets exploited symbols in poetry of rich suggestiveness rather than explicit signification; they sought to evoke, rather than to describe, using symbolic imagery to signify the state of the poet's soul and to evoke particular states of mind in readers.

Aestheticism was the counterpart to French symbolism in the English circle, a 19th century European movement that emphasized aesthetic values over moral or social themes in literature, fine art, the decorative arts, and interior design.

The emergence of aestheticism was also a response to, and a rejection of, 19th century industrialism and its accompanying utilitarianism. Its doctrine was described by the slogan "art for art's sake", and the idea that "art had no social responsibility that it was an end in itself", that "the object of art and indeed of life for the aesthete was the appreciation and cultivation of beauty". (Beasley, 2007:22) The artist held that art should provide refined sensuous pleasure, rather than convey moral or sentimental messages, believing that art did not have any didactic purpose but need only be beautiful and art should exploit symbolic suggestion so as to achieve pure and absolute beauty.

Though symbolism and aestheticism exert significant influence on modernism, modernist poetry, modern in its sense, departs from its predecessors in many aspects. The difference, first of all, consists in the perception of poetic self. Symbolists regard the poet as a seer or a dreamer and poetry as his magical, inspired creation. By contrast, modernists stress the objectivity of poetic self who presents rather than represent, by building simple and precise objective imagery in economic and concise diction. The poetry is no longer "the spontaneous outpouring of one's soul". (Painter, 2006:96) Modernists pursue "defined precision" in imagery in contrast to "indefinite musicality" symbolist seek in it. Modernists seek diction of "concise simplicity" rather than "solemn obscurity" in symbolist poetry. (Painter, 2006: 96) Modernists reject the obscurity in language, replacing the heavy lexicon and convoluted syntax in many symbolist works with straightforward language. Symbolists support the idea that poetry should be indistinct through vague language and enigmatic imagery, which modernist poets revolt against with their prose-like clarity and sharp precision. Pound the modernist rebukes the "Symbolist-Impressionist" for their thinking about "the empirical of ego-centric perceiver". (Kim, 2003:165)

Secondly, in an age of awakening self-consciousness of individuals, modernist poets seek the representation of germinal consciousness of subjective poet in their works. The modernist Hulme notes the changing of themes from the ancient to the modern: "The old poetry dealt essentially with big things, the expression of epic subjects leads naturally to the anatomical matter and regular verse... But the modern is the exact opposite of this, it no longer deals with heroic action, it has become definitely and finally introspective and deals with expression and communication of momentary phrases in the poet's mind". (Hulme, 1994:53) Pound advances the building of image with such intensity as to reflect what the poet feels at the moment and to inspire in the readers emotions of the same intensity. In Pound's works, the focus is not on the magnificent, the mythical but on the universal. In his translation of the Chinese poetry, his selection of 19 from the 159 poems is a reflection of the purpose as the selected ones are mainly about the universal experiences of the ordinary, about war and love, loneliness and longing. Pound wears different masks to express the feelings for the individuals, from the distinguished poets in various cultures to common people in face of harsh life, the soldiers in desolate frontiers longing to go home, the loving wife in deserted house yearning for the return of the husband. Pound, through his building of imagism, promotes the modernist poetry in the representation of the poet's momentary consciousness and of the individual mind of the ordinary people.

Thirdly, modernists make innovations in language as embodiment of modernity. Modernists believe in new forms as fit means of expression for the modernized society. The old "fixed and artificial form", the old effort to "to attain the absolutely perfect form of poetry", (Hulme, 1994: 53) the old dominance of meter and regular syllables as the element of perfect form should be discarded. The modernist Hulme is aware of "the fluidity of the world and of its impermanence" and appeals to the artists for the abandonment of the fixed form and "the elaborate rules of regular metre" for the dynamic world. (Hulme, 1994: 52) In the ever-changing modern society, modernist poets have to desert the fixed form for "the maximum of individual and personal expression" and grasp the unique moments of beauty in nature, the intense moments of emotions in our consciousness "the production of a general effect" instead of "minute perfections of phrase and words", which will then "take away the predominance of metre and a regular number of syllables as the element of perfection in words". (Hulme, 1994:53) Thus, innovative forms emerge in modernist poetry with colloquial speech language against the excessive ornamentation of Romantist poetry. Pound adopts free verse in his translation of strictly-rhymed Chinese poetry for the general aesthetic effect. The new form wins popularity and produces many great works of modernist poetry, such as *Adam's Curse* by Yeats with its dramatic everyday talk dialogues, and T. S. Eliot's *The Waste Land*, in simple and austere free verse generating great energy and intensity.

3. 2 Decentralization of Ego

The industrialized modern world of iron and steel, along with the dominant profit-oriented capitalism, exiled humans from the center of the universe and thus left the human consciousness astray. In the field of philosophy, the psychoanalysis developed by Sigmund Freud generated the objective study of the self and the unconscious. Human mind became an object of study as scientific as nature, possibly to be traced and analyzed as to the previously intangible and intractable motivations and emotions. In tune with new perceptions and conceptions of the modern era, Pound introduced the concept of de-centered poetic self to modern poetry, against the previous modes of personal epic centering on the poet's mind. Pound marginalized the poetic self from the center by wearing different masks and telling "the tale of the tribe" (Pound, 1973:194) as a de-centered scripter. Pound's translations from different cultures and times were more elaborate masks for him to decenter the self. Pound's decentralization of ego, therefore, consisted in the depersonalization of objective reality, that is, the concrete image in concise language, and the depsychologization of objective reality, that is, the restraint in emotional expression, and finally, the defiance of authorial presence.

3.2.1 Depersonalization of Objective Reality — Concreteness

Pound denounces abstraction and generalization and advances concreteness in image and in language. He warns the poets to "go in fear of abstraction" as the abstract expression like "dim lands of peace" "dulls the image" when it "mixes an abstraction with the concrete". (Pound, 1968: 5) In his belief that "natural object is always the adequate symbol" and "language is made out of concrete things... general expressions in non-concrete terms are a laziness", (Pound, 1971: 49) Pound stresses the concreteness of images as precise reflection of natural objects. He rejects his predecessors' approach to the mythical, to the spiritual, to the cosmic, to the realm beyond the empirical. Before Pound, the modernist T. E. Hulme advances earthliness in poetry denouncing the depiction of the other world, of the mythical as a "drug", exhorting the poet to renounce "infinity" and turn to "the contemplation of finite things". (Painter, 2006:128) Like Hulme, Pound lays emphasis not on the idealized or metaphysical associations of objects abundant in symbolist poetry, but on the earthly objects themselves, portraying them as they are in the natural world. His attention is on the object and its immediate, earthly surroundings. For him, "the rose once again has become beautiful in itself, in its petals, scent, and color, and not in its imagined resemblances to mystical love or some other such thing". (Painter, 2006:48-49) He will not reject the concrete flower to reveal its association with beauty or with myths or merely to depict the spiritual experience. He will try to look upon the concrete anew, seeking the emotional intensification through the precise depiction of the earthly flower itself. The scholar Kirsten Painter mentions in his book of the feature in Imagist poetry: "In their depiction of earthly reality and the everyday object/Have the monopoly on the everyday and the earthly/Still bringing the everyday squarely into poetry". (Painter, 2006: 125)

Pound's stress on the depersonalized depiction of objects is seen in many of his poetry translations. Take one example in his translation of Li Bai's poem *Seeing Off a Friend*:

The original line: 芳树笼秦栈,春流绕蜀城。

Ezra Pound: Sweet trees are on the paved way of the Shin,
Their trunks burst through the paving,
And freshets are bursting their ice
in the midst of Shoku, a proud city.

Fu Huisheng: Fragrant trees envelop suspension
wooden roads,
around Chengdu City the Jin River
flows.

From the comparison of the two versions, Pound has a impressively different approach in that he adds vivid natural objects to give emotional impact. The two images, the bursting of the tree trunks through the road and the bursting of the freshets through the surface of ice, animate the scene with vigorous force of life accompanying the advent of spring. It is eloquent evidence to the following lines of comment on the rise and fall of men's fates, whose wax and wane is similar to the seasonal change from desolation to vigor as shown in the natural world. Pound's addition of the natural images in his translation pumps force to his conclusion through the analogy.

Another example is from Pound's translation of Li Bai's departure poem:

The original line: 烟花三月下扬州

Ezra Pound: The smoke flowers are blurred over the river.

Witty Bynner: On your way to visit Yangzhou in the misty month of flowers;

Xu Yuanchong: For River Town green with willows and red with flowers.

Qiu Xiaolong: to Yangzhou, the mist covering
the water, the flowers making
a blaze of March colors

Tang Yihe: Sailing down to Yangzhou in the Third Moon
Amid the misty blooming flowers.

Pound's literal translation of "smoke flowers" seems to be a mistranslation because the expression originally depicts the blooming flowers in April, the abundance of which creates an illusion of blurry mist. Where all the other translators put in the metaphoric sense literally in their translations, such as Bynner's "the misty month of flowers", Xu's "red with flowers", Qiu's "the flowers making a blaze of March colors", and Tang's "the misty blooming flowers", Pound discards the metaphor like "mist" and "cloud" and "blaze" and puts it into "smoke flowers" , which becomes a concise and concrete natural image conjuring up in the reader' mind the exact scene of blurry blossoms. Such treatment echoes Pound's principle of "direct treatment of the thing", (Pound, 1968:3) that is, the depiction of earthly objects without any embellishment or ornament.

Similar examples abound in Pound's translation. "And if you ask how I regret that parting? /It is like the flowers falling at spring's end,/confused, whirled in a tangle". (from *Exile's Letter*) Where the original poem only mentions the falling of flowers in the end of spring, Pound adds an image of flowers "whirled in a tangle" in his translation, which renders the readers sorrowful with the uncontrolled fate of fallen flowers. The image creates the sympathy in readers with all its precise concreteness. For the original line:"木落秋草黄,登高望戎虏", Pound's translation goes as "Trees fall, the grass goes yellow with autumn. /I climb the towers and towers/to watch out the barbarous land". (from *Lament of the Frontier Guard*) As to the two characters in the original Chinese text as "climb" (登) and "high" (高), Pound uses the concrete image "tower" for the abstract concept "high" and with the repetition of the image in the line "climbing the towers and towers", he conveys the desolation of the place and the despair of the soldier. For the original line:"阳和变杀气,发卒骚中土", Pound's translation goes as "A gracious spring, turned to blood-ravenous autumn,/A turmoil of wars-men, spread over the middle kingdom" (from *Lament of the Frontier Guard*) It is a depiction of the battle scene when gentility turns into cruel hostility. When the original lines involve abstract terms for the change, "harmony" (阳和) and "atrocity" (杀气), Pound adds two natural images "spring" and "autumn" as perfect analogy of the changing scene in the battlefield.

Apart from the addition of natural images, Pound also simplifies or omits or rewrites the moral preach or emotional expression for the decentralization of self. For the two lines of the original poem in the sense that "temperament and emotion is developed and conventions entrench it", Pound simplifies it in his *South-Folk in Cold Country* into one short statement: "Emotion is born out of habit." And in the poem *The River-Merchant's Wife: A Letter*, he spares no effort to revive the depiction of natural scenes, yet when the sentimental comes along, that is, the young lady lamenting on how the sight breaks her heart and how she sits there worrying about the fading away of her rosy cheeks, the lapse of youth in sorrow (感此伤妾心，坐愁红颜老), Pound shortens that into two simple lines: "They hurt me, /I grow older". The simplification is deliberately creative for the retirement of the poetic self to achieve objectification.

Omission is also common practice for Pound's treatment of the subjective conveying of feelings. Take an example from Pound's treatment for Tao Yuanming's *Unmoving Clouds*. Where Fang Zhong put as "But how true the common saying goes, /That the sun and the moon rise and wane, /Shouldn't we rather sit close together, /To talk about life's shifting scenes?" for the original text of "人亦有言，日月于征。安得促席，说彼平生", Pound has two concise lines portraying the activity of the sun and the moon: "And men say the sun and moon keep on moving/because they can't find a soft seat." He cuts off the other two lines in his translation because they are the vague mental activities of the poet and contribute little to the objective depiction of reality and to the de-involvement of subjective self.

Pound also adopts the means of rewriting to convert subjective moralization in the original to an objective image so that the poetic self retreats from the scene. The following example is taken from his translation of the poem *The Unmoving Cloud* together with Fang Zhong's version in the same stanza.

The original text: 翩翩飞鸟，息我庭柯。敛翮闲止，好声相和。
岂无他人，念子实多。愿言不获，抱恨如何。

Ezra Pound: The birds flutter to rest in my tree,
and I think I have heard them saying,
"It is not that there are no other men
But we like this fellow the best,
But however we long to speak
He cannot know of our sorrow."

Fang Zhong: Fluttering, fluttering, the light birds
Come to rest on my garden branches,
Perching in quiet contentment;
Sweetly to one another they sing.
True it is I have other friends.
But now I think of you most.
What I wish I cannot get,

How vexed am I to think of this!

Fang Zhong's version is a literally faithful one for the original text, addressing directly to the friend about his contemplation on their deep friendship and on the futility of unfulfilled wish. Pound, in his creative translation, adopts a different way of expressing the subjective feelings, converting the poet's sentimental statement to that of birds. With the clear notes by Fenollosa, Pound could not mistake the meaning of the original text and his creative treatment seems deliberate with his consistently preached principle of reducing the subjective and decentering the poetic self. The subjective feelings and emotions become objective reality and the poetic self is hidden behind the seemingly emotionless exposition of subjective consciousness. In Pound's *Lament of the Frontier Guard* about a soldier in the frontier in sorrowful longing to go home, the sentiment is written more like the confession of the Personae about the states of his consciousness, "And sorrow, sorrow like rain. /Sorrow to go, and sorrow, sorrow returning". The feeling is depicted objectively like rising tides, pausing for a while yet coming back again with greater force. Therefore, Pound, in his modernist ideal, retires the poetic self by treating the phenomena in the universe, either external objects or internal consciousness, as the objective.

Pound left America for Venice in 1908 and then settled in London as a well-received poet but he soon detected the polished insincerity "bound by mass and time" in the continental poetry which he wanted to replace with American "Emersonian sincerity" through "irreverent, intuitive exactness" of depiction. (Makin, 1985:17) Hard facts, as Pound found out, could hardly be carried in a language "evolved to project penumbras of misty anti-fact". (Makin, 1985:22) Pound then began to discover the new style of language as a carrier of hard reality of iron and steel in the modern world. He was impressed by the virtues of prose written by realists like Stendhal, Flaubert and Maupassant and he believed that the hardness of prose language should be applied to poetry. He said: "Poetry must be as well written as prose... There must be no book words, no periphrases, no inversions. It must be as simple as Guy de Maupassant's best prose, and as hard as Stendhal's" (Pound, 1971: 48-49) Poetry, like prose, should run naturally as in natural speech with "no interjections", "no words flying off to nothing", "no clichés, set phrases, stereotype journalese". (Pound, 1971:49) Pound's "hard language" is composed of natural concrete words with each contributing certain exact sense to the whole and he defines the new style as the important goal for the artist: "Granted one can't get perfection every shot, this must be one's INTENTION". (Pound, 1971:49)

In the first place, hardness of language concerns the precision in depicting objective reality. In rejection of the previous trend of over-sentimentality in poetry and that "Tennysonianness of speech", Pound calls for objectivity in precise depiction, preaching in his essay that "The only escape from such is by precision.... Objectivity and again objectivity, and expression... nothing — nothing that you couldn't, in some circumstance, in the stress of some emotion, actually say" because "every literaryism, every book word, fritters away a scrap of the reader's patience, a scrap of his sense of your sincerity". (Pound, 1971: 49) Pound criticizes the way some artists slip into the practice of flowery ornamental language without the sincerity to express the true self and he preaches for simple language: "When one really feels and thinks, one stammers with simple speech, it is only in the flurry, the shallow frothy excitement of writing, or the inebriety of a metre, that one falls into the easy — oh, how easy! — speech of books and poems that one has read". (Pound, 1971:49) As opposed to symbolists' "inaccuracy,", "blurriness," and "mushy technique," Pound prescribes precision as an antidote, laying emphasis on the contributing function of each component —"having each word in its proper place in the line". (Pound, 1968:293) Each contributing word is interwoven into a skeletal framework of the image, as permanent as the rock in the universe —"as if it were there for a thousand years", (Pound, 1968: 293) yet as fresh as they have never existed before —"yet the reader hears it for the first time". (Pound, 1968:293) In this way, poetry serves as "rigid reflections of steel and stone" "as representative of the invisible skeleton of the visible world". (Hickman, 2005:96) In the simple shape of the image, the poet could present "dynamically forceful precision, frequently through qualities of hardness and severity and specifically through its capacity to suggest something skeletal and often metallic" (Hickman, 2005:45) and only "such forceful severity, precision, hardness, and rigidity" could combat "effeminacy on symbolic terrain". (Hickman, 2005:46) Precision, in Pound's eyes, is tantamount to force, suitable for the landscape of "machinery" and "steel and stone" of the modern urban environment.

Secondly, hardness concerns the plain, undecorated simplicity of language. Pound, with the distaste for the extraneous sentimentality of Romantists, seeks simplicity as a countermeasure. To him, the path to clarity and precision is through simplicity and brevity in language by replacing the verbose and redundant expressions with the concise and compact ones, as preached in Pound's famous words: "Use no superfluous word... which does not reveal something... don't... fill up the vacuums with slush". (Pound, 1968:4,7) The hardness of language could be achieved by discarding ornamental and decorative "superfluous" words. "Since the beginning of bad writing, writers have used images as ornaments... One is tired of ornamentations, they are all a trick". (Pound, 1968: 446) Chinese poetry appeals to Pound as an exemplar of hard language against the prevailing didacticism in English poetry of the time. In his translation of Chinese poetry, Pound is seen to revive the original hardness in language. Take an example of the use of adjectives from translations of Li Bai's poem *The River-Merchant's Wife: A Letter*:

The original text: 门前迟行迹,一一生绿苔。苔深不能扫,落叶秋风早。

Ezra Pound: You dragged your feet when you went out.
By the gate now, the moss is grown, the **different** mosses,
Too **deep** to clear them away!
The leaves fall early this autumn, in wind.

Xu Yuanchong: **Green** moss now overgrows before our door,
Your footprints, **hidden**, can be seen no more.
Moss can't be swept away, so **thick** it grows,
And leaves fall early when the **west** wind blows.

W. J. B. Flectcher: Before the door, where stood your **parting** feet,
The prints with **verdant** moss are covered **high**.
Deep is that moss! It will not brush away.
In **early** autumn's gale the leaflets fall.

C. Gaunt: Where we bade each the other farewell at the gate
The footprints are **green** with moss now,
Deep moss that clings fast to the **unswept** steps.
How early the wind strips the bough!

Pound uses the least adjectives among four versions, the mere two adjectives "different" and "deep" to describe "mosses", each revealing something to the readers. Xu uses four, "green" and "thick" to modify "moss", "hidden" for "footsteps" and "west" for "wind". Fletcher uses five, "verdant", and "deep" for "moss", "parting" for "feet", "high" for "footprints" and "early" for "autumn". Gaunt uses three, "green" and "deep" for "moss", "unswept" for "steps". Pound's use of the simple adjective "different" to modify "mosses" is unique, the compact word fully expressive of the relentless elapse of time by indicating the accumulation of layers of mosses on top of layers. Where other translators resort to the verb "overgrow" (Xu) or the prolonged clause "The prints with verdant moss are covered high" (Fletcher) to give the original sense of "mosses growing one by one" (一一生绿苔), Pound uses a concise adjective to reveal the image of thick mosses in the dynamic process of layers covering layers, which indicates the long lapse of time when the changing seasons bring back the mosses over and over again. When the mosses become "different", how about the parting lover? The word is simple yet indicative and expressive enough to inspire the sympathy from readers. Pound does not use the color word "green" or "verdant" as Xu and Fletcher and Gaunt do, because for him, mosses are green as a certainty and thus the adjective "does not reveal something" (Pound, 1968: 4) and becomes "superfluous". (Pound, 1968: 4) The comparison reveals that Pound's language is "hard to the bone", yet creates the image that conforms to the overall tone of the poem.

3.2.2 Depsychologization of Objective Reality — Restraint

Against the over-unleashed sentimentality in Romantist poetry, Pound has the practice of depsychologization of objective reality, that is, the depiction of the objective to evoke feelings and emotions instead of the direct statement. The presence of "I" in the poem is not the direct referent of the poet himself but the mask that hides the poetic self. Such derepresentation of "I" is a prominent feature in modernist poetry, and especially in Pound's poetic principles and translation practices.

As to the detachment of "I" from the poet's self, Pound uses two main methods. In the first method, "I" becomes an image in the poetry as the mask for the poet to de-center his poetic self. In the second one, "I" stands for the voice of the master, the storyteller in ancient times and thus "I" becomes the scripter. Pound discards his poetic self with these foreign or ancient masks through his voracious learning of foreign cultures and works and arduous translation of them into English. Pound, in his poetic career, attempts to discover new faces in various cultures. By adopting a wide range of Personae, he steers his poetry to the new terrain. Chinese poetry, with its restrained emotions, reinforces his conviction in the derepresentation of the poetic self. The "mask" technique is used even further in his epic *The Cantos*, the fragments of historical events and historical figures and cultural treasures juxtaposed throughout the epic with little presence of the poetic self.

Firstly, "I" becomes an Image, as an objective being in the poetry that inspires the emotional interpretation of the poet and of the readers. The "I" is not a static solitary entity but an agglomeration of different beings. In his early poem *The Tree*, Pound claims that "I stood still and was a tree amid the wood,/ knowing the truths of things unseen before". (Pound, 1990: 3) The poet and the tree merge into one and "I" is a specific image of its own. In his poem *La Fraisne*, Pound had another mask as "*a gaunt, grave councilor*": "For I *was a gaunt, grave councilor*/Being *in all things wise, and very old*". (Pound, 1990:4) In *Marvoil*, Pound converts himself to "a poor clerk": "A poor clerk I, 'Arnaut the less' they call me". (Pound, 1990:21) In his widely acclaimed translation collection *Cathay*, "I" in many cases is the protagonist of a dramatic narrator rather than the poet himself. In *The River-Merchant's Wife: A Letter*, "I" is the female protagonist in southern China. She recalls her innocent childhood growing up together with her future husband, a cute little girl with the hair just covering the forehead with the boy in the neighborhood coming around on bamboo horse and playing in all innocent happiness. Several years later, the formerly little girl becomes the boy's bride, lowering her head in silent shyness. The married life is blissful with their passionate love growing with each day and the wife desires to mingle her dust with his in the coming world. Yet the marital bliss lasts only a year when the husband is forced to be away from hometown to make a living in the most dangerous section of the Yangtze River buried with numerous rocks. The wife spends the days in solitary distress and apprehension for months and months. The moss on the path that used to be tramped by the husband, the leaves that falls in the autumn wind, the paired butterflies in the garden all remind the protagonist of the absence of her beloved one. In the end of the poem, she says she is willing to go a long way to meet the husband if ever he would go back home. Throughout the poem, a delicate Chinese girl is telling her story, extraordinary passion and fidelity in ordinary daily life. Pound, in his translation, narrates from the perspective of the protagonist in free verse to copy her innocent unaffected tone. The precise copying of the girl's tone creates the classic image in America poetry. It is the same case with the mask in Pound's translation *The Jewel Stairs' Grievance*, Pound uses "I" as the subject of the non-subject lines of the original non-subject poetry. He again narrates the sorrow and grief at the desertion of the protagonist through his derepresentation of "I".

The original text: 玉阶生白露，夜久侵罗袜。却下水晶帘，玲珑望秋月。

Ezra Pound: The jeweled steps are already quite white with dew,
It is so late the dew soaks my gauze stockings,
And I let down the crystal curtain
And watch the moon through the clear autumn

Witter Bynner: Her jade-white staircase is cold with dew;
Her silk soles are wet, she lingered there so long...
Behind her closed casement, why is she still waiting,

Watching through its crystal pane the glow of the autumn moon?

Qiu Xiaolong: Waiting, she finds her silk stockings
soaked with the dew drops
glistening on the marble palace steps.
Finally, she is moving
to let the crystal-woven curtain fall
when she casts one more glance
at the glamorous autumn moon.

Sun Dayu: Dew drops on the gem steps fall'n cool
Through her flimsy silken socks seep;
Stepping down through the screen of crystal beads
She at the sparkling autumnal moon doth peep.

Among the four translators of the poem, Pound is the only one that uses "I" instead of "she" as the agent of the activities. "I" again becomes a mask for Pound to hide his own poetic self. Where Bynner and other translators add "she" as the missing subject for the original, Pound adds "I" as the counterpart. Pound himself becomes the abandoned lady in court and watches through her eyes the desolate night scenes. The voice is not Pound's but the lady's in the poem. With the adoption of "she", the poet is present at the scene watching and depicting. The initial "her" in two lines in Bynner's version first intrudes the picture with the protagonist, arousing the readers to wonder her identity and circumstances at the very beginning. And Bynner assumes his authorial presence with his question of "why is she still waiting?" Pound, in contrast, depicts the natural scene and then presents the protagonist's activity from her perspective. Then the prior natural scenes take the same perspective and becomes the lady's perception of the external world. The poem is expressed in the voice of the lady with the poet retiring from the stage. Also, in the poem *Lament of the Frontier Guard*, Pound identifies "I" with the soldier in defense of the country in the barbarous desert frontier: "By the North Gate, the wind blows full of sand, /Lonely from the beginning of time until now! /Trees fall, the grass goes yellow with autumn. /I climb the towers and towers/to watch out the barbarous land."

Secondly, "I" becomes the scripter in history. In his poem *Piere Vidal Old*, Pound takes the voice of a well-known figure in the Provence tales. He writes in profuse passion: "When I but think upon the great dead days/And turn my mind upon that splendid madness, /Lo! I do curse my strength/And blame the sun his gladness; /For that the one is dead/And the red sun mocks my sadness. /Behold me, Vidal, that was fool of fools! /Swift as the king wolf was I and as strong/ when tall stags fled me through the alder brakes... " (Pound, 1990:28) For the readers to interpret the poem properly, Pound reveals the identity of the scripter and the circumstances concerning the character in the preface: "It is of Piere Vidal, the fool par excellence of all Provence, of whom the tale tells how he ran mad, as a wolf, because of his love for Loba of Penautier, and how men hunted him with dogs through the mountains of Cabaret and brought him for dead to the dwelling of this Loba of Penautier, and how she and her Lord had him healed and made welcome, and he stayed some time at that court". (Pound, 1990:28) When Pound claims passionately in his poem: "Is your hate, then, of such meaure? /Do you, truly, so detest me? /Through all the world will I complain/Of how you have addressed me", the "I" in the poem is not his poetic self, but Heine's, because he translates and then adapts it from Heine. In *Three Cantos* published in 1917, he begins it with the story of "I": "Hang it all, there can be but one Sordello! /But say I want to, say I take your whole bag of tricks,/Let in your quirks and tweeks, and say the thing's an art-form. /.../I stand before the booth, the speech; but the truth/Is inside this discourse — this booth is full of the marrow of wisdom. ..." It is the voice of Odysseus through Pound. He is telling the story, depicting the history through his knowledge from other authors and his poetic self fades in the disguise of such masks. For Pound, the sentimentality of the poet himself is not the focus of the poetry that requires ornamental and profuse statement. In his eye, "I" is part of the universe, objective in nature and forceful in origin. Thus, the objective depiction of "I" is essential. "The I, as Pounds asserts, is a passive receptacle through which the fluid force of the natural world presents itself". (Kim, 2003:167)

The Victorian poetry is marked by its profuse sentimentality, so overflowing as to be represented often by interrogatives and exclamations. There is the opening rhetoric question by John Keats in *Ode on a Grecian Urn*: "Who are these coming to the sacrifice? /To what green altar, O mysterious priest,/Lead'st thou that heifer lowing at the skies,/And all her silken flanks with garlands drest?" There is the closing rhetoric question by Percy Bysshe Shelley in his *Ode to the West Wind*: "The trumpet of a prophecy! O Wind,/If Winter comes, can Spring be far behind?" There are the effluent lauds to God Pan by Elizabeth Barret Browning in her *A Musical Instrument*: "Sweet, sweet, sweet, O Pan! / Piercing sweet by the river! /Blinding sweet, O great god Pan!" There are the repetitive beckonings to the sea by Alfred Tennyson in his *Break, Break, Break*: "Break, break, break,/On thy cold gray stones, O Sea!" However, such rhetoric display of emotions is a rarity among modernists. A look at Pound's poetry and his translations will reveal the rarity of such exclamations and interrogatives. The modernist poetry, as Pound advocates, should be as objective as it can in the description of the natural world, in which human emotions don't assume superiority but remain an objective part.

Pound's translation collection *Cathay* contains no exclamations for the overflowing poetic feelings. The absence of inundated emotions marks a typical feature of modernist poetry, which focuses more on the objective depiction rather than the subjective sentimentality.

Interrogatives are necessary somewhere in the poetry, but Pound's interrogatives function differently. Previously, they are often used introvertly as a means of self-reflection such as in William Wordsworth's *The Solitary Reaper*: "Or is it some more humble lay,/Familiar matter of to-day? /Some natural sorrow, loss, or pain,/That has been, and may be again?" Or they are used to capture the attention of the readers to usher in the surging emotions of the poet in the following lines as in Byron's *The Eve before Waterloo*: "Did ye not hear it? — No; 'twas but the wind,/Or the car rattling o'er the stony street ;/On with the dance!" Or sometimes they are used to shed intellectual insight on some abstract concept such as in John Keats' To Autumn: "Where are the songs of Spring? Ay, where are they? /Think not of them, thou hast thy music too". Pound's interrogatives, by contrast, are seldom the introvert reflections but the direct statement by the protagonist in the poetry as part of the depiction of the objective circumstances as shown in *Song of the Bowman of Shu*: "Here we are, picking the first fern-shoots/And saying: When shall we get back to our country? /... We grub the old fern-stalks. /We say: Will we be let to go back in October? /... Our mind is full of sorrow, who will know of our grief?" In such interrogatives, the poet himself is invisible but an indirect narrator of their feelings. The readers are moved not by the subjective overflow of the poet himself, but by the natural flow of events as just the bystanders of the world. It is the same case in *The River Merchant's Wife: A Letter* when the female protagonist is in her yearning for her husband's return: "Forever and forever and forever. /Why should I climb the look out?" Pound, the poet himself, as the readers, is just bystanders of his protagonist's mentality. Sometimes the questions are raised to reach their own answers: "What flower has come into blossom? /Whose chariot? The General's" (from *Song of the Bowman of Shu*) "Who brought this to pass? /Who was brought the flaming imperial anger? / Who has brought the army with drums and with kettle-drums? /Barbarous kings" (from *Lament of the Frontier Guard*) There are the mere interrogatives in the whole poetry collection *Cathay*, from which we find Pound's tendency to depict objectively the world around us instead of resorting to the subjective consciousness of the poet himself, asking questions to explore the spiritual realm.

While other translators tend to use the exclamations or interrogatives, Pound often states the fact directly. The following example is in his translation of Chinese poet Tao Yuanming's *The Unmoving Cloud*.

The original text：翩翩飞鸟，息我庭柯。敛翮闲止，好声相和。
岂无他人，念子实多。愿言不获，抱恨如何。

Ezra Pound：
The birds flutter to rest in my tree,
and I think I have heard them saying,
"It is not that there are no other men
But we like this fellow the best,
But however we long to speak
He cannot know of our sorrow."

Burton Watson：
Flutter flutter, birds on the wing,
they light on the limbs in my garden,
fold their wings, rest peacefully,
blending their beautiful cries.
Not that there are no others,
but I think of you so very often.
With longings unfulfilled,
brooding on my sorrow, what shall I do?

Fang Zhong：
Fluttering, fluttering, the light birds
Come to rest on my garden branches,
Perching in quiet contentment;
Sweetly to one another they sing.
True it is I have other friends.
But now I think of you most.
What I wish I cannot get,
How vexed am I to think of this!

Wang Rongpei：
The birds that fly on wings at ease
Have come to rest on garden trees.
There they perch and sit abreast,
Singing lyrics at their best.
I do have other friends to boast,

But now I think of you the most.
However, you are far away
And I am filled with deep dismay!

Compared with versions of other translations, Pound is unique in his treatment of the feelings of the poet as the monologue by the birds ("It is not that there are no other men/But we like this fellow the best,/But however we long to speak/He cannot know of our sorrow."). Burton Watson describes the mental state of the poet (brooding on my sorrow) and give a rhetoric question at the end (what shall I do?). Fang Zhong also resorts to the exclamation to express the subjective feelings (What I wish I cannot get,/How vexed am I to think of this!). Wang Rongpei gives a direct explanation of the poet's feeling (I am filled with deep dismay) and adds the reason of sorrow (you are far away). Pound could not have misinterpreted the original meaning when Fenollosa's notes for the poem indicate clearly the explicit expression of feelings, yet he deliberately changes it to the monologue of birds, morphing the sorrow of the poet to the sorrow of the birds. The motive behind all the conversions, explicit from the ultimate effect, is Pound's preach of expressing the subjective from the objective when he renders the sorrow of birds reflective of the poet's sadness instead of directly giving the melancholy exclamation.

3.2.3 Defiance of Authorial Presence

In the modern age marked by immense scientific advance, Pound takes a scientific perspective in his poetic practice. He parallels arts to science in that science deals with the objects and art with human consciousness, and both are to reveal the general nature in the universe but in different respects: "As the abstract mathematician is to science so is the poet to the world's consciousness. Neither has direct contact with the many, neither of them is superhuman or arrives at his utility through occult and inexplicable ways. Both are scientifically demonstrable". (Pound, 1973:332) Pound defies the "superhuman" authority of the poet, denouncing the superior capability of the poet to be enlightened by the supreme being and to announce the occult. He argues for the scientific nature of arts, when the individual voices, like minor mathematic facts, could be demonstrated and would reveal the universal truth in collection. The modernist T. E. Hulme also believes in the scientific nature of arts to "prolong the individual facts into general laws". (Hulme, 1994:192) Thus, the modernist poets are in constant search for the general truth by presenting individual voices with the poetic self invisible, which is in defiance of the previous overemphasis on the poet's omnipotent presence. Pound, in particular, renounces the authorial presence in poetry and instead, he seeks multiple masks to hide the self. He says: "I began this search for the real in a book called *Personae*, casting off, as it were, complete masks of the self in each poem. I continued in long series of translations, which were but more elaborate masks". (Pratt, 2007: 132) In his poetry, Pound frequently changes his personality, from the hero Ulysses in Homer's *Odyssey* in his first Canto to the delicate Chinese woman in *The River-Merchant's Wife: A Letter* who waits in sorrowful longing for her husband's return from a long journey, from the French glory-seeking troubadour to the deserted courtesan in *The Jewel Stairs' Grievance*. They are from different times, different places, of different sexes, with different moods, yet they are alike in one sense, all as the masks for Pound. And also, when it comes to the exposure of the poetic self, the modernists do not salute and acclaim but satire and mock. Pound's self-portraits in both *Hugh Selwyn Mauberley: Life and Contacts* and *Pisan Cantos* are more reflective than eulogistic. In the first one, Pound, at the age of 35, bids farewell to London in his poetry, thinking of how dilettantish he once was. The second one is a heavier one with his reflection in the American military camp prison over his Rome radio broadcasts of treason during the Second World War. He views the Second World War as the great human catastrophe, causing destruction to the world, and to the poet himself. "Pound himself means many other selves. Like his hero and alter ego, Ulysses, Pound was many-minded, a highly complex personality incorporating multiple individuals". (Pratt, 2007: 134) In his poems and his translations, Pound pulls down the authentic presence of the poet as a move in his modernist movement.

Multiple voices refer to Pound's assemblage of past voices in his translations and other poetic works. Firstly, Pound develops masks, personae in his term, to express his poetic self in the disguise of other narrators. The technique is developed from Robert Browning's famous dramatic monologue *My Last Dutchess*, a piece of spoken verse that offers insight into the profound feelings of the speaker. Pound, in his translations, selects the themes on ordinary individuals instead of epic heroes. In his translation collection *Cathay*, there are the descriptions of daily-life trifles, the records of a journey, the conveyance of grief or frustration, all of ordinary individuals. Pound believes the state of individuals is a manifest reflection of the general social truth just as scientists, with the discovery of atoms and molecules, could probe deeply into the general laws of the universe. Scientifically, just as the different particles constituting the mass, the different individuals constitute the humankind. What the artist should present is the unique individuality of each entity: "From the arts we learn that man is whimsical, that one man differs from another. That men differ among themselves as leaves upon trees differ. That they do not resemble each other as do buttons cut by machine". (Pound, 1968: 42) In his translations, Pound becomes different Personae in their unique state of mind and state of existence. In *Song of the Bowmen of Shu*, the poet wears the mask of a soldier who fights away from home for many years and yearns for the return to the homeland. The *Beautiful Toilet* portrays a young lady in the futile longing for the return of her husband. *The River-Merchant's Wife: A Letter* is narrated from the perspective of a young girl who recalls the memory from her childhood, about her transformation from a little girl to a loving wife and of her lonely yearning after her husband's departure. *The Jewel Stairs' Grievance* is a vivid portrayal of a neglected court lady sorrowful in abandonment. *Lament of the Frontier Guard* delineates the frontier soldier in deep sorrow in the desolate fields. *Sennin Poem by Kakuhaku* and Tao Yuanming *The Unmoving Cloud* are about the hermit life. *A Ballad of the Mulberry Road* is about a beauty that draws attention of every passer-by. Every personality is unique with Pound's meticulous imitation of the tone and the pursuit of precision in depiction. For example, in *Song of the Bowmen of Shu*, short simple clauses are used in succession without logic connection. It is an imitation of the speech by the soldier seeped in sorrowful longing for return: "Sorrowful minds, sorrow is strong, we are hungry and thirsty. /Our defence is not yet made sure, no one can let his friend return." Similar examples are found in another poem that depict the sorrow of the soldier *Lament of the Frontier Guard*. In the poem, Pound wears the mask of a soldier in the frontier and interrogates directly the cruelty of barbarous kings for their suffering: "Who brought this to pass? /Who has brought the flaming imperial anger? /Who has brought the army with drums and with kettle-drums? / Barbarous kings." For the original declarative statements, Pound converts them to interrogatives so that he, in the voice of the soldier, directly inquires the fate about the root of their suffering. The parallel interrogatives, each longer than the previous one, build up the force that impels the readers to sense their misery. And the following lines, in the short fragments, are a vivid simulation of the sorrowful sobbing of the persona: "Three hundred and sixty thousand,/And sorrow, sorrow like rain. /Sorrow to go, and sorrow, sorrow returning. / Desolate, desolate fields,/And no children of warfare upon them,/No longer the men for offence and defence." In *The River-Merchant's Wife: A Letter*, Pound imitates the tone of the young girl in her happy memories of the puppy love in their childhood with the frequent use of small simple words: "While my hair was still cut straight across my forehead/I played at the front gate, pulling flowers./ You came by on bamboo stilts, playing horse,/You walked about my seat, playing with blue plums./And we went on living in the village of Chokan:/Two small people, without dislike or suspicion." These unique personalities in Pound's poetry compose a panoramic mosaic picture of the human world that contributes to the unveiling of the universal human nature.. From his poetry, especially the translations of the ancient, Pound displays the concrete basics of human existence across history: love and war, friendship and departure, suffering and pleasure, emperors and soldiers, hermits and poets, all as universal ingredients of human culture with which any reader could identify. In many other translations, Pound establishes the distinctive perception of life by the individual, through the vivid imitation of the narrator's tone. Take an example from his translation of Li Bai's poem along with other versions.

The original text: 妾发初覆额,折花门前剧;
郎骑竹马来,绕床弄青梅。
同居长干里,两小无嫌猜。

Ezra Pound: While my hair was still cut straight across my forehead
I played about the front gate, pulling flowers.
You came by on bamboo stilts, playing horse,
You walked about my seat, playing with blue plums.
And we went on living in the village of Chokan:
Two small people, without dislike or suspicion.

Witter Bynner: My hair had hardly covered my forehead.
I was picking flowers, playing by my door.
When you, my lover, on a bamboo horse,
Came trotting in circles and throwing green plums.
We lived near together on a lane in Ch'ang-kan,
Both of us young and happy-hearted.

Amy Lowell: When the hair of your Unworthy One first began to
cover her forehead,
she picked flowers and played in front of the door.
Then you, my Lover, came riding a bamboo horse.
We ran round and round the bed, and tossed about the
sweetmeats of green plums.
We both lived in the village of Chang Kan.
We were both very young, and knew neither jealousy

nor suspicion.

Pound imitates the tone of a young lady in the recollection of her happy childhood when she and her husband played and grew up together. At that time, she was a lovely little girl with her hair just covering the forehead who loved playing the flowers at the door. The boy next door often came by riding on a bamboo like riding a horse and went around the little girl. It is the most innocent stanza of the poem as the protagonist recalling the innocent days in her life. Pound uses three parallel sentences about the playful activities by the two small children: "I played about the front gate, pulling flowers. /You came by on bamboo stilts, playing horse, /You walked about my seat, playing with blue plums." In the three independent lines, he adopts simple monosyllable verbs of "play" (for three times) and "come" and "walk" and "pull" to imitate the childlike innocence at the time. As compared to Pound's simple version, Bynner combines the activities into one sentence with "when" to highlight the suddenness of the boy's emergence. And his use of the verb phrase "trot in circles" is not common in daily speech. The parallel structure of "trotting in circles" and "throwing green plums" as the accompanying activities of "coming on a bamboo horse" is a little clownish. Lowell changes the subject too often from "she" to the direct addressing of "you" and then to "we", which is quite rare in the narration of simple facts. It creates a sense of complexity in life as contrasted to the original simplicity. And with the additional word "then", Lowell stresses the activities in succession. Pound's version is like the separate shots flashing across the girl's mind that in combination creates the sense of innocence and sympathy. In the last line of the stanza, Pound's version of "two small people" is amusingly vivid when the little kids foster intimate friendship in their playful days. It builds a tone of strong reminiscence as people often chuckle at the innocence of the childhood days, at the smaller version of their grown-up bodies yet in much naive minds. Take another stanza as an example:

The original text: 十六君远行，瞿塘滟滪堆。五月不可触，猿声天上哀。

Ezra Pound: At sixteen you departed,
You went into far Ku-to-en, by the river of rolling eddies,
And you have been gone five months.
The monkeys make sorrowful noise overhead.

Witter Bynner: ... Then when I was sixteen, you left on a long journey
Through the Gorges of Chu-t'ang, of rock and
whirling water.
And then came the Fifth-month, more than I could bear,

And I tried to hear the monkeys in your lofty far-off sky.

Amy Lowell: When I was sixteen, my Lord went far away,
To the Cu'u T'ang Chasm and the Whirling Water
Rock of the Yu River.
Which, during the Fifth Month, must not be collided with;
where the wailing of the gibbons seems to come from the sky.

Pound uses the three separate sentences beginning with the protagonist's direct addressing to her husband, shifting the tone to the sorrowful anxiety. The direct addressing from the wife conveys her genuine concern for her husband's safety. When Pound uses the present perfect tense "you have been gone five months", her worry, though not directly stated, is presented to the reader who could conjure up the image of her counting the days of her husband's departure in apprehension. Lowell uses two relative clauses to form a complex statement. It is not in any way the form of daily speech and thus more of a written description than oral confidence. Bynner's addition of "more than I could bear" is a direct statement of the moods, turning the lines into more of a complaint than anxious concern. The example is evident proof to Pound's intention to produce distinctive masks, developing personalities of vigour and sincerity, as an essential means for the artist to create works of lasting influence. Pound's translation of works from Latin, Anglo-Saxon, Italian, Chinese and Japanese cultures enables him to "synthesize a series of Englishes into a personal idiom" (Brooker, 1979:34) and cultivate images striking in themselves and "subdued to his spirit". (Homberger, 1972) From each unique voice of multiple personalities, Pound endows the personalities with such power that "from the first to the last lines of most of his poems he holds us steadily in his own pure, grave, passionated world". (Homberger, 1972)

The poet's voice is invisible when there is no subjective evaluation or comment, nor hints of the poet's appreciative or depreciative preference. Pound, in his translations, mutes the voice of the poet and delegates the authoritative poet to the unbiased presenter of objective reality. Take the example from Pound's translation *The Beautiful Toilet* along with other versions.

The original text: 荡子行不归,空床难独守。

Ezra Pound: Who now goes drunkenly out
And leaves her too much alone.

Arthur Waley: The wandering man went, but did not return.
It is hard alone to keep an empty bed.

Burton Watson: A wanderer who never comes home,

It's hard to sleep in an empty bed alone.

Wang Rong-pei： As he wanders in an unknown zone，
It's hard for her to go to bed alone.

When other translators use the word "hard" in literal correspondence to the original character（难），Pound has the unique approach of omission. The clause involving "it's hard" gives the comment of the poet，demonstrating the clear authorial presence. Pound，by comparison，adopts a more objective approach by merely stating the fact，without any evaluation from the poet.

3.3 Self-consciousness of Poet

Modernist poetry is modern in thought，character，and practice. The late 19th century and the early 20th centuries witnessed dramatic changes in Western society which precipitated new literary trend to accommodate to it. The traditions underwent inevitable changes under the impact of industrialization in urban environment and revolution in philosophy and psychology. Modernist poetry highlights the self-consciousness of the poet as the effective means to portray and reflect the ever-changing reality.

Consciousness of the artist was either neglected or indulged in previous trends. Prior to modernism in literature，the Enlightenment in the 18th century advocated reason as the primary source and the legitimate justification of authority. Under the influence of Newtonian natural philosophy，the Enlightenmentalists appreciated the perception of the orderly，regular，logical physical world subject to universal laws and enhanced human rational capacity to penetrate the mysteries of nature to the new height. Without the faculty of reason，man's senses and impressions amounted to nothing. In some sense，the Enlightenment glorified reason as common human possession. The mechanic perception of the physical universe was to Modernists the rigid suppression of the artist's individualistic quality. The successive Romantism in the 19th century opposed to deposing the individual consciousness by stifling imagination，sensitivity，feelings，spontaneity and freedom，by blocking the emotions and creativity. Romantists advocated self-consciousness as the key element to find the existence of God，which was evident in all forms of life. The return of God to Nature led to a revival of the unseen world，the supernatural and the mysterious. Romantists went to the other extreme with their redundant presentation of sentimental emotions and their lifting the poetic self to the exaggerated height.

Modernists，in face of the disruption of old order in politics and economy and morality, felt the urge to reshape the traditional systems to restore order and come to terms with the seemingly untetherable rapid changes. They departed from the tradition of the Enlightenment, laying emphasis on the intuition as the direct means of poetic experience and on the individualistic quality. They also drew a line from the Romantism, stressing objective reality as the only effective means to reveal the subjective. Man was no longer the soulless, mechanical, logical and unfeeling thinking machines in the Enlightenment. Nor was he the carrier of God's discipline authorized with the overflow of instinctive depiction in the direct statement of intense emotions as Percy Bysshe Shelley put it in *Prometheus Unbound*: "The joy, the triumph, the delight, the madness! /The boundless, overflowing, bursting gladness,/The vaporous exultation not to be confined! /Ha! Ha! The animation of delight/Which wraps me, like an atmosphere of light,/And bears me as a cloud is borne by its own wind." The passion was burning yet to modernists, leaned too much on intuitive flashes and feelings. Modernism trusted the individual intuition and consciousness to perceive and present, cultivating the objective truth in the universe and abandoning the means of imagination for unbridled emotion.

3.3.1 Abandonment of Religion

With the recognition of the complexity of the world, and with critical scrutiny over the old "final authorities", Modernists reject reason as the all-solving panacea and Creator as the compassionate, all-powerful existence. Darwin's theories of evolution, the rise of positivism and scientific materialism all undermine the faith in the Christianity. Pound has the distaste for Christianity. He believes that "Christianity is verminous with Semitic infections". (Pound, 1973:71) He appeals for the renunciation of Christianity, condemning the conscious Christian mind as "the root of all evil": "Christianity has become a sort of Prussianism, and will have to go. All the bloody moral attacks are based on superstition, religion, or whatever it is to be called". (Pound, 1971:97-98) To him, all religions would breed evil because "Every religion is ... an attempt to enforce a type or a cliché; an attempt to impose a thought-mould upon others". (Kim, 2003:61) The rigid matrix of Christianity stifles individual intuition and perception by succumbing to supreme authority and rejects the physical world by escaping to the spiritual world. Pound seeks "the real" in the nature and in man, lifting self-consciousness as the salient characteristic of the modernists with his stress on the individual poetic experience.

In his translation of the ancient Anglo-Saxon poem *The Seafarer*, Pound shows the distaste for religious preach by eliminating the last nine lines of the poem with Christian reference, the moral instruction and a hymn to God. At other places, Pound makes similar alterations by eliminating Christian moralizing. At various times throughout the poem, *The Seafarer*, that is, the downtrodden exile at the sea, in all his loneliness, begins to sing for the wonders and greatness of God, of Christian virtue, which Pound does not preserve in his translation, but alters the passage where men are preached to combat the malice of devils. The images of devils and angles make no recurrence in his translation. Pound, with his purpose of representing the modern, alters the reference of Christianity boldly even at the cost of faithful translation, "altering the very nature of the poem" (Nadel, 2008: 45) by replacing Christian values with "something almost barbaric". (Nadel, 2008:45) But to the modernist Pound, it is an imperative practice to showcases the modern spirit when "defiance was a keynote of modernists". (Pratt, 2007:119)

3.3.2 Abandonment of Reason — Germinal Consciousness

Modernists differ from their predecessors in the emphasis of awakening individual consciousness, unlike the Enlightenmentalists who stress intellectual reason, unlike the symbolists who gives supreme prominence to the perceptive power of human mind, unlike the Romantists who overemphasizes the spiritual power of the poet self. With the advent of modern philosophy and psychology, the artists seek new styles to fit modernism. In philosophy, Schopenhauer argues that man should dismiss reason and surrender to perceiving natural objects as the eternal form, that is, the objectification of the thing-in-itself. Bergson argues that intuition, rather than analysis, can achieve a penetration into a reality by making the distinction between intellect and intuition, between the rational consciousness of everyday life and the deeper consciousness of immediate experience. He says: "There is one reality, at least, which we all seize from within, by intuition and not by simple analysis. It is our own personality in its flowing through time — our self which endures". (Lierbregts, 2004: 83) Intuition rather than symbols or concepts, Bergson says, is the only means to give the essence of our self and intuition enables us to grasp the mobile reality because our inner life is "a continuous flux, a succession of states, each of which announces that which follows and contains that which precedes it". (Bergson, 2002, 35) The major means to attain the truth is to shun away from abstract concepts and rationality of "Being" and to employ the intuitive power to have the immediate experience of "Becoming", as Bergson notes, since the abstract concepts are unable to represent the inner life of duration, a constant flow of conscious experiences which constitutes our true selves. T. E. Hulme, a modernist pioneer, substantiates the argument: "Our eye perceives the features of the living being merely as assembled, not as mutually organized. The intention of life — a simple movement which runs through the lines and binds them together and gives them significance — escapes it. This intention is just what the artist tries to regain in placing himself back within the object by a kind of sympathy and breaking down by an effort of intuition the barrier that space puts between him and his model". (Hulme, 1994: 192) The aesthetic intuition is for Hulme an effective means not merely to attain the individual fact, but to point out the direction through this external perception and "prolongs the individual facts into general laws". (Hulme, 1994: 192) Pound the modernist also stresses the importance of active consciousness to seek general truth of the universe. He does not focus on the mere going-on in the human mind or the mere inquiry of questions to be replied by the spiritual self, but on the consciousness in combination with the material world, the objective universe. Yet active consciousness is not the mere receptacle of the objective, but a "higher" consciousness as compared to the passive one. Pound coins the term "germinal consciousness" because it could enable the poet to see the "universe of wood alive, of stone alive", (Pound, 1971: 92) and the "thoughts are in them as the thought of the trees is in the seed, or in the grass, or the grain, or the blossom". (Pound, 1971: 92) With germinal consciousness, the poets can link themselves to the vital universe through the awareness of their true selves. Modernists, to Pound, should make constant search "in his own soul" and embody the things through his genuine perception and intuitive poetic experience.

Intuitive power is the energy source of poetry, liberating the mind of the poet and of the readers in the precise report of objective facts. Pound asserts that "the serious artist is scientific in that he resents the image of his desire, of his hate, of his indifference... as precisely the image of his own desire, hate or indifference. The more precise his record the more lasting and unassailable his work of art". (Pound, 1968: 46) Pound once wrote about his experience in writing his famous poem *In a Station of the Metro*: "Three years ago in Paris I got out of a 'metro' train at La Concorde, and saw suddenly a beautiful face, and then another and another, and then a beautiful child's face, and then another beautiful woman, and I tried all that day to find words for what this had meant to me,... " (Pound, 1974: 86-7) Pound seized this intuitive impact on him and restored the similar impact in his poem. He selected the image of "Petals on a wet, black bough" that would represent exactly what he felt at the sight of the beautiful faces in the gloomy crowd. It is the accurate and clear denotation of a world outside the poetic self yet to the immediate access of all separate selves.

The power of intuition also lies in the uniqueness of difference selves that engenders multifarious perceptions. The world provides the facts to determine "that one man differs from another. That men differ among themselves as leaves from a tree differ. That they do not resemble each other as do buttons from a machine". (Pound, 1968: 42) Against the degradation of humans as uniform machinelike workers in the modern era of industrialization, the modernists call for individuality. Pound, in his essay *The Serious Artist*, preaches: "No perfect state will be founded on the theory, or on the working hypothesis that all men are alike. No science save the arts will give us the requisite data for learning in what ways men differ." Art, especially poetry, is an effective means to demonstrate the difference of men, "touching the nature of man, of individuals". (Pound, 1968:47) Thus, Pound, in his works, endeavors to reveal the individual lives and thoughts in different protagonists. There are the forlorn seafarer he translates from the ancient Anglo-Saxon text, the sorrowful abandoned lady, the desolate frontier soldiers he translates from the classical Chinese poetry, the ancient hero of Odysseus he adapts from Homer's epic. The artist Pound tries to demonstrate the true state of life and of mind through different individuals, just as the serious scientist deals with "the relations of abstract numbers, of molecular energy, of the composition of matter" (Pound, 1968: 47) to find the scientific truth.

Active consciousness also means "cosmic consciousness", (Lierbregts, 2004:42) the fresh perception of the image to represent true reality. Pound's poem *The Tree* is fresh perspective of the image to reflect the subjective experience: "I stood still and was a tree amid the wood, /Knowing the truth of things unseen before; /Of Daphne and the laurel bow/And that god-feasting couple old/that grew elm-oak amid the world. /'Twas not until the gods had been/Kindly entreated, and been brought within/Unto the hearth of their heart's home/That they might do this wonder thing; /Nathless I have been a tree amid the wood/And many a new thing understood/That was rank folly to my head before." In the poem, Pound's poetic self is merged with the entity of tree. From that new perspective as a tree, all the divine beings become tangible reality instead of the imaginary myths. The poet transforms the ancient myths into reality "out of flashes of cosmic consciousness" and in that metamorphosis,

Pound reveals to himself "the inner matter of the Daphne story". (Lierbregts, 2004:42-43) The attempt to merge with the cosmic consciousness is seen in many of his works. The poem *A Girl* is another typical one: "The tree has entered my hands,/The sap has ascended my arms,/The tree has grown in my breast —/ Downward,/The branches grow out of me, like arms." The persona in the poem has the sensation of converting herself as a part of the natural world and experiences it in that germinal consciousness.

Pound's emphasis on germinal consciousness for good poetry is also demonstrated in his interest in Chinese ideograms. Pound, impressed by Ernest Fenollosa's insight in the essay *The Chinese Written Character as a Medium for Poetry* that Chinese ideograms are "something much more than arbitrary symbols" "based upon a vivid shorthand picture of the operations of nature" and assumes "the quality of a continuous moving picture", (Fenollosa, 1936: 12) adopts the etymological visibility of the ideogram in his translations. He believes that the pictorial nature of the ideogrammic character reveals the nature of the universe and enables the readers to be in direct contact with the conscious experience. Later Pound even goes further with his etymological practice in his translation of Confucian works and his experiment in translation by this intuitive grasp by restoring the visibility of the Chinese characters. For example, for the original line "日居月诸", Pound gives the translation "Sun, neath thine ancient roof, moon speaking ancient speech", (Pound, 2003:768) where he decodes the Chinese character "居" in its two components that means "house" and "ancient" respectively. For the original line "昊天有成命", Pound's version is "light above heaven focused the decree", (Pound, 2003: 966) where the Chinese character "昊" is interpreted in its two ingredients that means "sun" and "heaven" respectively. Also, Pound puts the original line "渐渐之石,维其高矣" into "Where the torrent bed breaks our wagon wheel/up, up the road", (Pound, 2003:909) in which the Chinese characters "渐渐" indicating the immensity of the stone in the original is interpreted by Pound in the combination of its ingredients of "water" and "wagon". Many of such practices reflect Pound's intention to sense the ancient works with his intuition instead of following the conventional established rules for the semantic content.

3.4 Free Verse

The modernist Hulme notes that "there is an intimate connection between the verse form and the state of poetry at any period" and "each age must have its own special form of expression, and any period that deliberately goes out of it is an age of insincerity". (Hulme, 1994: 50-51) The modern age, with the transformed landscape by the industrialization and the deeper exploration of human consciousness, calls for a new form of expression rather than the "fixed and artificial form" (Hulme, 1994: 52) of regular metre. The old form has developed from the initial freedom to the following decay and then become the manacles for the poetic feelings. A variety of forms over the decades, the Elizabethan poetic drama and the following heroic couplet and the lyrical poetry with all its sentimentalism, have been emerging and fading. "After being too much used their primitive effect is lost. All possible tunes have been played on the instrument". (Hulme, 1994:50) The old forms are no longer appropriate for the new age and there must be some new forms "deliberately introduced by people who detest the old ones". (Hulme, 1994:51) Free verse, at that call, becomes the main form of the new age and Pound is the pioneer.

As the name suggests, free verse is a modern form of poetry of using more irregular cadences instead of following any specific rhyme or metrical scheme. Free verse, vers libre in French term, is generally believed to derive from the practices of 19th century French poets such as Gustave Kahn and Jules Laforgue who launch the vers libre movement in their revolt against the tyranny of strict French versification. Its popularity in English could be traced back to such notable poets as Walt Whitman, whose signature collection *Leaves of Grass* is composed of free verse poetry, pulling away from the restrictions of the traditional patterns of meter and rhyme. Since Walt Whitman, modernists embrace free verse poetry as an effective means to express unbridled passionate emotions. Free verse poetry continues to evolve throughout the 20th century, adopted and spread by poets such as Carl Sandburg and Robert Frost, and especially Ezra Pound, the pioneering figure in modernism and a master of free verse in his renowned translation of Chinese poetry *Cathay* and then a mentor to many of the 20th century's most famous authors and poets.

Free verse emerges as a form close to the modern speech to reflect the dramatic changes in the modern era and as a response to the immense information and the complex consciousness in the modern world. Pound asserts the necessity of vers libre in his *A Retrospect*: "I think the desire for vers libre is due to the sense of quantity reasserting itself after years of starvation". (Pound, 1968:3) Pound is ready for contemporary speech as his new poetic language, the language with rhythms "closer to the patterns of speech" (Beasley, 2007:26) when he finds "a vast number of subjects cannot be properly rendered in symmetrical forms". (Carpenter, 1988:170) The new form of free verse is the combination of "the words and the word-order such as anyone might naturally use" (Moody, 2007:208) "freed from all conventional constraints". (Moody, 2007:208) With free verse, the poetry marches forward with more realistic content of the modern society and more experimental form of colloquial speech against the previous ornamental poetic language. Pound believes that free verse represents progress in poetry. Free verse is not the lazy escape from the deliberate conception of exquisite meters, but a form adopted in necessity when the meter becomes an obstacle to the smooth expression of emotion, as Pound put it: "I think one should write vers libre only when one 'must', that is to say, only when the 'thing' builds up a rhythm more beautiful than that of set meters, or more real, more a part of the emotion of the 'thing', more germane, intimate, interpretative than the measure of regular accentual verse; a rhythm which discontents one with set iambic or set anapaestic". (Pound, 1968:12) Nor is Free verse exactly free from any restrictions and unbound by any principles because "No vers is libre for the man who wants to do a good job". (Pound, 1968:12) Pound devotes himself to the experimentation of free verse and enables it to "reach its classical stage". (Homberger, 1972:117) G. W. Cronin in his article *Classic Free Verse* in 1917, highly acclaimed the poetic achievement of Pound in the use of free verse:"No longer, as in Whitman, an instinct, an iconoclasm, it has learned, by way of the French symbolists, to do remarkable stunts, acquired a technique and a system all its own, and become deliberate, exquisite, self-assured and positive. One of those rare periods we designate auriferously. The Golden Age. The Golden Age of Vers libre!" (Homberger, 1972:117)

3.4.1 Colloquial Language

Free verse, first of all, contains colloquial speech in poetry. The two prominent figures stimulating Pound's new approach, Ford Madox Ford and Flaubert, both argue for the modernity of language in literature, with Ford calling for rendering the concrete in contemporary speech and Flaubert advancing *le mot juste*, that is, the exact word striped of all associations. Pound, under their influence, disdains the traditional metric system: "Surely all systems of metric... have been a vulgarity & a barbarism, and their beautiful results have been due to genius & accident & not to any virtue inherent in the system". (Carpenter, 1988:164) He realizes that "a vast number of subjects cannot be... properly rendered in symmetrical forms" and the solution is colloquial speech in poetry for "the trampling down of every convention that impedes or obscures".

(Carpenter, 1988:170) To Pound, the freedom of form will give free rein to the profound content. Pound believes the way to depict a thing matters as much as what is depicted. He is impressed by the freedom of expression in Japanese hokku: "A great hokku poem never makes us notice its limitations of form, but rather impresses us by the freedom through mystery of its chosen language, as if a sea-crossing wind had blown in from a little window". (Bell, 1981:10) Inspired by the method, Pound uses free verse in his translations of oriental poetry to unleash the emotions without the restrictions of English metrics. Before Pound, James Legge and Herbert Giles adopt in their translations of Chinese poetry "the mainstream Victorian poetic treatment", with the result that the translated Chinese poems seemed "well within normative English poeticism", with "familiar features of meter, rhyme, and poetic diction", yet at the cost of the "strangeness and otherness" in the original Chinese, except in some exotic names persons and places. (Xie, 1999:5) Other Chinese translators in the period include Charles Budd, Launcelot A. Cranmer-Byng, and W. J. B. Fletcher, creating translations invariably continuing the Victorian tradition of poetic treatment established by Legge and Giles, and "the debased Tennysonian and Pre-Raphaelite line of archaic diction and exoticism". (Xie, 1999: 5) Pound revolutionizes poetic language with free verse translations of Chinese poetry, developing the poetic diction from archaism to colloquial speech, "the language he felt appropriate to purpose and context". (Wilson, 2005:129) T. S. Eliot praised him to be "the inventor of Chinese poetry for our time" (Alexander, 1979:100) and with the new technique of extending rhythmic control over longer lines in simple colloquial language, the beauty of the poems strikes the reader and wins Pound widespread acclaim. A comparison of the different versions by Giles and Pound will reveal the difference in rhyme and in style.

Herbert Giles: A singing-girl in early life,
And now a careless roué's wife...
Ah, if he does not mind his own,
He'll find some day the bird has flown!

Ezra Pound: And she was a courtesan in the old days,
And she has married a sot,
Who now goes drunkenly out
And leaves her too much alone.

Giles uses tetrameter for each line, and rhyming them with the regular "life" and "wife", "own" and "flown" at the end of lines. But he adds a metaphor that is absent in the original and makes the last two lines the rewriting of the original instead of faithful translation. It is justifiable in that rhyming is difficult in English and the adding and cutting of the original words for the regular rhyme and meter has to be a frequent practice. Giles version deviates completely because of his eagerness for rigid rhyme. Pound, however, uses colloquial English to translate the stanza. The frequent use of "and" highlights the flavor of spoken English. And he employs a large number of single syllable words to reinforce the feature. Another simple comparison between Pound's version in free verse and other versions in metric forms will reveal the superiority of free verse in the translation of Chinese poetry.

The original poem: 妾发初覆额,折花门前剧;
郎骑竹马来,绕床弄青梅。
同居长干里,两小无嫌猜。

Ezra Pound: While my hair was still cut straight across my forehead
I played about the front gate, pulling flowers.
You came by on bamboo stilts, playing horse,
You walked about my seat, playing with blue plums.
And we went on living in the village of Chokan:
Two small people, without dislike or suspicion.

W. J. B. Fletcher: When first o'er maiden brows my hair I tied,
In sport I plucked the blooms before the door.
You riding came on hobby-horse astride,
And wreatherd my bed with green-gage branches o'er.
At ch'ang-kan Village long together dwelt
We children twain, and knew no petty strife.

Xu Yuanchong: My forehead covered by my hair cut straight,
I played with flowers pluck'd before the gate.
On hobbyhorse you came upon the scene,
Around the well we played with plumes still green.
We lived, close neighbors on Riverside Lane,
Carefree and innocent, we children twain.

C. Gaunt. When the curls first began to o'ershadow my brow
I was plucking the flowers by the gate.
When lo! There rode up a venturous knight
On a bamboo charger he sate;
Together we played, village boy and maid,
Nor suspected the schemings of fate.

First of all, in the translation versions with regular metric forms, there are more archaic words no longer used in the contemporary speech. Fletcher and Xu, when translating the sense of "two youngsters", put that as "we children twain", in which "twain" is no longer in spoken language now. Pound's version, in contrast, apart from the proper word "Chokan", is made up of words commonly in use in everyday life in the modern world. Also, the syntax in version with regular metric forms is in unnatural order to meet the requirement of rhyme and meter. There is the inversion such as "There rode up a venturous knight" by Gaunt, the postponement of verbs till the end of the sentence such as "When first o'er maiden brows my hair I tied" by Fletcher, the separation of subject and predicate with participles such as "You riding came on hobby-horse astride" by Fletcher, the fronting of adverbials to the initial or middle position of the sentence such as "In sport I plucked the blooms before the door" and "At ch'ang-kan Village long together dwelt" by Fletcher, "On hobbyhorse you came upon the scene,/Around the well we played with plumes still green" by Xu, "On a bamboo charger he sate" and "Together we played, village boy and maid" by Gaunt. Pound, in contrast, resorts to no sentence in irregular order, each of the sentences following the simple pattern of "subject + predicate + object + adverbial". The poetry flows with the natural mobility of activity and phenomena. What's more, Pound's version in free verse cut down the redundant modifiers of noun phrases so that the language flows naturally. Xu, for regular rhyme in his version, adds long participle attributives such as "covered by my hair cut straight" to modify "my forehead", "pluck'd before the gate" to modifier "flowers". The past participle are used as the modifiers of the noun phrase prior to it. The postponement of the modifier "still green" after the noun "plums" is quite rare in spoken language. Pound, on the contrary, seldom uses long modifiers after the noun phrases, only one among the eight noun phrases in the stanza, "the village of Chokan" and all the other noun phrases are short and simple ones as we use in spoken language: "my hair", "the front gate", "flowers", "bamboo stilts", "horse", "my seat", "blue plums". Besides, Pound's version commands greater number of verbs than other versions. In the depiction of the playful activities of the boy and the girl, Pound uses three similar sentences composed of main clause and the present participle as the accompanying action: "I played about the front gate, pulling flowers. /You came by on bamboo stilts, playing horse,/You walked about my seat, playing with blue plums." The six verbs he uses correspond exactly with the six verbs in the original poem. Pound the translator is a good mediator between the different conventions of Chinese language in which a sentence with multiple verbs is common, and

English language in which a sentence is with one main verb. The other translators adopt much fewer verbs than Pound does, Fletcher using four ("plucked", "riding", "came" and "wreathed"), Xu using three verbs ("played", "came" and "played"), Gaunt using three ("plucking", "rode", "sate"). Pound's purpose is not only to be faithful to the original in expression, which he actually does not follow rigidly, but to create the sense of colloquialism with the large number of verbs. Lastly, Pound uses more small words made up of three to four letters and more single-syllable words are found in Pound's version. Among the 52 words in the stanza, 40 are one-syllable words, the two or three syllable words are still colloquial ones including "across", "forehead", "about", "flowers", "bamboo", "about", "village", "Chokan", "people", "without", "dislike" and "suspicion". Fletcher, in a total of 44 words, 34 of them have only one syllable, three of them are compound words (hobby-horse, green-gage, ch'ang-kan), one three-syllable word and 8 two-syllable words including the uncommon ones in modern English: "o'er", "maiden" and "astride". Gaunt uses similar number of one-syllable words (41 in the total of 51), yet with the greatest number of three-syllable words including the rarely-used ones in spoken English like "o'ershadow" and "venturous", and another two-syllable word "schemings" is also far from colloquial. Besides, where Pound uses one-syllable simple verbs like "play" and "pluck" and "walk" and "pull", Gaunt uses two-syllable verbs including "began" and "suspected". Xu, among the 46 words, uses 36 one-syllable words, the multi-syllable words including similar nouns yet with two compound words: "hobbyhorse" and "Riverside". Thus, Pound has achieved his touch of colloquialism with his selection of simple colloquial words.

3.4.2 Simplicity and Austerity of Language

Free verse represents the modern era with its simplicity and directness. The simplicity and austerity of the verse are "the essential components of the modern idiom" in which "language became like a pane of glass, a window to meaning whose perfection consisted in not claiming any attention to itself". (Preda, 2001: 87) Exquisite language itself is not the purpose of the artist, but what the language reveals and presents is. Simple but forceful language is effective to delineate the image for the readers to decode while flowery ornamental language draws too much attention to the diction itself and obscures the image. "Modernist ideology is visible in the simplicity of the diction leading to the essential, the true, the universal". (Preda, 2001: 78) Pound's cultivation of precise language marks the deviation from the traditional sentimentalism and over-decorative language. Pound is against the overflow of passion in Victorian poetry and calls for the new poetic style in the modern society. He said in his essay of *Retrospect*: "As to Twentieth century poetry, and the poetry which I expect to see written during the next decade or so, it will, I think, move against poppy-cock, it will be harder and saner, it will be what Mr Hewlett calls 'nearer the bone'. It will be as much like granite as it can be, its force will lie in its truth, its interpretative power (of course, poetic force does always rest there); I mean it will not try to seem forcible by rhetorical din, and luxurious riot. We will have fewer painted adjectives impeding the shock and stroke of it. At least for myself, I want it so, austere, direct, free from emotional slither". (Pound, 1968:11) Pound uses the translations to establish and reinforce the new style of abandoning the decorative language to the hard language "nearer the bone". The Chinese poetry is representative of its "reductionist poetics" with the "language beyond metaphor". (Pound, 1973: 158) Pound's translation of Chinese poetry *Cathay* "provides new possibilities and new forms for development for American poetry" and its influence on American New Poetry Movement "is unmatched by any other versions of translations". (赵毅衡, 1985:177-178)

In the first place, simplicity of language is set for the universal emotions. A general look at the themes in Pound's translation collection of Chinese poetry *Cathay* will reveal its simplicity in the expression of the ordinary and the universal emotions. *Song of the Bowmen of Shu* reflects the sorrow of a soldier who fights for years away from home and yearns for the return to the homeland. *The Beautiful Toilet* is the longing of a young lady for the return of her husband. *The River Song* is the depiction of the glorious pleasure and the lament on man's fate. *The River-Merchant's Wife: A Letter* is the memory of a young girl of the love story between her and her husband, about her transformation from a little girl to a loving wife and of her longing for her husband's return through the letter. *Poem by the Bridge at Ten-Shin* depicts the decadence at court. *The Jewel Stairs Grievance* is about the sorrow of a neglected court lady. *Lament of the Frontier Guard* again shifts to the theme of the sorrow of soldiers at war. *Four Poems of Departure* is about the affectionate friendship, the profound sorrow at the departure of friends. *The City of Choan* and *South-Folk in Cold Country* are about the vicissitudes of life by the reflection on the past. *Sennin Poem by Kakuhaku* and To-Em-Mei's *The Unmoving Cloud* are about the hermit life. *A Ballad of the Mulberry Road* is about a beauty that draws attention of every passer-by. *Old Idea of Choan* by Rosoriu again revolves around the theme of the decadence at court. The sorrow at war, on departure, for longing, over reflection is so common to men at any time and place of the universe that the very simplicity of the theme strikes the readers and arouses sympathy.

Secondly, simplicity of language means the condensed force with the omission of unnecessary words. In his pursuit of simplicity and brevity in poetic language, Pound reiterates his aim to replace the decorative language with the concise. One of his three tenets for imagism reads: "To use absolutely no word that does not contribute to the presentation". (Pound, 1968: 3) "Use no superfluous word... which does not reveal something... don't... fill up the vacuums with slush". (Pound, 1968:4,7) Pound achieves the economy of diction by renouncing flowery "ornament". He advises the artist to "use either no ornament or good ornament". (Pound, 1968:5) He speaks most sharply on the abuse of ornament in language: "Since the beginning of bad writing, writers have used images as ornaments... One is tired of ornamentations, they are all a trick". (Painter, 2006: 98) Take an example from Pound's translation of Li Bai's poem *The River-Merchant's Wife: A Letter* along with some metric counterparts by three other translators.

The original text: 八月蝴蝶黄,双飞西园草。感此伤妾心,坐愁红颜老。

Ezra Pound: The paired butterflies are already yellow with August
Over the grass in the West garden;
They hurt me. I grow older.

W. J. B. Fletcher: I sit and wail, my red cheeks growing old,
September now! — the butterflies so gay
Disport on grasses by our garden wall.
The sight my heart disturbs with longing woe.

C. Gaunt. In the eighth moon the butterflies pale their bright hues,
But in pairs they flit through the west glade,
With a pang I remember it, sitting alone,
Old in heart though my cheek does not fade.

Xu Yuanchong: The yellow butterflies in autumn pass
Two by two o'er our western garden grass.
This sight would break my heart and I'm afraid,
Sitting alone, my rosy cheeks would fade.

Pound's simple statement of "I grow older" depicts a lovable young lady of innocence lamenting on the long lapse of time in parting with her husband. It is amusing as she is reflective of her sorrow in the longing of her husband's return though still in her teenage years as the prime of youth. Pound depicts a natural scene of the paired butterflies in the garden and the simple state of mind in the teenage lady at the sight of it. Both the natural scene and the human mind are portrayed in the concrete language of simplicity to inject a sense of the objective. The readers are amused spectators of the naivety of the lady yet with empathy for her yearnings. Fletcher uses a murky name for the emotion as "longing woe" and gives the direct statement of the feeling from "my heart" which is "disturbed". Gaunt also goes to the depiction of the consciousness with his expression of "with a pang I remember it". He uses "old" to be the literal translation of the original yet adds the unsaid "old in heart", which becomes the statement of the lady's mental activity instead of Pound's depiction of it as some objective truth, some natural phenomenon in the world, that is, the aging of humans and hence it loses the amusement and in turn the sympathy that might be inspired in readers. Xu also employs the abstract statement of the consciousness (This sight would break my heart and I'm afraid), the breaking of heart and the fear in heart both the blurry description of the mental state that Pound does not support, who believes that natural world is "the adequate symbol". For the image of butterflies, Pound uses a mere color adjective "yellow" where Fletcher goes to the abstract adjective "gay", intending it to create a contrast between the joy of butterflies and the lonely sorrow of the lady yet with a little artificiality. Also, Pound uses economic diction where the other translators spare no efforts to reinforce the joy in the activities of butterflies, Fletcher using the verb "disport" and the modifier "gay", Gaunt the verb "flit". Where Gaunt emphasizes the color with four words "pale their bright hues", Pound uses the simple literal correspondent of "yellow". Where Xu stresses the love in the natural world with words "pass two by two", Pound has a simple adjective "paired" to depict.

Take his translation of Li Bai's poem *Seeing Off a Friend* as an example, as compared to the versions in metric form by two other translators.

Line 1：青山横北郭，
Line 2：白水绕东城。
Line 3：此地一为别，
Line 4：孤蓬万里征。
Line 5：浮云游子意，
Line 6：落日故人情。
Line 7：挥手自兹去，
Line 8：萧萧班马鸣。
Ezra Pound： Blue mountains to the north of the walls,

White river winding about them;
Here we must make separation
And go out through a thousand miles of dead grass.
Mind like a floating white cloud,
Sunset like the parting of old acquaintances
Who bow over their clasped hands at a distance.
Our horses neigh to each other
as we are departing.

Herbert A. Giles: Where blue hills cross the northern sky,
Beyond the moat which girds the town,
'Twas there we stopped to say Goodbye!
And one white sail alone dropped down.
Your heart was full of wandering thought;
For me,— my sun had set indeed;
To wave a last adieu we sought,
Voiced for us by each whinnying steed!

W. J. B. Fletcher: Athwart the northern gate the green hills swell,
White water round the eastern city flows.
When once we here have bade a long farewell,
Your lone sail struggling up the current goes.
Those floating clouds are like the wanderer's heart,
You sinking sun recalls departed days.
Your hand waves us adieu; and lo! You start,
And dismally your horse retiring neighs.

Chinese poetry possesses the beauty in symmetry. In this poem, line 1 and line 2, line 5 and line 6 form perfect symmetry in Chinese, where "blue mountains" and "white waters", "stretch" and "wind", "north" and "east", "wall" and "city", "floating clouds" and "setting sun", "the wanderer's thoughts" and "the friends' feelings" are symmetric, each of the words matching exactly with that in the neighboring line. Giles, for the perfect rhyme in English poetry, converts the first two lines into different structures, line one becoming a subordinating clause to indicate the place where the activity emerges, the second line, though another adverbial, in the form of a prepositional phrase with relative clause embedded in it. (Where blue hills cross the northern sky,/Beyond the moat which girds the town) Another conversion of the symmetric to the irregular is in his version in line 5 and line 6. Giles dropped the metaphoric images in the original, the floating clouds and the setting sun and instead, he went to the abstract, directing stating the mental activity of the friend: "Your heart was full of wandering thought" and converting the original concrete image of setting sun to a different metaphor of the mental state of the poet himself: "For me, — my sun had set indeed". The motivation behind all the changes is evidently the pursuit of regular metric form, where he could convey the poetic sense in the rigid tetrameter. Also, Giles, to create a rhyme with the third line, discarded the original sense "city wall" and adopted "sky" which strays from the faithful interpretation even the lines are rhymed. There is a similar deliberate change in the image in line 4, where Giles uses the image of "one white sail" against the original image of a kind of grass that will fly with the wind, a metaphor for the lonely friend to leave for a faraway place as if blown by the wind. Giles adoption of the image aims at the following verb phrase that might form the rhyme with line 2, "down" and "town". Fletcher, in similar efforts to build rhyme, creates unsymmetrical lines different from the original. He, in particular, loves the inversion in sentences, where verbs go at the end of the lines. The prepositional phrases are put at the initial position or in the middle before the verbs as in line 1 and line 2: "Athwart the northern gate the green hills swell,/White water round the eastern city flows." Or there might be the object before the verb as in line 4: "Your lone sail struggling up the current goes." His purpose in his efforts is clear as he could render a sense of the arcane to correspond to the times of the poem and most importantly, the rhyme with line 2, "goes" for "flows". Another asymmetry lies in his version for line 5 and line 6. Where line 5 is a faithful correspondent to the original poem, line 6 is a complete departure with his addition of senses and words absent in the original: "You sinking sun recalls departed days." The concrete image of the setting sun as an analogy for the poet's reluctance to part with the friend just as the sun setting slowly down is unwilling to leave the western sky. Fletcher turns it into the metaphor for the friend and adds what is not stated in the original, the recalling of departed days. His purpose, again, is obvious: to form a rhyme with the last line as "days" and "neighs" are perfect match in phonemes. Fletcher also added "You start" in line 7 for its rhyme with the ending word "heart" in line 5. Such addition of words for rhyme at the expense of the sense is unavoidable in the translation of Chinese poetry into English poetry in regular meter and rhyme. Apart from that, the cutting of words, the inversion in sentences are all devices some translators use to achieve rhyme, yet to the detriment of the original sense, which Pound, on the contrary, attaches the greatest importance to. In his version, Pound focuses on the preservation of the image and the music in English. The minor changes he makes might not transform the original sense or aesthetics, "blue mountains" and "white water" put at the very beginning of the lines to be parallel to each other, to the north of the walls, "Mind like a floating white cloud" and "Sunset like the parting of old acquaintances" as obvious parallel structure with the same linking word "like" to indicate the analogical relation. From the comparison, it's possible to see the superiority of free verse to regular meter in the conveying of poetic sense.

3.4.3 Influence of Free Verse

Vers libre marks revolutionary departure from traditional practices that brings freshness and freedom to the otherwise languishing poetic language. Pound, with his successful translation in free verse, enables the classical Chinese poetry to exert immense influence upon the development of modernist poetry. His success in the translation justifies free verse and popularizes it in modernist poetry. "In particular, one of the 20th-century English poetic styles, imagist vers libre, might have been devised deliberately to give the translator from the Chinese just what he wants and needs to perform intelligently". (Xie, 1999:4) Pound perceives the rigidity of meters and rhymes in Victorian poetry and describes the common verse of Britain from 1890 to 1910 as "a horrible agglomerate compost", "a doughy mess of third-hand Keats, Wordsworth, fourth-hand Elizabethan". (Pound, 1968:205) Pound's Skopos to liberate poetry from the manacles of traditional form leads to the adoption of free verse. Pound clarifies his motive to write in free verse, saying that the beauty of ancient works lies in vers libre and rigid meters are restrictive chains to bind artists: "No one is so foolish as to suppose that a musician using 'four-four' time is compelled to use always four quarter notes in each bar, or in 'seven-eighths' time to use seven eighth notes uniformly in each bar. He may use one 1/2, one 1/4 and one 1/8 rest, or any such combination as he may happen to choose or find fitting. To apply this musical truism to verse is to employ vers libre". (Pound, 1968:93) The translation of poetry through free verse then becomes mainstream thanks to Pound's contribution in his translation.

And Pound's translation also promotes a new trend in verse translation, the strategy that puts stress not chiefly on form but on content. In the translation, Pound makes free inventive adaptation in verse form. James Holmes, the great translator of poetry and distinguished scholar of translation produces three basic categories for verse translation: mimetic form (the reproduction of the form of the original in the target language), analogical form (the form with equivalent function of the original form), organic form (the form with the semantic material of the source text shaping itself), and deviant or extraneous form (a new form with no signal in the source text either in form or content). Holms put Pound's strategy in translating Chinese poetry into the third category because in his translation, "the form is seen as distinct from the content, rather than as an integral whole". And according to James, such freedom in form, under Pound's lead, has come to be "the dominant strategy in the twentieth century, fuelled also by the development of free verse". (巴斯内特, 2001: 62-63) For the modernist poetry, the most remarkable revolution lies in its language, the adoption of vers libre. In the eyes of many readers, free verse is tantamount to modern poetry. The new poetry movement prompts free verse into wider popularity. Pound's use of free verse in his poetry translation, along with the practice of many other translators such as Arthur Waley promotes the development of the free verse movement in America.

Pound's overthrowing of conventional metric translation of Chinese poetry is more deliberate than experimental. He is a revolutionist in poetry with all his experiments in poetic form, "moving from Anglo-Saxon alliterative rhythm to French vers libre to Greek and Latin hexameters to Italian sonnets to Chinese ideograms or verbal pictures". (Pratt, 2007:10) Pound shatters the fetters of the limitations of conventional metric forms and regular rhyme and explored the uncommon form as he put it, "Any mind that is worth calling a mind must have needs beyond the existing categories of language". (Hickman, 2005 : 9) Free verse is the most influential modern one among his experiments. He, more than any poet, breaks "the heave of the pentameter", (Pratt, 2007: 10) making his poetry "a set of poetic exercises, every poem in a different and unique form". (Pratt, 2007: 10) It is stunning at the beginning because the sound was unfamiliar, the ears of the readers unused to them. Yet even the harshest critic has to admit that "also, you come upon some lyric that is beautifully simple in form and utterance, that orbs itself easily and naturally". (Homberger, 1972: 54) As a leader of imagist movement, he aims to modernize the poetry, and the scholar Stephen Spender is justified in his conclusion: "The aims of the imagist movement in poetry provide the archetype of a modern creative procedure". (Pratt, 2007:10)

Chapter 4 Skopos of History Rejuvenation

Pound is an heir to traditions since his translations spans continents and millennia, covering a myriad of cultures across time and space including ancient Greek, ancient China, French, Italy, Japan and many others. Cognitive sciences justify the idiosyncratic translational practices in that the translators' reception of the original text is determined by their respective cognitive environments, which are individually formed by "translators' external environments, the cultures in which they live, with their traditions and values". (Bowler, 2007:75) Pound is unique in his translational strategies, influenced and even determined by his values, especially values on tradition. He tries to take essence from traditions and discover the remedy for the social chaos. He is also an innovator with "Make It New" as the recurrent and "fitting slogan for his translations" (Park, 2008: 23) and with his radical experimentation in the poetic form, projecting vigor into the stagnant lifeless poetry at the time.

4.1 Skopos of Restoration of Order

In face of the social disorder after the world war, the economic turmoil during the Great Depression, and the uncertainty of ego after Freud's revolutionary exploration into human consciousness, Pound feels the responsibility of the poet in the guidance of order restoration for society, and as a poet-historian, he is to "discover and reveal the right orders of the germinal universe". (Kim, 2003:65) In *The Cantos*, Pound declares Confucianism as "a medicine for the ills of Western civilization". (Qian, 2003:96) Pound believes social harmony lies in order, in an elegance revealed by Confucian canons, particularly those in the Confucian classic *Da Xue*. His mission is like that of Prometheus, "carrying forward the light of Chinese philosophy" and "rejuvenating Western poetry with its ideal". (Qian, 2003:96)

4.1.1 Social Chaos as Background of Pound's Translations

Since the end of 19th century, the western society has witnessed tremendous revolutionary changes. The dramatic advances in urbanization and industrialization transformed the outlook of the world towards complexity and estrangement, which in turn spurred the solitude and isolation of individuals. The situation was even more complicated by the breakout of two world wars in the first half of 20th century. The unswerving traditional beliefs were doubted and revolted. Moreover, breakthroughs in psychology and philosophy such as Freud's psychotherapy, Bergson's Intuitionism and demarcation between psychic time and spacial time, opened new vista by overthrowing the conventional ideology but caused disorientation in human mind.

Two world wars exerted catastrophic impact on society. World War I, with more than 70 million military personnel involved and more than 15 million people killed, lasting from 1914 to 1918 and involving most of the world's great powers, was one of the largest military conflict which transformed the layout of Europe and led to social turmoil. World War II was another global military conflict that involved most of the world's nations and the mobilization of over 100 million military personnel. Over 70 million people, the majority civilians, were killed, making it the deadliest conflict in human history. Many civilians died because of disease, starvation, massacres, bombing and deliberate genocide. Such mass slaughters caused social trauma in a resulting chaotic and inhumane world that affected human ideology in different ways. The nationalists supported the sole force of military strength in chaos; the soldiers returned home disillusioned from the horrors of the war. For many years, the world was unable to recover from the war, people mourning the dead, the missing, and the disabled. Following such historic catastrophe, psychic trauma was caused with the syndromes of ego damage, regression, and relative helplessness across society. Then in the 1930s, Pound's native land, America suffered from the Great Depression, which later spread to almost every country in the world and became the longest, most widespread, and deepest depression of the 20th century. The Great Depression had devastating effects across the world, personal income, tax revenue, profits and prices plunging and unemployment soaring in virtually every country. The era of financial crisis produced poverty and hardship that led to emotional trauma and spurred the resurgence of social realism

In the realm of psychology and philosophy, Sigmund Freud developed his original creation — psychoanalysis and his life's work focused on its exploration, investigation, and constant revision. Freud's model of the mind was a challenge to the enlightenment model of rational agency, which exerted a revolutionary impact on human consciousness. Bergson was another powerful philosophical influence during Pound's time. Bergson argued that the real entity consisted not in things or intellect, or free will, but in the changing and moving "current" in time. It was not the current in its literal sense, but the process of continuous activities in various forms with factors interweaving and substituting and presenting themselves. The activities were psychological rather than physical, temporal rather than spatial, mobile and fluid rather than static, which, in continuity, comprised the basics of the universe and which, in essence, formed an original impulse in life endless and unpredictable. His process philosophy shed fresh light on conventional topics as time and identity, perception and change, memory and consciousness, language and the limits of reason, redefining the relations between intelligence and intuition, and insisting on the necessity of increasing thought's possibility through the use of intuition, which, according to him, alone approached a knowledge of the absolute and of real life. Bergson believed that time was neither a real homogeneous medium nor a mental construct, but possesses what he referred to as *Duration*, which, in his view, was creativity and memory as an essential component of reality. "In reality, the past is preserved by itself automatically. In its entirety, probably, it follows us at every instant; all that we have felt, thought and willed from our earliest infancy is there, leaning over the present which is about to join it, pressing against the portals of consciousness that would fain leave it outside". (Bergson, 2002:173) To Bergson, the real time was psychological time equivalent to his *Duration* with strength but not quantity, presenting itself as continuous and interactive yet eternal and intuitive. The philosophical emphasis on human consciousness was an antithesis to the conventional faith in human intellect and in sacred enlightenment and it threw the intellectuals into profound consideration and further exploration while rendering the general public bewildered at the newly-discovered and unleashed subjective power.

4.1.2 Restoration of Order against Chaos

In the society with chaos both physical and psychic, Pound, who upheld the poet's responsibility to seek light in darkness and to guide the benighted public towards enlightenment through poetry, came to the translation of multiple works in ancient civilizations "to develop and enunciate ideals — aesthetic, social, and philosophical — to respond to the various forms of turmoil, public and personal, that they confronted in the 1930s and early 1940s". (Hickman, 2005:12) The restoration of order, as Pound detected from his extensive reading in Chinese philosophy, could be achieved through the dissemination of Confucius ethical ideology. Pound's concern with Confucius dated from 1914 till the Second World War, during it, and after it. In the foreword of his translation of Confucius' philosophy *Ta Hio*: *The Great Learning of Confucius*, Pound expressed his reverence for Confucius who started in humility but rose to be Prime Minister and governed the country with his wise philosophy: "His analysis of why the earlier great emperors had been able to govern greatly was so sound that every durable dynasty, since his time, has risen on a Confucius design and been initiated by a group of Confucians. China was tranquil when her rulers understood these few pages. When the principles here defined were neglected, dynasties waned and chaos ensued. The proponents of a world order will neglect at their peril the study of the only process that has repeatedly proved its efficiency as social coordinate". (Pound, 2003: 615) Confucius' work, and that of Mencius, "remained a constant stronghold of order and repose in his mind amidst threatening chaos". (Pound, 1973: 91) It was Pound's consistent belief that Confucianism would offer a solution to the West in chaos and disorder from its political institutions to its economic system. In the translation of Confucian works, Pound envisioned an earthly paradise where people and nations lived in harmony through the pursuit of individual integrity and rapport with nature.

Pound believed that it was Confucianism that secured peace and harmony in Chinese society for thousands of years and Confucian works ignited his hope for social order. He quoted Confucian works *Da Xue* in the epic *The Cantos* and made the comprehensive translation titled *Ta Hio*: *The Great Learning*. When personally inquired by T. S. Eliot of his belief, Pound gave the explicit answer: "I believe the *Ta Hio*" (*Da Xue*). Pound was convinced that a fair world order could only be built on the principles preached in the book, with the following words echoing Pound's deepest beliefs: "wanting good government in their states, they first established order in their own families; wanting order in the home, they first disciplined themselves; desiring self-discipline, they rectified their own hearts; and wanting to rectify their hearts, they sought precise verbal definitions of their inarticulate thoughts; wishing to attain precise verbal definitions, they set to extend their knowledge to the utmost. This completion of knowledge is rooted in sorting things into organic categories". (Pound, 1973: 92) In the translation of *Book of Songs*, another classic Confucian works evaluated by Confucius as being pure in thought and as the best means to educate the public for social peace and harmony, Pound expressed his wishes to learn from history and reform his contemporary society in unrest.

The original text: 絺兮绤兮,凄其以风。我思古人,实获我心!

（《诗经·绿衣》）

Ezra Pound: Nor fine nor coarse cloth keep the wind

from the melancholy mind;
Only ancient wisdom is
solace to man's miseries. (Pound, 2003:767)

The original poem expresses the husband's mourning of his beloved wife at the sight of the green dress of hers. The poem explores from without to within, developing from the dress to the texture, to the weaving of the dress, to the capability of his bereaved wife, and then to his grief of losing her. In the original poem, the Chinese character that means "old" today is the substitute for "bereaved", but in Pound's translation, he put it as "old" and preaches his political ideal that "Only ancient wisdom is solace to man's miseries". Pound's purpose of restoring an orderly society by learning from the past is often the motivation behind his creative translation.

Another example also comes from *Book of Songs*.

The original text: (瞻彼淇奥,绿竹猗猗。有匪君子,如切如磋,如琢如磨。)
瑟兮僩兮,赫兮咺兮,有匪君子,终不可谖兮!
(瞻彼淇奥,绿竹青青。有匪君子,充耳琇莹,会弁如星。)
瑟兮僩兮,赫兮咺兮,有匪君子,终不可谖兮!
(瞻彼淇奥,绿竹如箦。有匪君子,如金如锡,如圭如璧。)
宽兮绰兮,猗重较兮,善戏谑兮,不为虐兮!

(《诗经·淇奥》)

Ezra Pound: he careth his people's weal,
stern in attent,
steady as sun's turn bent
on his folk's betterment
nor will he fail.

…
his acumen in debate
splendid, steadfast in judgment-hall
he cannot fail us
nor fall.

…
stern in his amplitude,
magnanimous to enforce true laws, or lean
over chariot rail in humour
as he were a tiger

with velvet paws. (Pound, 2003:782)

The original poem is a eulogy of personality, of a man of integrity. The division of the empire in ancient times brings misery on the common people, who then wish for the emergence of the man of integrity to lead society to unity and peace. In the poem, the gentleman is well educated with distinguished capacity, with high moral standard, with tolerant mind, with modest manners and with agreeable humor. The second and fourth stanzas are repeated to reveal the solemn manners, the high stature and the last stanza stresses his width of mind and his humor. Pound's translation borders on adaptation, in which he expresses his wish for a capable leader to steer the world out of mire. Pound's ideal of the gentleman "careth his people's weal", "bent on his folk's betterment", "splendid" in "acumen in debate" and "steadfast in judgment-hall", "stern in his amplitude" and "magnanimous" to enforce true laws. For the main character in the last line which means humor in Chinese, Pound creates a metaphor in his translation to indicate the sternness of the ideal leader like "a tiger with velvet paws", that is, seemingly gentle but actually strict. The metaphor stems from Pound's etymological method, that is, the dissembling of the notions into individual components and the analysis of the new composite meaning. It is anything but the original image of humorous gentleman, but demonstrates Pound's political proposition of strict law and order and his desire for an iron-handed leader.

Pound's purpose of restoring order against is firstly seen in his advocacy of rapport with nature. Pound looks for the remedy for social disorder, which to him, lies primarily in sharpening aesthetic sensitivity, "perception of the beautiful" (Kim, 2003:64) since the evil could only reign over the good when people are unable to sense the beautiful. For Pound, the beauty besprinkles the natural world, which, merged with its spiritual inspiration "to reveal the physical life-force", (Kim, 2003:68) is a powerful means to restore order in the chaotic physical world. Through his contact with Chinese philosophy, Pound develops an obsession with the profundity of the time-honored Tao values on nature. The Western poet tend to look upon nature as "the eloquent handiwork of a Supreme Being" above man's creation, the Chinese poet sees nature as "the embodiment of the Absolute itself" in which "Every element in the landscape, from the most sublime to the lowliest, is equally a manifestation of the Tao" and man is one of the elements rather than "the lord and caretaker of creation". (Watson, 1984:7) In his essay *Immediate Need of Confucius*, Pound criticizes "the West's ego-centric consciousness which erases the alterity of Nature". (Pound, 1973:86) He criticizes Greek philosophy of rationality as "almost an attack upon nature" but praises "the Confucio-Mencian ethic or philosophy" for it doesn't "splinter and split away from organic nature". (Pound, 1973: 86-7) Pound advocates Taoist rapport with nature in his poetry translations, leaving nature as it is and man as part of the landscape. Take an example of the translations of Li Bai's poem.

The original text: 浮云游子意,落日故人情

Ezra Pound: Mind like a floating white cloud,
Sunset like the parting of old acquaintances

Witter Bynner: I shall think of you in a floating cloud;
So in the sunset think of me.

W. J. B. Fletcher: Those floating clouds are like the wanderer's heart,
You sinking sun recalls departed days.

Herbert Giles: Your heart was full of wandering thought;
For me, — my sun had set indeed;

Xu Yuanchong: With floating cloud you'll float away;
Like parting day I'll part from you.

Amy Lowell: The floating clouds wander everywhither as does man.
Day is departing — it and my friend.

Different from other versions, Pound revives the original juxtaposition of the two relatively concrete images in his translation, the floating clouds as an analogy of the wanderer's feeling and the setting sun as the reluctance to part with a friend. Four concepts in the original are treated like parallel entities in Pound's translation, with the effect of montage where the juxtaposition of two separate shots creates more rather than a sum of its parts. There is a perceivable resemblance of a wanderer's drifting life to the floating clouds, both transitory with no permanent place to settle down. Nor will the readers fail to find the similarity of the setting sun to the sorrow and reluctance in the parting of old friends. Man and nature are in the parallel plane in the syntactically uncommitted structure in Pound's translation. Giles put nature as a metaphor for human feelings in his translation "my sun had set". Fletcher also personates natural object to prompt human activity in the translation "You sinking sun recalls departed days". Xu explicitly links nature and man in the repetition of words "float" and "part", as the action of floating is identical in the friend and the clouds and the action of parting is the similar for the friends and the days. Lowell has the similar treatment in her translation to point out the similarity the clause for comparison "as does man" and the parallel construction of "it (day) and my friend". Pound, among the lists translators, is the only one to give four noun phrases as independent images with equal status in the construction, which is a proof to his principle of "direct treatment of the thing" (Pound, 1968: 4) and man's rapport with nature with each playing a part in the universe.

Chinese poetry is the prototype of the dynamic operations of nature with human activities as an element in the dynamic universe. Take another example of Pound's translation *Song of the Bowmen of Shu* as an example.

The original text: 采薇采薇,薇亦作止。曰归曰归,岁亦莫止。……
采薇采薇,薇亦柔止。曰归曰归,心亦忧止。……
采薇采薇,薇亦刚止。曰归曰归,岁亦阳止。……

Ezra Pound: Here we are, picking the first fern-shoots
And saying: When shall we get back to our country?
. . .
We grub the soft fern-shoot,
When anyone says "Return," the others are full of sorrow.
. . .
We grub the old fern-stalks.
We say: will we be let to go back in October?
There is no ease in bitter, but we would not return to our country.

James Legge: Let us gather the thorn-ferns, let us gather the thorn-ferns;
The thorn-ferns are now springing up.
. . .
Let us gather the thorn-ferns, let us gather the thorn-ferns;
The thorn-ferns are now tender.
. . .
Let us gather the thorn-ferns, let us gather the thorn-ferns;
The thorn-ferns are now hard.

In Pound's translation, the elapse of time is embodied in the growth of the fern-shoots from the tender to the hard, yet the soldiers are still unable to return home. The contrast built in the translation strikes strong emotions in the readers, of pity and indignation and emphatic sorrow. Pound gives three adjectives "first" (in "Here we are, picking the first fern-shoots"), "soft" (in "We grub the soft fern-shoot") and "old" (in "We grub the old fern-stalks") to describe the natural process of the lapsing seasons and the growing landscape of natural beings. James Legge, in comparison, gives the literal translation to the original with all the repetition. Pound's translation is creative in his translation instead of the literal transference of linguistic units, integrating the human activity of picking ferns with ferns' natural growing process. They combine to form the harmonious static pictures to reveal the dynamism of the universe.

Pound's intention to restore order is also embodied in his preach of name rectification in his translations. Pound witnessed the decline of western civilization after two world wars and the ideological wasteland in the chaos of society where conflicts intensified between man and society, man and man, the displayed ego and the suppressed ego, and damped people's confidence in traditional values, turning Europe into disorderly barren wilderness. Pound turned his eyes to the oriental Confucianism as a remedy for the plagues of western society and found in *Ta Hio* the beauty of harmony and order. And among all the Confucian ideas, he appreciated Confucian "ch'ing ming", "right naming" or "rectification of names", which in his eyes would provide the cure for the confused names as the fundamental cause of social evil.

Pound launched the right-naming campaign for the restoration of order "as a weapon against forms of public political deception and hence exploitation". (Qian, 2003: 121) As a poet with political enthusiasm for social reform, he regarded the confusion of names as the reason for the corrupt political system and there were "manipulations of the public mind" carried on by "false naming". (Qian, 2003: 120) For example, the *U. S. Constitution* said Congress should control the issuance of money and the value, but the actual manipulator of the purchasing power of the dollar was Federal Reserve Bank whose directors were private bankers or, put in a Pound's term, "thieves", who caused the disruption of the financial system. Pound believed that "a man should not be called controller of currency unless he really controls it" (Qian, 2003: 121) and to prevent these theft, it was necessary to avoid ambiguity and implement clarity, precision, explicitness in public language. Pound, convinced the evil of society lay in the inaccurate naming, constantly stresses his advocacy of "right naming". In Pound's version of *The Analects*, a dialogue between Confucius and his disciples goes as follows: "Tze-Lu: The Lord of Wei is waiting for you to form a government, what are you going to do first? Kung: Settle the names (determine a precise terminology). Tze-Lu: How's this, you're divagating, why fix 'em? Kung: You bumkin! Sprout!... If words (terminology) are not (is not) precise, they cannot be followed out, or completed in action according to specifications". (Qian, 2003: 120) It is an illustration of Pound's convictions, which are conveyed through Kung's words, that action is impossible without precise terminology. Another illustration is taken from Pound's translation *Ta Hio: The Great Learning of Confucius*.

The original text：知止而后有定，定而后能静，静而后能安，安而后能虑，虑而后能得。

Ezra Pound： Know the point of rest and then have an orderly mode of procedure; having this orderly procedure one can "grasp the azure," that is, **take hold of a clear concept**; **holding a clear concept** one can be at peace [internally], being thus calm one can **keep one's head** in moments of danger; he who can **keep his head in the presence of a tiger** is qualified to come to his deed in due hour.（Pound, 2003:618）

James Legge： The point where to rest being unknown, the object of pursuit is then determined; and, that being determined, **a calm unperturbedness** may be attained. To that **calmness** there will succeed a tranquil repose. In that repose there may be **careful deliberation**, and that **deliberation** will be followed by the attainment of the desired end.（理雅各，1992:3）

Legge's version is a literal faithful to the original text. Compared to that, Pound's version is creative in his treatment of the Chinese character "静"（quiet）. Where Legges states as "calm unperturbedness" for the character, Pound put it with his unique interpretation "take hold of a clear concept" and "holding a clear concept". It is obviously Pound's deliberate choice as propaganda of his concept of clarified language, of his belief in the right naming as the guidance of the individuals and the government as the fundamental means to achieve internal peace. Many of Pound's adaptive approaches in his translation are justified from the perspective of his name-rectifying purpose. The following examples are manifest indicator of Pound's Skopos in translation.

The original text：欲正其心者，先诚其意；欲诚其意者，先致其知。

Ezra Pound： ... and wanting to rectify their hearts, they sought **precise verbal definitions of their inarticulate thoughts** [the tones given off by the heart]; wishing to attain **precise verbal definitions**, they set to extend their knowledge to the utmost.（Pound, 2003:619）

James Legge： Wishing to rectify their hearts, they first sought to **be sincere in their thoughts.** Whishing to be sincere in their thoughts, they first extended to the utmost their knowledge.（理雅各，1992:3）

A comparison of the two versions reveal the difference in the interpretation of the Chinese character "诚"（sincerity）. Legge literally puts it into "be sincere" as many other translators do, but Pound's choice is uniquely different, with "precise verbal definitions" as the corresponding translation. To make the concept clearer, he even adds the word "inarticulate" before "thoughts". That is what exactly Pound believes in, the necessity to express clearly and accurately what is vaguely and abstractly defined. His purpose to carry forward the spirit of precise language is carried all along and reflected in his translation, to assume authority as the words of Chinese sage Confucius.

The original text: 物格而后知至,知至而后意诚,意诚而后心正,心正而后身修,……

Ezra Pound: When things had been classified in organic categories, knowledge moved toward fulfillment; given the extreme knowable points, **the inarticulate thoughts** were defined with **precision** [**the sun's lance coming to rest on the precise spot verbally**]. Having attained this **precise verbal definition** [***aliter*, this sincerity**], they then stabilized their hearts, they disciplined themselves; (Pound, 2003:619)

James Legge: Their knowledge being complete, their thoughts were **sincere.** Their thoughts being **sincere**, their hearts were then rectified. Their hearts being rectified, their persons were cultivated. (理雅各, 1992:35)

Again, while Legge uses "sincere" and "sincerity" to interpret the Chinese character, Pound translates as "precise verbal definition", "extreme precision" and what should be noted that he justifies his translation with the disintegration of the Chinese character as "the sun's lance coming to rest on the precise spot verbally". In the sixth chapter of *Ta Hsio: The Great Learning*, Pound stresses more emphatically his purpose of "precise verbal expressions for the heart's tone, for the inarticulate thoughts" (Pound, 2003: 625): "Thus the mind becomes your palace and the body can be at ease; it is for this reason that the great gentleman must find the precise verbal expression for his inarticulate thoughts" (Pound, 2003:624-625) for the original text "富润屋,德润身,心广体胖。故君子必诚其意". Another exemplification of Pound's "right-naming" purpose in translation comes from his disintegration of the Chinese character "明" (bright, luminous).

The original text:《大甲》曰:"顾諟天之明命。"

Ezra Pound: It is said in the *Great Announcement*: He contemplated the **luminous** decree of heaven, and found **the precise word wherewith to define it.** (Pound, 2003:620)

James Legge: In the *Tai Jia* it is said, "He contemplated and studied the **illustrious** decrees of Heaven". (理雅各, 1992:5)

Apart from the literal correspondence of the character "luminous", Pound amplifies the translation with the additional idea "the precise word wherewith to define it" as an emphasis of his ideology of preciseness in language. It is deliberately creative compared with the literal translation of Legge's and Pound's treatment in his translation reveals his distinct purpose of propagating his "right-naming" ideology to address social ills.

Pound is convinced that right-naming is essential for peace and harmony in individuals as well as in the world. And the way to achieve right-naming is through precision of language: "The right-naming campaign was a campaign for precision in the use of individual words". (Qian, 2003: 120) Pound consistently advocates precise language, as illustrated in his epic *The Cantoes* "But down on the word with exactness" (XCIX) and he believes that the precise language is able "to denominate the world accurately, forcefully, sharply, closest to presence". (Preda, 2001: 132) To Pound, the right expression possesses the power to pinpoint the signified and reveals the genuine order of the world itself that dispels all the confusion and corruption to restore justice and harmony in society. In a letter to Bunting, Pound writes: "The poet's job is to define and yet again define till the detail of surface is in accord with the root in justice". (Pound, 1971: 277) For the precision of expression, Pound sometimes lays too much emphasis on the construction of words in his translation of Confucian works, presenting the detail of surface so as to revive the original meaning, to propagate his ideology of precision, to reinforce "ideas of order" (Preda, 2001: 131) through the harmony of the signifier and the signified.

4.2 Skopos of History Preservation

Pound values tradition, declaring that "without history one is lost in the dark, and the essential data of modern history cannot enlighten us unless they are traced back". (Kim, 2003:91) Pound searches for ancient voices to preserve the past and reform the present, a search for his own voice in the midst of the precedent great voices, a search that yields translations from various languages and for different historical phases. He strives to "resuscitate the dead art" of poetry, and to "maintain the sublime in the old sense". (Lierbregts, 2004:80) In the translations, Pound strives to preserve the cherished tradition in different cultures, and out of his "reverence for tradition and novelty", (Lierbregts,

2004:80) he makes constant efforts to seek the unchanging standards of literary excellence that prevails regardless of time, place, and language. Pound's preservation of history is unique in that he aims at establishing his own principles in poetry with his comprehensive knowledge of older poetry and the innovative experimentation in the translation. He, through "the active re-creation of those past voices into his own voice", (Lierbregts, 2004:82) polishes the old tradition so that it shines with new luster under his pen.

Pound, first of all, preserves the best traditions in poetry which will, in integration, contribute to his imagist poetics. His translation of Calvacanti is to promote the clear and precise poetic language to reverse the sentimental and ornamental poetry in the late Victorian era. His translation of the old Anglo-Saxon poem *The Seafarer*, though critically under attack for its diversion of meaning in certain poetic lines, is acclaimed for its faithful preservation of the alliterative rhyme. The Japanese Noh plays strikes Pound with its unity of image, which he gives intensive prominence to in his translation. Also, Pound's translation of ancient Chinese poetry is hailed for its beauty when Pound highlights the precise and concise images, the austerity of language, the restraint of emotions, which are exactly the best traditions of Chinese poetry.

Pound also borrows from tradition, through his translation, what could reflect the contemporary society and address the current problems. Pound lived his life in an era of chaos in the western world, where the two world wars caused devastation, grief to the families of the bereaved soldiers and widespread panic and debased values to the general public, and the Wall Street Crash of 1929, quickly followed by the Depression, shook the world more about the doom of capitalism. Pound believes in the responsibility of poets to restore order in society as art is to him not a distraction but a value for society, an essential, central valuable public service that merits appreciation, celebration and support. Therefore, he turns to the translation of the works in various civilizations for the cure of social evils in the western world. For Pound, translation has a twofold function in cultural production: "restorative in relation to past knowledge" and "critical with regard to present value formations". (Lan, 2005:16) He aims the translation of classic works to restore valuable insights lost in the bygone pages so as to benefit the current society. With such Skopos, Pound adopts "unconventional and even violent means" (Lan, 2005:16) to overcome linguistic barriers in the original perceptions built up in the course of history. The distractors of Pound's idiosyncratic approach in Confucian translations would be enlightened if they look at the translations from the perspective of Pound's ideological motivations. In the essay on Guido Cavalcanti responding to criticisms of his problematic translations, Pound asserts: ' As to the atrocities of my translation, all that can be said in excuse is that they are, I hope, for the most part intentional, and committed with the aim of driving the reader's perception further into the original than it would without them have penetrated". (Pound, 1968:172)

4.2.1 Selection of Translation Works

Pound's purpose in history preservation is seen in his meticulous selection of translation texts. His gathering of international experts over a wide range of time and space is never blind or random but deliberate, intending the translations for the rejuvenation of tradition. To revive and promote precise language, Pound comes to the works of Danial and Cavalcanti, because in the art of Danial and Cavalcanti, he has seen "that precision" "that explicit rendering, be it of external nature, or of emotion". (Pound, 1968:11) He is stimulated by Japanese Haiku for translation to develop the new Imagist juxtaposition structure in short poems. He is impressed by Chinese poetry for translation just as what he notes in his editing and publishing Fenollosa's *The Chinese Written Character as a Medium for Poetry*: "Chinese poetry... speaks at once with the vividness of painting and with the mobility of sounds". (Fenollosa, 1936:13) Pound's encounter with the exactness of Chinese poetry propels his translation in *Cathay* (1915) and "reaffirms his drive toward precision". (纳代尔, 2008:38) For Pound, the universal principles exist in the enduring traditions and when recovered, would enlighten the modern society.

Pound also makes meticulous selection in his translation works as a window to the valuable traditions to echo the present circumstances. The translational scholar Bassnett points out the importance of the selection of themes "relevant to the social system" for the work of literature to be noticed because the role of literature to the social system as a whole is an indispensable component of the poetics. (巴斯内特, 2004:26) Pound's approach is creative adaptation, not to literally copy the individual words in the original works but to illuminate the present society with preserved traditions, to inspire and enlighten the readers in the modern circumstances. Pound received from Fenollosa's widow the notes of 150 Chinese poems, yet he chose only a few of them into his translation collection *Cathay* published in 1915. A glimpse at the themes of selected works would reveal Pound's intention behind his translation. Against the general background of social turmoil during the First World War, Pound selected the tiny fraction from the notes that carried the particular emotions of sorrow and regret, with the themes embracing departure, exile, estrangement, separation, love, war, travel, escape, heroism and war as the most prominent theme. The Pound scholar David Moody made an theme analysis of the first seven prominent poems found them "arranged into a closed or ring sequence" (Moody, 2007:269):

a. *Song of the Bowmen of Shu* — of the sorrow of war
b. *The Beautiful Toilet* — neglected ex-courtesan
c. *The River Song* — decadence at court
d. *The River-Merchant's Wife: A Letter* — a love letter
c. *Poem by the Bridge at Ten-Shin* — decadence at court
b. *Jewel Stairs' Grievance* — a neglected court lady
a. *Lament of the Frontier Guard* — of the sorrow of war

The 19 translated poems were not selected randomly but to make up "a single, multifaceted image of a great empire in a dysfunctional phase", (Moody, 2007: 269) the scenario mirroring the contemporary situation in Pound's times of the western world in the phase marked by the disruption of order. In *Cathay*, Pound revealed the state at war with the barbarians on its borders: "By the North Gate, the wind blows full of sand, /Lonely from the beginning of time until now! / Trees fall, the grass goes yellow with autumn. /I climb the towers and towers/to watch out the barbarous land: /Desolate castle, the sky, the wide desert. /There is no wall left to this village. /Bones white with a thousand frosts, /High heaps, covered with trees and grass" (from *Lament of the Frontier Guard*) Pound exposed the court in a condition of high decadence: "The lords go forth from the court, and into far borders. /They ride upon dragon-like horses, /Upon horses with head-trappings of yellow-metal, /And the streets make way for their passage. /Haughty their passing, /Haughty their steps as they go into great banquets, /To high halls and curious food, /To the perfumed air and girls dancing, /To clear flutes and clear singing; /To the dance of the seventy couples; /To the mad chase through the gardens. /Night and day are given over to pleasure/And they think it will last a thousand autumns, /Unwearying autumns" (from *Poem by the Bridge at Ten-Shin*). He also depicted soldiers dying and forgotten far from the court and from their homes: "A gracious spring, turned to blood-ravenous autumn, /A turmoil of wars-men, spread over the middle kingdom, /Three hundred and sixty thousand, /And sorrow, sorrow like rain. / Sorrow to go, and sorrow, sorrow returning, /Desolate, desolate fields, /And no children of warfare upon them, /No longer the men for offence and defence." (from *Lament of the Frontier Guard*) Pound's selection of themes was based on the relation between Rihaku's China and the British Empire in 1914. In both cases, there were barbarians to be fought off by soldiers suffering in the battlefield, decadent government incapable of giving enlighened direction, the common people having the hard time from separation from families and friends. In his selected translation, Pound instilled widespread sympathy among his contemporary readers because separation and sorrow, the pervasive theme of *Cathay*, also constituted the prevailing emotional tone of the war-plagued society. Pound expressed his antipathy in the unequivocally anti-war details in related themes like domestic neglect or desertion, unwanted exile resulting in departure and loneliness and nostalgia, the "details whose contemporary relevance must have been obvious to readers at the time". (Wilson, 2005:144) Pound sent his translations of some war poems to his friend Gaudier-Brzeska in the battlefield and his friend replied: "The poems depict our situation in a wonderful way. We do not yet eat the young nor old fern shoots, but we cannot be over victualled where we stand". (Pound, 1974:58) The Pound scholar Hugh Kenner, in his book *The Pound Era*, cited the vividness of poems in *Cathay* to reflect the modern world: "Dating from the first winter of the war, it is like a poem abstracted from the departure of troop trains. ... Its exiled bowmen, deserted women, levelled dynasties, departures for far places, lonely frontier guardsmen and glories remembered from afar, cherished memories, were selected from the diverse wealth in the notebooks by a sensibility responsive to torn Belgium and disrupted London". (Kenner, 1972:202)

4.2.2 Time Perspective of Universality

Pound never doubts the permanent nature in objects and in humanity. From the beginning, he is clear about the vision: "I believe in a sort of permanent basis in humanity". (Bell, 1981: 138) Such permanence is represented in Pound's translation through his demonstration of universality of time and place. He presents visions from other ages and civilizations as occurrence in "here and now" instead of that from remote time and place. Pound deliberately adopts "the universalistic stance" (Preda, 2001: 78) erasing local and historical allusions because his aim is not to transmit cultural and local messages but to go beyond the original text to represent the universal fact in the world that would apply to both the East and the West. For Pound, "the original is the end and the beginning" and "he doesn't aim to go beyond it". (Preda, 2001:78)

Pound's universal stance is first demonstrated in the universality of time in his translations, the ahistorical treatment of something archaic and remote. His poetry translation *Cathay*, through the simple diction, the scientific approach and the restrained emotions, the concrete human existence across history of love and war, friendship and enmity, suffering and pleasure, emperors and soldiers, reveals the universal ingredients of human culture with which any reader could identify. Pound digs for the essential, the true, and the universal. The poems in *Cathay* are not archaic or modern, but "simply ahistorical". (Preda, 2001:78) Pound tries to preserve and revive history believing that the past is open to knowledge and investigation and effective to inspire and instruct. With his deliberate treatment of universal time in his poetics, he keeps trace of the lost time and reveals that "it (history) is not irretrievably lost, and that the combination of remaining fragments can still be meaningful and full of beauty". (Preda, 2001:122)

The ahistorical Skopos is achieved by Pound by the temporal marker of present tense to transform the specific historical situation to the timeless fact. For example, in the war poem of *The Lament of the Frontier Guard*, originally about a particular war in history, Pound adopts the ahistorical tone, changing the historical event to the universal indication of any similar event: "By the North Gate, the wind blows full of sand,/Lonely from the beginning of time until now! /Trees fall, the grass goes yellow with autumn. /I climb the towers and towers/to watch out the barbarous land:/Desolate castle, the sky, the wide desert." In another example of Pound's translation *Song of the Bowmen of Shu*, Pound uses the present tense throughout the poem to convert what happened to what continually happens. A comparison between the translation by Pound and by Arthur Waley will perspicuously reveal the different time perspectives.

The original text: 采薇采薇,薇亦作止。曰归曰归,岁亦莫止。
……
采薇采薇,薇亦柔止。曰归曰归,心亦忧止。
……
采薇采薇,薇亦刚止。曰归曰归,岁亦阳止。

Ezra Pound: Here we are, picking the first fern-shoots
And saying: When shall we get back to our country?
...
We grub the soft fern-shoot,
When anyone says "Return," the others are full of sorrow.
...
We grub the old fern-stalks.
We say: will we be let to go back in October?

Arthur Waley: We plucked the bracken, plucked the bracken
While the young shoots were springing up.
Oh, to go back, go back!
The year is ending.
...
We plucked the bracken, plucked the bracken
While the shoots were soft.
Oh, to go back, go back!
Our hearts are sad,
...
We plucked the bracken, plucked the bracken
But the shoots were hard.
Oh, to go back, go back!
The year is running out. (Waley, 1978:122-3)

Where Waley uses past tense, Pound uses present tense to reveal the present situation in the depiction of the ancient one, which is one of the major purposes of his translation. Hugh Kenner points out *Cathay* poems have remained vital for over half a century because that "They say, as so much of Pound's work says, that all this has happened before and continually happens". (Kenner, 1972:202)

Apart from the universality of time, Pound also achieves his ahistorical stance by converting the diachronic images into the simultaneous ones, that is, placing historical events and historical figures and ancient works at the same temporal plane. Pound emphasizes the visual nature of poetry in his poetics. His technique of collage is "a form with no history and allowing of no history" (Preda, 2001:123) by diluting sequentiality. Though not revealing actions in a logical development and narrating coherent and continuous stories, Pound creates original poetry in his *Cantos* with juxtaposition of such personalities in different historical phases as Confucius, Jefferson, Adams, which, in "a form that flattens temporal levels", (Preda, 2001: 123) creates fascinating reading. He preserves history through placing the ancient works of various civilizations on the current temporal level of the modern narrator in the unique approach of collage, adopting the a-syntactical structure, the simple juxtaposition of images, to represent profound emotions.

Pound, inspired by the prototypical collage method in Chinese poetry, tries to restore the original style with the creative method of disconnected image juxtaposition. Chinese poetry, like Chinese painting, conforms to the ancient philosophy of Taoism that maintains the equal status of man and nature, and places things and humans on the same plane in parallel relationship. The Chinese poetry scholar Wai-lim Yip notes the universal stance in space in the Chinese poetry, saying that Chinese poetry presents the totality of views from different angles, "releasing them from the restrictive concept of time and space, letting them leap out directly from the undifferentiated mode of existence instead of standing between the reader and the events explaining them, analyzing them". (Yip, 1997: 7) The simple juxtaposition of images represented in "the asyntactical and paratactical structures" in Chinese poetry promote "a kind of predicative condition wherein words, like objects in the real world, are free from predetermined relationships and single meanings and offer themselves to readers in an open space" and enable readers to "move freely and approach the words from a variety of vantage points to achieve different perceptions of the same moment". (Yip, 1997: Preface) Chinese poetry is characterized by loose syntactical structures without connective prepositions or conjunctions so as to reinvent a "free-floating activity" in which the objects could "maintain their multiple spatial and temporal extensions". (Yip, 2008:164)

Pound revives in his translation the detachment from the objects through the syntactic flexibility of poetic lines. The syntactic flexibility is mainly demonstrated in the absence of subjects and sometimes verbs, the indefinite part of speech and the lack of connectives. Pound realizes in his growing knowledge of Chinese language that when the subject retreats from the dominating position, the nature is able to display itself as it is. Without "I" in the primary position, all the creatures can present themselves, their lives, activities and rhythms, all as they are in real life, in real world, yet with the capacity to elicit subjective sympathy. Take an example in Pound's translation of *Book of Songs*:

The original text: 日月告凶，不用其行。
四国无政，不用其良。
彼月而食，则维其常；
此日而食，于何不臧。

（《诗经·十月之交》）

Ezra Pound: Sun, moon, foretell
evil? run wild.
State without rule,
good men exiled.
Moon's gnawed out in normal course.
What imprecise force
swallows the sun. (Pound, 2003:756)

James Legge: The sun and moon announce evil,
Not keeping to their proper paths.
All through the kingdom there is no proper government,
Because the good are not employed.
For the moon to be eclipsed
Is but an ordinary matter.
Now that the sun has been eclipsed,—
How bad it is! (Legge, 2011:496)

In the original poem, the poet expresses his misgivings about the country through association of the solar eclipse, the lunar eclipse with the corruption of the court. The ancient people believed that the eclipses were the warnings sent by gods, which predicted disasters in the empire. The poet, through his description of abnormal natural phenomena, conveys his apprehension for the country's future. Pound's translation is perspicuously different from Legge's syntactically coherent version. Pound depicts four objects in parallel in five lines without any logical connectives to show the relations between objects, inspires the profound thought among readers about the relationship between the political situation and the natural abnormalities. "Sun, moon, foretell/evil? run wild,/ State without rule,/good men exiled/Moon's gnawed out in normal course", these lines are only fragments in the language, which are connected by mere commas by Pound. They seem like the murmuring of the poet to himself yet conveys the dismantled unsettlement within.

In the perception of collage to spur intense aesthetic experience, Pound makes deliberate use of the method in his translation and then in his poetic works. In his epic *The Cantos*, Pound develops the method of collage even further through the juxtaposition of particulars, putting Odysseus, Divus, and the modern narrator on the same plane. Pound wrote to his father in 1927, describing the three elements of *The Cantos* as "Live man goes down into world of Dead" "the repeat in history", "the magic moment or moment of metamorphosis bust thru from quotidian into divine or permanent world." That is, Pound, by collecting the fragments in the past, seeks to discover the repetitive cycle in history, the rhyme of events to illuminate the present society. Pound registers history by a documentary means, with the collage of fragments like Jefferson, Adams, John Quincy Adams, Van Buren, Douglas, Mussolini for the theme of fighting the developing financial criminality in the previous centuries in Cantos XXXI, XXXII, XXXIII, the collage of abundant examples of 22 successive dynasties of China in *Cantos* LII-LXXI to seek harmony and order for the contemporary world. He also puts the translations of illuminating ideologies from the distinguished philosophers and writers of different civilizations like shattered sparks in the camp fire of his tome. With the technique of collage, Pound thrusts the blizzard of historical facts and figures, trivial or significant, in the same plane to inspire the intelligent conclusions from readers, with these discontinuous glimpses of history, sometimes in leaps, sometimes in contrast. The collage approach of documental facts is not intended as story-telling, but to plant seeds that might flower in the reader's imagination. Pound develops the documentary method to bring history into art, "to show that divinity and beauty — or the 'timeless' — were not defeated by an awareness of fact and time" and ultimately, "to show how the timeless was attainable within time". (Makin, 2006:104)

Pound's intention to preserve the culture is also seen in the generalization and foreignization of cultural allusions in his translations. The translation of culture-specific items often poses problems because of "the nonexistence or to the different value of the given item in the target language culture". (阿尔弗雷斯, 2007:58) Pound is creative in his alteration of cultural allusions in his translation for the universal acceptance of the message. Myths and legends and other cultural allusions are to Pound time-specific or space-specific but the timeless emotions in the poetry will be carried on to readers in modern times. The Western world has the similar technical genres of translation towards "maximum acceptability", "reading as an original", or as what Venuti terms, "a labor of acculturation which domesticates the foreign text, making it intelligible and even familiar to the target-language reader, providing him or her with the narcissistic experience of recognizing his or her own cultural other". (阿尔瓦雷斯 & 比达尔, 2007:54) In Pound's translations, the allusions carrying an aura of culture-specific associations is "decontextualized from the source field and dehistoricized, then re-contextualized and re-historicized in the target field"(赫曼斯, 2007:100) so that they will be more acceptable to the English audience. Many illustrative examples can be found in his translation of Chinese poetry with cultural messages "more remote from him than the Greek". (Pratt, 2002:3) For example, in his translation *The River-Merchant's Wife: A Letter*, the original line "常存抱柱信，岂上望夫台? (often/hold/hug/column/credibility, how/mount/look/husband/pavilion)" is drastically deprived of its cultural allusions into the simple lines of "Forever and forever and forever. /Why should I climb the lookout?" The first allusion "抱柱信" (the credibility of hugging the column) comes from Chinese philosopher Zhuang Zi, who writes about a man named Weisheng getting himself drowned by the swelling flood when waiting under the bridge post for his love. Weisheng loved the girl at the first sight and they decided to elope against the obstruction of her parents. He kept his promise of meeting at the wooden bridge but the girl didn't make her appearance. The gathering cloud and roaring thunder was followed by the pouring rain and then the torrential flood which soon covered the bridge and Weisheng, who embraced the post to wait until he was drowned. The girl, who had been captured by her parents, escaped to the bridge only to find her deceased lover and threw herself into the flood. The tragedy of love forges the character Weisheng as a symbol of credibility recurring in many of the later literary works. The second allusion "望夫台" refers to the pavilion to look out for the husband. In Three Empire Period, Liu Bei, the later emperor of Shu Empire, bid farewell to his beloved wife to fight for his noble cause in conquering the remote central plain area. The wife, in all her eagerness for the return of her husband, ascended the hill every day, longing to see her husband returning in triumph but in vain. The lookout pavilion then became a symbol of marital fidelity. A comparison of varying English versions will reveal the different approaches and Skopos of the translators.

The original text:　常存抱柱信，岂上望夫台？

Ezra Pound:　Forever and forever and forever.
Why should I climb the lookout?

Witter Bynner:　That even unto death I would await you by my post
And would never lose heart in the tower of silent watching

W. J. B. Fletcher:　My troth to thee till death I keep for aye:
My eyes still gaze daring on my lord.

S. Obata.:　You always kept the faith of Wei-sheng,
Who waited under the bridge, unafraid of death,
I never knew I was to climb the Hill of Wang-fu
And watch for you these many days.

Amy Lowell:　I often thought that you were the faithful man who
Clung to the bridgepost.
That I should never be obliged to ascend to the
Looking-for-Husband Ledge.

C. Gaunt:　We swore to be true with a "beam-clasping" faith,
And the thought of his absence was pain.

Xu Yuanchong:　Rather than break faith, he declared he'd die.
Who knew I'd live alone in tower high?

Among the seven versions, one gives the allusion of Wei-sheng as by S. Obata and one depicts the image of the ancient man without mentioning the name by Lowell as "the faithful man who clung to the bridge post", one gives the literal presentation of the moral as "'beam-clasping' faith" as by Gaunt, and two others merge the allusive meaning into the context as the narrator's feelings as by Bynner (That even unto death I would await you by my post) and by Fletcher (My troth to thee till death I keep for aye). Pound is unique in his version with no trace of the cultural allusion, but emphatic in the emotional force with the repetitive vows of "forever". As to "望夫台 (Pavilion to look out for the husband)", Obata gives the cultural origin literally as "the Hill of Wang-fu", Lowell makes semantic explanation of the function as "Looking-for-Husband Ledge", Bynner deletes the cultural message and generalizes the image into "the tower of silent watching" and Xu explains the cultural allusion of solitary loneliness in the general image of "living alone in tower high". Fletcher makes complete omission of the cultural reference, simplifying it into the action of "gazing" and Gaunt makes similar attempt to cut the image into the direct statement of emotional pain. Pound, unlike Obata and Lowell to restore the original cultural image and unlike Fletcher and Gaunt to delete the image, generalizes the image as "the lookout" to demonstrate the protagonist's yearning for her lover's return. In Pound's version, cultural allusions are transformed into the general facts, first into the lovers' commitment of eternal love (forever and forever and forever) and then into the questioning of her lover for his unfulfilled promise that leaves her all alone. Take another example from Pound's translation *Taking Leave of a Friend*.

The original text: 渭城朝雨浥轻尘,客舍青青柳色新。
劝君更尽一杯酒,西出阳关无故人。

Ezra Pound: Light rain is on the light dust.
The willows of the inn-yard
Will be going greener and greener,
But you, Sir, had better take wine ere your departure,
For you will have no friends about you
When you come to the gates of Go.

Witter Bynner: A morning-rain has settled the dust in Weicheng;
Willows are green again in the tavern dooryard. . .
Wait till we empty one more cup —
West of Yang Gate there'll be no old friends.

Xu Yuanchong: No dust is raised on the road wet with morning rain;
The willows by the hotel look so fresh and green.

I invite you to drink a cup of wine again;
West of the Sunny Pass no more friends will be seen.

In the poem, Wei City and Yang Pass are not simple naming of places but rich in historical allusions. Wei City is the region north of Wei River which is the main battlefield for the ancient Chinese military forces to fight off barbarians. Yang Pass is one important western passes of the Great Wall and one of China's western frontier defense outposts that protects the country from invasion from the northwest. It has been the place of desolation and sadness since ancient times when it was the last stop to see off a friend where they would be unable to contact each other ever since. Yang Pass is a symbol of the demarcation line between civilization and barbarism, the boundary that borders on forlorn desolation, a place that implies the distressful unknown prospect of the possible separation between life and death. The literal proper nouns of "Weicheng" or "Wei City", "Yangguan" or "Yang Pass" or "Yang Gate" make no resonance in English readers because the specific time and specific space that constitute this specific situation add the significance to the consciousness of the Chinese audience but these specific associations cannot be felt by the English audience. Pound omits Wei City completely and also the cumbersome local associations. He also ingeniously turns "Yang Pass" into "the gates of Go" in his translation. For Pound, what should dominate the poem is the essential emotion of distressful reluctance in friends' separation and the term "the gates of Go", apart from its musical achievement in alliteration, could create a sense of desolate sorrow in departure. It inspires greater emotional impact than the simple translation into "Yang Gate" by Bynner, or the semantic transference By Xu into "the Sunny Pass". A similar example is found from Pound's poem *The City of Choan* in *Cathay*. The original text "吴宫花草埋幽径，晋代衣冠成古丘" is teemed with cultural associations, among which the empire of Wu is one of the most powerful ones in Three Empire Period known for its power and prosperity in Chinese history and Jin Dynasty lasted from 265 AD to 420 AD, a period that witnessed great development in unification under the rule of 15 emperors over 156 years. In the Chinese poem, Li Bai ponders over the vicissitudes of life when all these signs of glory and power have been lost in history and forgotten. The Chinese translator Sun uses the literal translation of Wu Palace. Xu rejects the use of the proper noun and resorts to the literal translation as "the ruined palace". Pound, in his unique way, conveys it as "the dynastic house of the Go". The proper noun "Go" is a creative effort deliberately adopted by Pound to indicate the dissipation of past glory as it contains the semantic content in itself. In another case, the original text "烟花三月下扬州" carries intense cultural associations as Yangzhou is a place with rich association in Chinese history referring to the huge area south of the Yangtze River with abundant resources and prosperous life in Tang Dynasty. At the intersection between the canal and the long Yangtze River running across the country, Yangzhou used to be the business, shipping, economic and cultural center of the country abundant with merchants and poets and scholars. The cultural connotations are impossible to be conveyed through the transliteration as many translators do, either Yangzhou or Yangchou making no association of the thriving city it used to be. Pound, in the belief to "use no superfluous word" (Pound, 1968:4) that "represent nothing", (Pound, 1968:4) leaves out the proper noun with the mention of the location by "the river".

Pound is in constant quest of the precise revival of the poetic spirit instead of the literal translation of the superficial sense. Poetry of a far-off time or place requires a translation not only of word and of spirit, but of "accompaniment", (Preda, 2001:87) that is, that the modern audience must in some measure be made aware of the mental content of the older audience, and of what these others drew from certain fashions of thought and speech. And Pound deliberately makes his alteration of the original text to reach the ideal translation that combines all the elements contributive to the poetic sense, just as he himself says that the "atrocities" (Pound, 1968:172) of the translations are in great part intended.

Paradoxically, foreignization in Pound's translations also contributes to the timeless perspective. Literary works are often accompanied by the myths and legends in relation to it. "The resonance of the works comes from the ancient, the modern, the foreign, forming a massive orchestra playing overwhelming symphony". (Yip, 2006:63) The problem of the translation, then, is the finding of available expression for the experience seemingly arcane and mystic that belongs to a certain culture. Chinese poetry, for example, has its particular conventions along its long history of development. Burton Watson, in the translation of Chinese poetry, notes the difficulty in the preface: "... Chinese poetry, like that of the West, has its body of myths and legends that it draws upon, and it especially fond of employing allusions to the famous events and personages of the nation's lengthy past. All such mythical and historical allusions, of course, require some degree of explanation to be intelligible to the foreign reader". (Watson, 1984:3) The poetry scholar J. S. Holmes, in his book *Rebuilding the Bridge at Bommel* explores the limits of translatability, noting the three different levels in poetry, the first being in the linguistic context with the expressive lexical means to convey the meaning, the second in the "literary intertext" in which "a poem is written interaction with a whole body of poetry existing within a given literary tradition, and the rhythm, meter, rhyme, and assonances of the poem, but also its imagery, themes, and topic, are intimately linked with those in that whole array of other texts", (霍姆斯, 2007: 47) and the third in the socio-cultural situation which is never exactly the same in different societies or cultures. To convey all the features in the three levels is an impossible mission for most of the time and requires careful consideration and deliberate selection and rejection and the translators often find themselves in the dilemma between "exoticizing" and "naturalizing". (霍姆斯, 2007: 48) While many translators like Watson resort to the lengthy explanations for the allusions, Pound his unique approach in face of the dilemma and develops the method of simple conversion of the allusive terms into the proper nouns in English, writing in what Berman calls "a readable and vigorous target language that nevertheless retains some trace of the source-language text's strangeness, otherness, foreignness, alterity" as opposed to "opaque literalism" (鲁宾逊, 2006: 84) and sparing the supplementary explanations and emanating an exotic flavor in his translation. Berman points out that "translation that assimilates the foreign text to reductive and ethnocentric target-language norms, that erases all trace of foreignness, otherness, alterity — is impure or bad translation". (鲁宾逊, 2006: 83) Pound's approach is controversial but justifiable when the literary works are too complex to be translated with all its aesthetic features.

Pound's renunciation of complicated allusions unintelligible to western readers bears close relation to his timeless perspectives in myths and legends in history, signifying the difference of the foreign text as "a way of respecting the integrity of the original". (Qian, 2003: 37) For Pound, the mythical is "more aesthetic than religious". (Pratt, 2002: 3) He reiterates "the permanence base of humanity", regarding the myths as the reflection of the psychic experience, "an attempt to express a sensation or perception" (Lierbregts, 2004: 42-43) by the ancient people. He says: "I believe that Greek myth arose when someone having passed through delightful psychic experience tried to communicate it to others and found it necessary to screen himself from persecution". (Bell, 1981: 138) For him, mythical figures are the natural entities in history and the mythical culture is "metamorphic tradition of visionary experience" (Pratt, 2002: 3) existing as the psychic experience of the ancient people. Myths are not the record of the supernatural, but the psychic reality just like the natural phenomena that require no further associations for its interpretation. Thus, Pound, in his translation, tends to return to the original images without supplementary explanation, convinced that "a return to origins invigorates because it is a return to nature and reason" and the artist returns to the origin to "behave in the eternally sensible manner", "naturally, reasonably, intuitively". (Pound, 1968:93)

Pound's unique timeless approach of culture is demonstrated in his transliteration for richly-connoted proper names, such as "the north of Rakuhoku" in *Exile's Letter*, "Sen-Go" as the city name in *Exile's Letter*, "Choan" for the ancient capital name in China in *Old Idea of Choan* by Rosoriu and *The City of Choan*, "Kan-Chu" for the middle land in Han empire in *The River Song*, "Sennin" for immortals in *The River Song*, "the Choyu song" for a famous poetry in *The River Song*, "Kutsu" for the well-known patriotic writer Qu Yuan, "Rihoku" for the name of a gallant general in *Lament of the Frontier Guard*, "Rishogu" for the nickname of another great general as "the flying general" in *South-Folk in Cold Country*. Another specific example goes as follows:

The original text: 故人西辞黄鹤楼

Ezra Pound: Ko-jin goes west from Ko-kaku-ro,

Witter Bynner: You have left me behind, old friend, at the Yellow Crane Terrace,

Hope: Here he is, my good old friend!
He's at Yellow Crane Terrace on a western departure.
And — we're saying goodbye, goodbye.

Xu Yuanchong: My friend has left the west where the Yellow Crane towers

Sun Dayu: Mine old friend leaveth the West
From the Yellow Crane Tower.

Qiu Xiaolong: Leaving the Yellow Crane Pavilion,
you set out to the east,

Yellow Crane Tower is a famous historic tower on the Snake Mountain overlooking the Yangtze River in China. Legends have it that an immortal rode off on a yellow crane from the mountain and then the tower was built in commemoration of him. Another anecdote says about the man who saw an immortal landing from above the yellow crane and rode off with him after leisurely drinking. Reference to the tower also abounds in literature, and the most famous one comes from an 8th century poem called *Yellow Crane Tower*, reading as: "Long ago a man rode off on a yellow crane, all that remains here is Yellow Crane Tower. Once the yellow crane left it never returned, for one thousand years the clouds wandered without care." It is a poem reflective of the distress of the poet, the reminiscence of the home town, the melancholy over vicissitudes of life at the sight of the tower standing still for over one thousand years. Thus, Yellow Crane Tower brings associations of the historic and the occult. The Chinese translators, Xu, Sun and Qiu, translate the proper name by giving the semantic content of each Chinese character. The two English translators, Bynner and Hope adopts the same approach, with the only alteration from "tower" or "pavilion" to "terrace", which is more familiar to the westerners. Pound is different from any of them, adopting the transliteration of Ko-kaku-ro for the name, which bears no allusive associations for the western readers but adds eastern flavor to the poem. It is the same case with his bewildering translation of "the old acquaintance" to "Ko-jin", an apparently foreign name to the western readers. Pound's distinctive practice is deliberate because Fenollosa's notes present the term clearly as "the old acquaintance" or "the old friend". It is out of his consideration of poetic music as "Ko-jin" and "Ko-kaku-ro" forms perfect alliteration, and at the same time, out of his timeless perspective to preserve the historical moment in the exotic culture.

As to the cultural allusions intelligible to the Chinese readers but obscure to the western ones, Pound adopts the unique approach, focusing on reviving the universal emotions known to the consciousness of all and also preserving the exotic historic moments as they are.

4.3 Skopos of "Make It New"

Innovation is the keynote of Pound's poetics. Pound, along with other contemporary writers and thinkers such as T. S. Eliot, T. E. Hulme, regard themselves as the representatives of the modern era, an era marked by pervasive modernity with the invention and popularization of the telephone, the cinema, the automobile and the airplane, together with intellectual novelties such as Freud's psychoanalysis and Einstein's relativity theory, which, on the whole, transform the landscape of the world and require new forms of literature as the fit reflection of the changing appearance and in-depth consciousness. To fit the distinctively modern consciousness, Pound is in quest of something new, something that will alter the past to reflect the present and then to stretch into the future. He builds the slogan for innovation as "Make It New", which appears in *Canto* 53:

"Tching prayed on the mountain and
Wrote MAKE IT NEW
on his bath tub

Day by day make it new
cut underbrush
pile the logs
keep it growing."

Actually, earlier in 1934, Pound used "Make It New" as the title of his essay collection together with the Chinese ideograms on the title page. Pound writes an essay on the Confucian precepts which ends in "Make it new, make it new as the young grass shoot" followed by the Chinese ideograms for being new. In his translation of Confucian works, Pound's intention of innovation is manifest with his capitalized words for emphasis on innovation. For the original text:"汤之《盘铭》曰:'苟日新,日日新,又日新。'"James Legge's literal version goes as follows: "On the bathing-tub of Tang, the following words were engraved:—'If you can one day renovate yourself, do so from day to day. Yea, let there be daily renovation.'"(理雅各,1992:5) Pound's translation is more eye-catching with all the capitalizations:

"In letters of gold on T'ang's bathtub:
AS THE SUN MAKES IT NEW
DAY BY DAY MAKE IT NEW
YET AGAIN MAKE IT NEW" (Pound, 2003:620)

Pound repeats the phrase "MAKE IT NEW" thrice to preach his loud slogan to renovate the conventions. Pound has the ambition to develop the modern poetics different from his predecessors, different both in form and in content. With the modern spirit, he wants to discover the undiscovered, notice the unnoticed, examine the unexamined. He expounds elaborately how a modern artist should be: "His forbears may have led up to him; he is never a disconnected phenomenon, but he does take some step further. He discovers, or, better, 'he discriminates'. We advance by discriminations, by discerning that things hitherto deemed identical or similar are dissimilar; that things hitherto deemed dissimilar, mutually foreign, antagonistic, are similar and harmonic". (Pound, 1973: 25) Pound's advocacy for innovation is also reflected in his essay *Psychology and Troubadours* in his support for the active germinal consciousness to change against the passive mimetic consciousness to copy. Pound believes art should not be the mere mimetic copy of the world, but draw vigor from it to grow just like a tree grows with the nourishment from the root. With germinal consciousness, man is more than a physical mechanism to reflect his surroundings or a passive receptor of the circumstances, but can see the "universe of wood alive, of stone alive" (Pound, 1973:92) and conceive a fresh world with the true self blended in the vital universe.

Pound's advocacy to conceive and to innovate rather than merely inherit and copy, is well reflected in many of his translations. Pound's translations have profound influence on the American poetry. His poetic experiments reignite the vigor of poetry then fettered by the conventions of the previous century. Pound is experimental in making innovations to shatter the shackles of obsolete conventions because he believes that "The tradition is a beauty which we preserve and not a set of fetters to bind us". (Pound, 1968:91) He, in his translations from various cultures and from literary predecessors, draws the essence even at the risk of defying the established conventions in English literature. In the translation of the ancient Anglo-Saxon poetry, he is creative in his preservation of the unique rhythm in alliteration, coarse, rough but forceful. In the translation of the French and Italian poetry, he fosters precision as his imagist tenet against the previous sentimentalism. In the translation of the Chinese and Japanese poetry, he introduces the distinctive method of image juxtaposition to prompt intense emotional response. Pound's poetic experiments have introduced treasures of different cultures into American poetry.

4.3.1 "Make It New" against Poetic Stagnation

Though the Victorian era witnessed the flourishing of novels with masters such as Charles Dickens and William Thackeray, Poetry was in a sense stagnant and stale subsiding from the passion of the previous Romantist era. The Tennysonian style was exquisite at the beginning yet degenerated into hackneyed clichés after years of emulation, just as Pound detected in his essay: "For every 'great age' a few poets have written a few beautiful lines, or found a few exquisite melodies, and ten thousand people have copied them, until each strand of music is planed down to a dullness". (Pound, 1968: 244) In the Vicotrian poetry, the reclaiming of the past was the major theme, delineating the heroic, chivalrous stories of knights in the hope to regain the nobility and to impress it upon the people in the wide empire of England. Tennyson's *Idylls of the King*, for example, was a blend of the stories of King Arthur and the contemporary concerns and ideas. When many works drew on myth and folklore, the art became the sentimental extol of the old facts and the abstract beauty detached from the modern society. Pound, impressed by the remarkable changes in the modern society but concerned with the malaises accompanying the modern age, expresses his distaste for the rigid conventional approach in art. He believes the serious artist should be a mirror of the contemporary because "Artists are the antennae of the race... a nation's writers are the voltometers and steam-gauges of that nation's intellectual life" (Pound, 1968:59) and it is the responsibility of a serious artist to depict the development in each stage of civilization. Pound says: "By good art I mean art that bears true witness", (Pound, 1968:42) and "true witness" means the theme of literature should include the delineation of ugliness apart from the depiction of the beauty. Pound argues for it as follows: "The cult of beauty is the hygiene, it is sun, air, and the sea and the rain and the lake bathing. The cult of ugliness, Villon, Baudelaire, Corbiere, Beardsley are diagnosis. Flaubert is diagnosis. Satire, if we are to ride this metaphor to staggers, satire is surgery, insertion and amputations". (Pound, 1968:45) And when beauty is the theme, Pound detests the vague pompous style of old Victorian poetry: "I mean beauty, not slither, not sentimentalizing about beauty, not telling people that beauty is the proper and respectable thing". (Pound, 1968:45) The decorative pompousness and sentimentality in Victorian poetry is no longer appropriate since the modern audience lose their interest in the large speech. The scientific nature of the modern age calls for the scientific language and style in art, which, to Pound, means precision and clarity deprived of redundant expressions so as to reveal the fundamental truth in the universe: "Good writing is writing that is perfectly controlled, the writer says just what he means. He says it with complete clarity and simplicity. He uses the smallest possible number of words". (Pound, 1968:50)

In America, poetry was also in stagnation in Pound's time. The era of thriving local poetry drew to a close with the death of the great American poet Walt Whitman and "The years from 1880 to 1910 were something of a dark age for American poetry" when "poetry was pushed to the margins of the literary world" (比奇, 2006:7) by the thriving of novels by Mark Twain, Henry James, Theodore Dreiser, and other great writers. Poetry was in a predicament unable to compete with novels in importance and popularity and declined into "mediocrity of idea, form, and rhetoric". (比奇, 2006:7) Pound the modernist felt obliged to "break with tradition" against "the mediocrity of a given time" (Pound, 1968:227) when the poets embraced the artificial genteel tradition of English Victorian sonnets and odes as the dominant poetic of the American poetry. Pound called for the development of American poetry by abandoning the emulation of the dominant style of Victorian poetry and said: "I take it that the phrase 'break with tradition' is currently used to mean 'desert the more obvious imbecilities of one's immediate elders'". (Pound, 1968:227)

4.3.2 "Make it New" in Poetic Experiment

Against the hackneyed and stereotyped poetry, Pound takes the rebellion and experiments in the new poetics. He makes impelling statement for the necessity of experiments: "As for experiment: the claim is that without constant experiment literature dies. Experiment is one of the elements necessary to its life. Experiment aims at writing that will have a relation to the present analogous to the relation which past masterwork had to the life of its time". (Pound, 1973: 398) In his translation, Pound adopts the creative approach to present his new poetics and to inspire new poetry. In the translation of the canzoni by Arnaut Daniel, Pound focuses on the beauty of the poetry, giving prominence to "luminous detail". (Pound, 1968: 172) His translations of Cavalcanti and the ancient Anglo-Saxon poem *The Seafarer* are more adaptation than literal translation with his ingenious revival of the musicality at the cost of faithfulness. Pound mentions his motivation of the translation of Cavalcanti in his essay: "The melodic structure is properly indicated — and for the first time — by my disposition of the Italian text, but even that firm indication of the rhyme and the articulation of the strophe does not stress all the properties of Guido's triumph in sheer musicality". (Pound, 1968: 172) In the translation of the Anglo-Saxon poem *The Seafarer*, he deviates in some sense, but keeps the musical sound integral and faithful in his creative approach, cutting and converting the original semantic content for the revival of the musical quality of the poems. In the translation of ancient Chinese poetry, Pound is unique in his deliberate conversions, which yet steers the poetry in the new direction with the precise image and the hard language. T. S. Eliot praises that "Pound is the inventor of Chinese poetry for our time". (Wilson, 2005: 142) All in all, Pound aims not at the literal faithfulness in the translation but at the establishment and the promotion of his new poetics. He expounds it clearly in his essay: "As to the atrocities of my translation, all that can be said in excuse is that they are, I hope, for the most part intentional, and committed with the aim of driving the reader's perception further into the original than it would without them have penetrated". (Pound, 1968: 172) Pound, through his innovative translation, "brings the past alive into the present" (Xie, 1999: 144) and the Pound scholar Michael Alexander is justified in his praise of Pound: "... poetic courage and largeness, sustained creative enterprise, integrity in his art, the intense reflection of the light vouchsafed, these are not qualities lightly to be despised". (Alexander, 1979: 18)

Pound's innovation is firstly seen in the thematic adaptations in Pound's translations. Romanticism is the artistic movement against the modern Industrial Revolution and the scientific rationalization of nature. Romantist poetry features themes concerning the eulogy for the nature and the curse of the urbanization. The beauty of nature, in stark contrast to the ugliness of industrialized life, is the primary source of Romantist poetry and the artists' emotional retreat and the universal haven. For Romanticists, strong emotions are experienced in the confrontation of sublime beauty of nature, something as sublime as trepidation, awe and ecstasy. The movement places emphasis on imagination and intuition as the authentic source of poetic experience rather than the deductive reason in the Age of Enlightenment. The following aestheticism in the 19th century is the artistic movement that emphasizes aesthetic values over moral or social ones in literature. It is the reaction to the 19th-century industrialism and its philosophy, utilitarianism, and also a reflection of the universal dissatisfaction with social values and the artists' intent to escape from the ugly reality through artistic aesthetics. The aesthetes seek, as their slogan goes, "art for art's sake", believing that art has no social responsibility but is an end in itself and that the object of art is "the appreciation and cultivation of beauty". (Beasley, 2007:22) They hold that art should provide refined pleasure rather than convey moral and sentimental messages. They neglect the social reality of their times but focus on the realm of pure art.

Imagists, under Pound's leadership, transform the subjects away from the rejection of modern civilization. They believe with passion that the modern life bear its artistic value and poets should have modern sensitivity, adapting themselves to the modern world in the selection of modern materials and the adoption of new artistic forms. In their artistic works, they reveal their modern consciousness by diverting their eyes from the detached realm of art and nature into the modern world of steel and iron, the conflicts between man and society, between man and nature with the intrusion of industrialization and capitalism. Pound's famous Metro poem, as a touchstone of the new Imagist movement, is a demonstration of such modern sensitivity with its urban and modern setting — a crowded Paris subway station, normally dark and forbidding and ugly but soon transformed through Pound's original poetic form into something surprisingly beautiful, offering an unique and impressive aesthetic experience.

Pound's translation blazes new trails for poetry against Victorian conventions. It shifts the poetic theme from the ancient to the modern. *Cathy*, though the translation of ancient China, is considered an anti-war poetic collection under Pound's meticulous selection, mirroring the modern world in decadence where the soldiers fought in faraway places against the invaders, longing for homes and their beloved ones. Pound's theme deviates from the magnificent in tradition to the common in modernism, to the universal facts and feelings that resonate throughout history. "The old poetry dealt essentially with big things, the expression of epic subjects leads naturally to the anatomical matter and regular verse... But the modern is the exact opposite of this, it no longer deals with heroic action, it has become definitely and finally introspective and deals with expression and communication of momentary phrases in the poet's mind". (Hulme, 1994: 53) The poets in American New Poetry Movements regarded the themes of Chinese poetry as adequately modern. Though without modern skyscrapers and cars, these poetry reveals the permanent emotions and scenes in history, profound friendship, sorrow in separation, the natural scenes and everyday life as a replacement for the semi-god heroes in ancient epics. Pound, while preserving some exotic strangeness of cultures in different time and in different space, employs the universal emotions and ideals that strike the resonance among western readers. His purpose is to "enshrine a shared ideal" that promotes the development of modern poetry. (Park, 2008:24)

Pound's innovation is also seen in his experiment with poetic syntax in the translation. Chinese, an inflection-free language, is known for its flexibility and resilience in grammar without the limitation of number, tense, voice and gender. The subject and the predicate are sometimes absent and so are some elements indispensable in English grammar such as the articles, pronouns, connectives. The Chinese-English translator should determine in his translation, basically, whether the missed subject should be "I" or "he" or "she", the tense and aspect of the verb, the singular or plural form of the nouns, which seem to be minor factors yet affect the artistic conception of the poetry. Pound's translation goes through different phases, from the minor changes to bridge the gap between Chinese and English grammar, to the literal conversion of the paratactic syntax directly into English, then to the application of such seemingly non-syntactical structure to his own poetry. The experiment is an innovation on the tradition of English poetry and has profound influence on modernist poets in the 20th century. Pound's syntactic innovation is demonstrated in three major aspects: juxtaposition of parallel phrases without connectives, spacing between lines and phrases, paratactic and anaphoric construction.

Firstly, the juxtaposition of parallel phrases, which seems to be unsyntactical in English, is a prominent feature in Pound's translation. The omission of the subject in a poetic sentence or even the verbs runs counter to the conventions of English grammar but faithfully reflects the ambiguous nature of Chinese grammar, which, through such ambiguity, creates an artistic experience unique and intense. The a-syntactic structure first emerges in his translation of Chinese poetry *Cathay*, such as "Mind like a floating white cloud,/Sunset like the parting of old acquaintances". Pound uses two zero-article noun phrases with the only preposition "like" as the only link between the analogical images. The fragmental treatment is common in Pound's translations, represented by the arrangement of independent short clauses without connectives such as "The generals are on them, the soldiers are by them/The horses are well trained, the generals have ivory arrows and quivers ornamented with fish- skin. /The enemy is swift, we must be careful. /We go slowly, we are hungry and thirsty" in *Song of the Bowmen of Shu*, by the linkless verbless clauses such as "Haughty their steps as they go into great banquets,/To high halls and curious food,/To the perfumed air and girls dancing,/To clear flutes and clear singing;/To the dance of the seventy couples;/To the mad chase through the gardens" in *Poem by the Bridge at Ten-Shin*, by the isolated fragmental noun phrases such as "Three hundred and sixty thousand,/And sorrow, sorrow like rain. /Sorrow to go, and sorrow, sorrow returning,/Desolate, desolate fields" in *Lament of the Frontier Guard* and so on. Or sometimes, the noun phrases are juxtaposed in one line with no other elements to form a conventional clause such as "Desolate castle, the sky, the wide desert" from *Lament of the Frontier Guard* and "Surprised. Desert turmoil. Sea sun" from *South-Folk in Cold Country*. The fragmental lines abound in Pound's translation of *Book of Songs*.

The original text: 维鹊有巢,维鸠居之。之子于归,百两御之。
维鹊有巢,维鸠方之。之子于归,百两将之。
维鹊有巢,维鸠盈之。之子于归,百两成之。

(《诗经 • 鹊巢》)

Ezra Pound:

Dove in jay's nest
to rest,
she brides
with an hundred cars.

Dove in jay's nest
to bide,
a bride
with an hundred cars.

Dove in jay's nest
at last
and the hundred cars
stand fast. (Pound, 2003:760-1)

James Legge: The nest is the magpie's;
The dove dwells in it.
This young lady is going to her future home;
A hundred carriages are meeting her.

The nest is the magpie's;
The dove possesses it.
This young lady is going to her future home;
A hundred carriages are escorting her.

The nest is the magpie's;
The dove fills it.
This young lady is going to her future home;
These hundreds of carriages complete her array. (Legge, 2011:29)

The original poem depicts the luxurious extravagance of marriage ceremony. The three stanzas begin with the natural image of dove in jay's nest, in accumulative intensity with the three different verbs from "live" to "coexist" to "fill". The first stanza is the beginning of the ceremony, with a hundred carriages to indicate the wealth of the bridegroom and the nobility of the bride. The second stanza indicates the way back and the third the end of the ceremony. Three typical scenes constitute the process of the marriage ceremony. James Legge's translation is composed of 12 independent sentences in 12 poetic lines. In contrast, Pound cuts the poetic lines into halves, and between the lines of natural image and human ceremony, there are few connectives to show the logical relation. Even the images are cut into syntactic fragments. "Dove in jay's nest" depicts the natural image, and fragmental phrases "to rest", "to bide", "at last" appearing in the second line of each stanza stress the gradual process of dove's occupation of jay's nest. Though without any linking devices in between, the visualized images in the three stanzas form the vivid depiction of the proceeding of marriage ceremony. Another example is also from *Book of Songs*:

The original text:谁谓河广？一苇杭之。谁谓宋远？跂予望之。

(《诗经·河广》)

Ezra Pound: Wide, Ho?
A reed will cross its flow;
Sung far?
One sees it, tip-toe. (Pound, 2003:787)

James Legge: Who says that the Ho is wide?
With a bundle of reeds I can cross it.
Who says that Sung is distant?
On tiptoe I can see it. (Legge, 2011:147)

The poem conveys the nostalgia of the poet who has been away from the homeland for long. Standing by the river that separates him from his hometown, he expresses his sorrow of the incapability to return. The poem begins with the rhetoric question to inspire the thinking of the reader and the obvious answer of the short distance reinforces his eagerness to go back home. Pound's translation is full of linguistic fragments compared with Legge's complete sentence in every poetic line. In Pound's version, the two fragmental questions "Wide, Ho?" and "Sung far?" represent the typical features of colloquial speech and take the ironic tone to imply the opposite fact from the question and the inability to return despite the short distance compounds the grief. Though achieving intense emotional impact, Pound is radically experimental in the syntax.

Apart from the a-syntactic structures, another syntactic innovation is the unusual spacing between lines and phrases. In his famous Metro poem, Pound originally spaced between phrases: "The apparition of these faces in the crowd: / Petals on a wet black bough." He intends each of the phrases as a phase of perception. The disconnected phases of perception then creates "a sense of simultaneity" (Yip, 1969: 61) and "the simultaneous flash upon the reader's screen of imagination" might "overlie and inter-define each other" (Yip, 1969: 62) to intensify the perceptive impressions into emotional experience. The spacing between lines, though absent in the original Chinese poems, is created by Pound intentionally in his translation. Take his *The Beautiful Toilet* as an example:

Blue, blue is the grass about the river
And the willows have overfilled the close garden.
And within, the mistress, in the midmost of her youth,
White, white of face, hesitates, passing the door,
Slender, she puts forth a slender hand.

And she was a courtesan in the old days,

And she has married a sot,
Who now goes drunkenly out
And leaves her too much alone.

The previous half of the poem is the depiction of the scenes with luxuriant grass, verdant willows, the beautiful lady in the house. The latter half of the poem is about the emotional thoughts and feelings of the lady, of her lament on her pathetic fate of marrying a sot, of being deserted, of her permanent loneliness. The spacing between the two sections marks an unexpected transformation of the beautiful landscape to the lady's woeful life, thus creating "dramatic irony" as it is called. (Yip, 1969:146) Similar examples abound in *Cathay*. Sometimes the moralizing part might also go in the bracket to distance it from the objective depiction as in his *The River Song*: "(If glory could last forever/Then the waters of Han would flow northward.)"

Moreover, Pound's innovation of syntax is also reflected in his frequent use of paratactic syntax in the movement of past recollection. The anaphoric construction and paratactic construction are prominent features in Pound's translation. The important poetic syntax as "anaphoric construction" in modernist poetry is a structure with "the simultaneous combination of the two models" mirrored in passages as "the anaphoric and adjunctive use of the conjunction 'and'". (Xie, 1999: 149) In Pound's *Cathay*, the extended paratactic use of the adjunctive 'and' is the predominant practice "by narrative parallel and expansion". (Xie, 1999:149) A prominent example of the anaphoric construction is Pound's poem *Exile's Letter*, a translation of Li Bai's poem:

Now I remember that you built me a special tavern
By the south side of the bridge at Ten-Shin.
With yellow gold and white jewels we paid for the songs and laughter,
And we were drunk for month after month, forgetting the kings and princes.
Intelligent men came drifting in, from the sea from the west border
And with them, and with you especially,
There was nothing at cross-purpose,
And they made nothing of sea-crossing or of mountain-crossing,
If only they could be of that fellowship,
And we all spoke out our hearts and minds, and without regret.
And then I was sent off to South Wei,
smothered in laurel groves,
And you to the north of Raku-hoku,
Till we had nothing but thoughts and memories in common.

And then, when separation had come to its worst
We met, and travelled into Sen-Go
Through all the thirty-six folds of the turning and twisting waters,
Into a valley of a thousand bright flowers,
That was the first valley;
And on into ten thousand valleys full of voices and pine-winds.
And with silver harness and reins of gold,
prostrating themselves on the ground,
Out came the East of Kan foreman and his company.
And there came also the 'True-man' of Shi-yo to meet me,
Playing on a jeweled mouth-organ.
In the storied houses of San-Ko they gave us more Sennin music,
Many instruments, like the sound of young phoenix broods.
The foreman of Kan-Chu, drunk, danced because his long sleeves wouldn't
 keep still
With that music playing.
And I, wrapped in brocade, went to sleep with my head on his lap,
And my spirit so high it was all over the heavens.
And before the end of the day we were scattered like stars or rain.
I had to be off to So, far away over the waters,
You back to your river-bridge.
And your father, who was brave as a leopard,
Was governor in Hei-Shu and put down the barbarian rabble.
And one May he had you send for me, despite the long distance;
And what with broken wheels and so on, I won't say it wasn't hard going,
Over roads twisted like sheep's guts.
And I was still going, late in the year,
 in the cutting wind from the North,
And thinking how little you cared for the cost,
 and you caring enough to pay it.
Then what a reception:
Red jade cups, food well set on a blue jeweled table,
And I was drunk, and had no thought of returning.
And you would walk out with me to the western corner of the castle,
To the dynastic temple, with water about it clear as blue jade,
With boats floating, and the sound of mouth-organs and drums,
With ripples like dragon-scales, going glass green on the water,

Pleasure lasting, with courtesans going and coming without hindrance,
With the willow-flakes falling like snow,
And the vermilioned girls **getting drunk** about sunset,
And the waters a hundred feet deep **reflecting** green eyebrows
— Eyebrows painted green are a fine sight in young moonlight,
Gracefully painted —
And the girls **singing** back at each other,
Dancing in transparent brocade,
And the wind **lifting** the song, and **interrupting** it,
Tossing it up under the clouds.
　　And all this comes to an end.
　　And is not again to be met with.
I went up to the court for examination,
Tried Layu's luck, offered the Choyo song,
And got no promotion,
　　and went back to the East Mountains White-headed.
And once again, later, we met at the South bridgehead.
And then the crowd broke up, you went north to San palace,
And if you ask how I regret that parting:
It is like the flowers falling at Spring's end,
　　Confused, whirled in a tangle.
What is the use of talking, and there is no end of talking,
There is no end of things in the heart.
I call in the boy,
Have him sit on his knees here
　　To seal this,
And I send it a thousand miles, thinking.

Pound makes abundant use of the adjunctive "and" to give the speaking voice in a natural way, linking the various units of memory and perception in the narrative into notable paratactic syntax. In many poetic lines, the adjunctive "and" starts the line, initiating and carrying forward the stream of narration in the stream of consciousness, along with lines beginning in "with" and having the verb in present participial form. The protagonist's vision is substantiated by many present participial constructions in the poem, forming the seemingly ungrammatical "dangling participles" but constituting the persona's stream of memory acted out in continuous retrospect. Pound makes conscious use of paratactic syntax in an attempt to convey in English the subtle and dramatic shades of feeling and emotion of the protagonist in the original Chinese poem.

Pound displays a wide variety poetic techniques and rhetorical structures in his *Cathay*, "especially in the use of paratactic and anaphoric constructions". (Xie, 1999: 155) In the study of Fenollosa's often detailed notes and literal versions, Pound has the intuitive sense of the importance and significance of paratactic structures in the original Chinese poems. Compared with other versions of Chinese poetry, Pound's versions carry the greater number of anaphoric constructions and paratactic constructions. Take another example that highlights such constructions in Pound's translations.

The original text: 总为浮云能蔽日,长安不见使人愁。

Ezra Pound: Now the high clouds cover the sun
And I can not see Choan afar
And I am sad.

Xu Yuanchong: As floating clouds can veil the bright sun from the eye,
Imperial Court now out of view saddens my heart.

Sun Dayu: It's all because the floating clouds could cover the sun;
The Imperial City hid from sight doth one dismay.

Tang Yihe: Floating clouds can always eclipse the sun.
How sorrowful I am I cannot see Chang An!

Pound cuts the last poetic line in the original text into two separate ones linked with the adjunctive "and", which is unusual as compared to other versions. Xu treats the lines in the relationship of cause and effect in his translation with the veiling of the sun by the clouds being the reason of the invisibility of the imperial court, which, in turn is the reason of the poet's sorrow. Sun and Tang do not stress the relationship of the covering of the sun and the invisibility of the city. Sun, using the city as the subject, that is, the agent of the feeling, makes more explicit the relationship of cause and effect. Tang, putting "I cannot see Chang An" as the subordinate of the main clause "how sorrowful I am" stresses the direct relationship between the fact and the emotion. Pound, however, uses the simple paratactic connective "and" as the linking device, turning the lines into separate images succeeding one another, the image of clouds covering the sun, and then the image of the poet trying to see the city in the far distance in vain, and then the image of the sad protagonist. Pound intends the images to inspire rather than explicate with the blank space between images that renders possible relationships and interpretations. Similar examples abound in the collection such as "The sea's colour moves at the dawn/And the princes still stand in rows, about the throne,/And the moon falls over the portals of Sei-go-yo,/And clings to the walls and the gate-top" from *Poem by the Bridge at Ten-Shin*, "The lone man sits with shut speech, /**He** purrs and pats the clear strings. /**He** throws his heart up through the sky, /**He** bites through the flower pistil/and brings up a fine fountain. /The red-pine-tree god looks on him and wonders. /**He** rides through the purple smoke to visit the sennin, /**He** takes 'Floating Hill' by the sleeve, /**He** claps his hand on the back of the great water sennin" from *Sennin Poem by Kakuhaku*, in which Pound continues the poetic lines with six repeated pronouns "he" as the subject and creates the separate images in the seeming monotony of the sentence pattern, which, in parallel, extends the continuity of the image of the hermit.

Pound also makes rhythmic creations in his translations. Absolute rhythm and free verse are other innovations that influence the later modernist poets. Pound denounces the rigid poetic form of rhyme and meter in the Victorian poetry, clamoring against the fossilized verse tradition: "The musical terms 'staccato' and 'legato' apply to verse. The common verse of Britain from 1890 to 1910 was a horrible agglomerate compost, not minted, most of it not even baked, all legato, a doughy mess of third-hand Keats, Wordsworth, heaven knows what, fourth-hand Elizabethan sonority blunted, half melted, lumpy. The Elizabethan 'iambic' verse was largely made to bawl in theatres, and had considered affinity with barocco". (Pound, 1968: 205) The mechanical use of inflexible rhyme is merely an impediment to the expression of the poetic feelings and emotions and the overstress on rhyme will "draw away the artist's attention from forty to ninety per cent of his syllables and concentrate it on the admittedly more prominent remainder" and "draw him into prolixity and pull him away from the thing". (Pound, 1973:42) Pound advocates the precise language in simplicity and austerity instead of the "decorative or rhetorical word" and without all the "pseudomagniloquence", the "puffed words". (Pound, 1968: 205) Chinese poems have the symmetric beauty and strict rules of rhyme, yet Pound resorts to free verse for his translation. Giles and Fletcher use the traditional metric forms to translate Chinese poetry, making fronting and postponement of words, adding and cutting of the semantic content to achieve regular rhyme and metre. In free verse, however, words can be arranged in accordance to the emotional heaving and ebbing of the poet and the translator is able to present the emotions of the poet more faithfully with the plasticity of the language. Pound argues that the discarding of rhyme is "not because one is incapable of rhyming neat, fleet, sweet, meet, treat, eat, feet, but because there are certain emotions or energies which are not to be represented by the over-familiar devices or patterns; just as there are certain 'arrangements of form' that cannot be worked into dados". (Pound, 1973:345) The free verse, with all its flexibility in expression, is more suitable for the expression of express the intense emotions without impediment. Translation can often be used considerably "to bring a literature out of lethargy or veritable cardiac arrest". (Rose, 2007:26) After Pound, free verse becomes the major means for the translation of Chinese poetry and the predominant form of modernist poetry.

Pound's free verse is not absolutely "free" since his poem translations are "held together from within by so many filaments, syntactic, sonoric, imagistic, that any change, as surely as change in a verse of Pope's, will be change for the worse". (Kenner, 1972:200) The "syntactic, sonoric, imagistic filaments" refer to the rhythmic phrases in the poetic line, "absolute rhythm" in Pound's term, an influential contributor to the development of modernist poetry combining the natural flow of emotions and music. Pound argues that poetry, as the carrier of emotions, should be in concordance with the emotional wax and wane in regular rhythm and it is good only "when this rhythm, or when the vowel and consonantal melody or sequence seems truly to bear the trace of emotion which the poem is intended to communicate". (Pound, 1968:51)

Pound's absolute rhythm is in essence rhythm in phrases. Absolute rhythm is composed of "words with a vague adumbration of music, words suggestive of music, words measured, or words in a rhythm that preserves some accurate trait of the emotive impression, or of the sheer character of the fostering or parental emotion". (Pound, 1968:51) Its merits consist in the selection and arrangement of poetic elements determined by emotion, thus unifying the use of words and the flow of emotions. Since the phrases are the smallest units in poetry and in many cases coinciding with the sense units, the display of musical quality is simultaneous to the unfolding of semantic content. The ongoing of the divided small phrases is also in compatibility with the breathing process, the natural inhaling and exhaling of air. The poetry then becomes a natural process of spoken language that facilitate readers' involvement in the process and simultaneous interpretation and appreciation that intensifies the poetic experience. Absolute rhythm is also rhythm in accent. The correspondence of each accent for a Chinese character and the arrangement of five to seven accents in a poetic line make the revival of the traditional Chinese five and seven-character poetry. Take his poem The Beautiful Toilet as an example. The original text is made up of five-character lines with reduplicative words in the initial position of the first six lines. Pound, with his subtle use and control of rhyme, revives the reduplication and creates the correspondence of rhyme to the original by accenting the words in accordance.

`Blue, `blue is the `grass a`bout the `river

And the `willows have `over`filled the `close `garden.

And wi`thin, the `mistress, in the `midmost of her `youth,

`White, `white of `face, `hesitates, `passing the `door,

`Slender, she `puts `forth a `slender `hand.

In each of the verse line, Pound stresses five to six words that are in strict accordance to the characters of the original poem. In the first line, the five stressed words are the exact equivalent of the five characters of the original line. In the second line, the double-stressed word "overfilled" is meant to be the correspondent of the reduplicative words of the verdant green of the willows. The repetition of "blue", "white" and the ingenious separation of "slender" in the fifth line revive the rhyme of the original.

Pound's adoption of free verse and invention of absolute rhythm has great influence on modernist poetry. His translation of Chinese poetry "encouraged subsequent translators of Chinese to abandon rhyme and fixed stress counts". (Kenner, 1972:199) Kenner summarizes Pound's achievement and contribution to poetry into three major criteria that change the nature of an English poem: "the Vers libre principle, that the single line is the unit of composition; the Imagist principle, that a poem may build its effects out of things it sets before the mind's eye by naming them; and the lyrical principle, that words or names, being ordered in time, are bound together and recalled into each other's presence by recurrent sounds". (Kenner, 1972: 199) Two of the principles of Pound's achievements concern the musical quality of language in poetry. Pound's free verse allows "a greater originality of expression than conventional metrical and stanzaic forms". (Beach, 2006: 26) Pound's absolute rhythm, based on free verse, is another original contribution. T. S. Eliot hails him to be "the inventor of Chinese poetry for our time" and Wai-lim Yip praises Pound to have "invented Chinese translation by phrase". (Alexander, 1979: 100) Pound's emphasis on the inner form instead of the superficially regular meter and rhyme shifts the focus of poetry more on internal emotions than on external rigid forms. When the traditional meter and rhyme becomes an impediment of poetic emotions, it is discarded by Pound in favor of the form that could represent the new vista of world. Absolute rhythm in poetry is elaborately composed and "each song finds and follows at every move its own inner form". (Moody, 2007: 208) The originality consists in the natural music of words developed in the poetry in measured and cadenced shapes that inspires and touches anyone with a fine ear for music in nature. Eliot praises Pound's translation as a phase in the development of Pound's poetry and it could even be "a phase in the development of English poetry". (Wilson, 2005:142) "When a literature is in a phase of expanding and including, it is likely to be looking for new subjects, new themes and new sounds. This phase may well make it receptive to translations that show their foreign origins". (Rose, 2007:28) Pound's innovational efforts are seen in his integration of the best traditions in various source languages into the target language of English to enrich it and they are well paid off in hailed acceptance by the western readers.

Bibliography

Alexander, Michael. 1979. The Poetic Achievement of Ezra Pound. London: Faber and Faber Limited.

Beasley, Rebecca. 2007. Theorists of Modernist Poetry: T. S. Eliot, T. E. Hulme, Ezra Pound. London and New York: Routledge, Taylor and Francis Group.

Bell, Ian F. A. 1981. Critic as Scientist: The Modernist Poetics of Ezra Pound. London and New York: Methuen Co. Ltd.

Bergson, Henri. 2002. Creative Evolution. Edited by Keith Ansell-Pearson, John Mullarkey, London: Continuum.

Bergson, Henri. 2002. Time and Free Will: An Essay on the Immediate Data of Consciousness. Authorized Translation by F. L. Pogson. London: Routledge.

Brooker, Peter. 1979. A Student's Guide To The Selected Poems of Ezra Pound. London: Faber and Faber Limited.

Carpenter, Humphrey. 1988. A Serious Character: the Life of Ezra Pound. Boston: Houghton Mifflin Company.

Catford, J. C. 1965. A Linguistic Theory of Translation. London: Oxford University Press.

Edwards, Paul. 2000. Blast: Vorticism 1914-1918, edited by Paul Edwards. Hampshire: Ashgate Publishing Limited.

Fenollosa, Ernest. 1936. The Chinese Written Character as a Medium for Poetry with a Foreword and Notes by Ezra Pound. London: Stanley Nott.

Frank, Stewart. 2004. The Poem Behind the Poem: Translating Asian Poetry. Washington: Copper Canyon Press.

Gentzler, Edwin. 2004. Contemporary Translation Theories (Revised Second Edition). Shanghai: Shanghai Foreign Language Education Press.

Hickman, Miranda. 2005. The Geometry of Modernism: The Vorticist Idiom in Lewis, Pound, H. D., and Yeats. Austin: University of Texas Press.

Homberger, Eric. 1972. Ezra Pound: The Critical Heritage. London and NewYork: Routledge.

Hulme, T. E. 1994. The Collected Writings of T. E. Hulme, edited by Karen Csengeri. Oxford: Clarendon Press.

Kayman. 1986. The Modernism of Ezra Pound: The Science of Poetry. London:

Macmillan Press.

Kenner, Hugh. 1972. The Pound Era. London: Faber and Faber.

Kim, Joon-Hwan. 2003. Out of the "Western Box": Towards a Mutlicultural Poetics in the Poetry of Ezra Pound and Charles Olson. New York: Peter Lang Publishing, Inc.

Lan, Feng. 2005. Ezra Pound and Confucianism: Remaking Humanism in the Face of Modernity. Toronto, Buffalo, London: University of Toronto Press.

Lewis, Ethan. 2007. Modernist Image: Rhythmic and Perceptual Resonance in the Works of Ezra Pound and T. S. Eliot. Lewiston • Queenston • Lampeter: The Edwin Mellen Press.

Lierbregts, Perter. 2004. Ezra Pound and Neoplatonism. Madison, Teaneck: Fairleigh Dickinson University Press.

Liu, James J. Y. 1962. The Art of Chinese Poetry. Chicago: The University of Chicago Press.

Makin, Peter. 1985. Pound's Cantos. London: George Allen & Unwin Publishers Ltd.

Makin, Peter. 2006. Ezra Pound's Cantos: A Casebook. New York: Oxford University Press Inc.

Moody, David. 2007. Ezra Pound: Poet (A Portrait of the Man and his Work) New York: Oxford University Press.

Nadel, Ira B. 2004. Ezra Pound: A Literary Life. New York: Palgrave Macmillan.

Nida, Eugene A. & Taber, Charles. 1969. The Theory and Practice of Translation. Leiden: E. J. Brill.

Nolde, John J. 1996. Ezra Pound and China. Maine: The National Poetry Foundation University of Maine.

Nord, Christiane. 1997. A Functional Typology of Translations. Philadelphia: John Benjamins Publishing Company.

Nord, Christiane. 2001. Translating as a Purposeful Activity: Functionalist Approaches Explained. Shanghai: Shanghai Foreign Language Education Press.

O'Connor, William Van. 1968. Ezra Pound. Minneapolis: University of Minnesota Press.

Painter, Kirsten B. 2006. Flint on a Bright Stone: A Revolution of Precision and Restraint in American, Russian, and German Modernism. California: Stanford University Press.

Park, Josephine. 2008. Apparitions of Asia: Modernist Form and Asian

American Poetics. New York：Oxford University Press.

Pound, Ezra. 1950. The Letters of Ezra Pound, edited by D. D. Paige. New York：New Directions.

Pound, Ezra. 1960. ABC of Reading. [1934.] New York：New Directions.

Pound, Ezra. 1964. Confucius to Cummings, An Anthology of Poetry. New York：New Dorectopms.

Pound, Ezra. 1968. Literary Essays of Ezra Pound：Edited with an Introduction by T. S. Eliot. London：Faber and Faber Limited.

Pound, Ezra. 1971. Selected Letters 1907-1941 of Ezra Pound. New York：New Directions

Pound, Ezra. 1973. Selected Prose 1909-1965, edited by William Cookson. London：Faber and Faber Limited.

Pound, Ezra. 1974. Gaudier-Brzeska. New York：New Directions.

Pound, Ezra. 1990. Personae：The Shorter Poems of Ezra Pound. New York：Lea Baechler and A. Walton Litz.

Pound, Ezra. 2003. Ezra Pound：Poems and Translations. New York：Literary Classics of the United States, Inc.

Pound, Ezra. 2005. Early Writings, Poems and Prose. Ed. Ira. B. Nadel. New York：Penguin.

Pratt, William. 2002. Ezra Pound, Nature and Myth. New York：AMS Press.

Pratt, William. 2007. Ezra Pound and the Making of Modernism. New York：AMS Press, Inc.

Preda, Roxana. 2001. Ezra Pound's (Post) Modern Poetics and Politics：Logocentrism, Language, and Truth. New York：Peter Lang Publishing, Inc.

Qian, Zhaoming. 2003. Ezra Pound & China. Michigan：The University of Michigan Press.

Qian, Zhaoming. 2008. Ezra Pound's Chinese Friends. New York：Oxford University Press Inc.

Reiss, Katharina. 2004. Translation Criticism：The Potentials & Limitations. Shanghai：Shanghai Foreign Language Education Press.

Tytell, John. 1987. Ezra Pound：The Solitary Volcano. New York：Archor Press.

Venuti, Lawrence. 1995. The Translator's Invisibility. London & New York：Routledge.

Waley, Arthur. 1978. The Book of Songs：Translated from the Chinese. New York：Grove Press, Inc.

Watson, Burton. 1984. The Columbia Book of Chinese Poetry from Early Times to the Thirteenth Century. New York:Columbia University Press.

Wilson, Peter. 2005. 庞德导读. 北京:北京大学出版社.

Xie, Ming. 1999. Ezra Pound and The Appropriation of Chinese Poetry:Cathay, Translation, and Imagism. New York and London:Garland Publishing, Inc.

Xu, Yuanchong. 1994. An Unexpurgated Translation of Book of Songs. Beijing: Chinese Literature Press.

Yip, Wai-lim. 1969. Ezra Pound' s Cathay. Princeton: Princeton University Press.

Yip, Wai-lim. 1997. Chinese Poetry:An Anthology of Major Modes and Genres. Durham and London:Duke University Press.

Yip, Wai-lim. 2008. Pound and the Eight Views of Xiao Xiang. Taiwan: National Taiwan University Press.

阿尔瓦雷斯(Alvarez, R.), 比达尔(Vidal, M. C. A.), 2007. 翻译,权力,颠覆(Translation, Power, Subversion). 北京:外语教学与研究出版社.

安德曼(Anderman, G.), 罗杰斯(Rogers, M.), 2006. 今日翻译:趋向与视角(Translation Today:Trends and Perspectives). 北京:外语教学与研究出版社.

巴斯内特(Bassnett, S.), 2004. 翻译研究:(第三版)(Translation Studies). 上海:上海外语教育出版社.

巴斯内特(Bassnett, S.),勒菲弗尔(Lefevere,A.), 2001. 文化构建:文学翻译论文集(Constructing Cultures:Essays on Literary Translation). 上海:上海外语教育出版社.

鲍克(Bowker, L.), 2007. 多元下的统一? 当代翻译研究潮流(Unity in Diversity? Current Trends in Translation Studies). 北京:外语教学与研究出版社.

比奇(Christopher Beach). 2006. 20世纪美国诗歌. 重庆:重庆出版社.

卞建华, 2006. 对诺德"忠诚原则"的解读.《中国科技翻译》第3期.

卞建华, 2006. 关于翻译目的论相关问题的讨论——与克里斯蒂安·诺德教授的四次网上交流.《中国翻译》第1期.

卞建华, 2008. 传承与超越:功能主义翻译目的论研究. 北京:中国社会科学出版社.

卞建华, 崔永禄, 2006. 功能主义目的论在中国的引进、应用与研究(1987-2005).《解放军外国语学院学报》第5期.

陈刚, 胡维佳, 2004. 功能翻译理论适合文学翻译吗? ——兼析《红楼梦》咏蟹诗译文及其语言学派分析.《外语与外语教学》第2期.

陈建军, 2004. "目的论"的角度看《波布族——一个社会新阶层的崛起》之中文译本.《中国翻译》第5期.

陈水平, 何高大, 2009. 目的论与歌曲翻译之标准.《外语教学》第4期.

陈小慰，1995. 简评“译文功能理论”.《上海科技翻译》第 4 期.
陈小慰，1996. 试论“译文功能理论”在应用文类翻译中的指导作用.《上海科技翻译》第 3 期.
陈小慰，2000. 翻译功能理论的启示.《中国翻译》第 4 期.
崔永禄，2003. 翻译理论教学与研究中的开放态势.《中国翻译》第 3 期.
邓隽，2010. 从目的论管窥严复译《天演论》.《上海翻译》第 2 期.
段峰，2008. 文化视野下文学翻译主体性研究. 成都：四川大学出版社，
范详涛，2003. 翻译层次性目的的多维描写.《外语教学》第 2 期.
范详涛，刘全福，2002. 论翻译选择的目的性.《中国翻译》第 6 期.
范勇，2005. 目的论观照下的翻译失误——一些大学网站英文版例析.《解放军外国语学院学报》第 1 期.
顾正阳，2006. 古诗词曲英译美学研究. 上海：上海交通大学出版社.
郭建中，2002. 当代美国翻译理论. 武汉：湖北教育出版社.
何庆机，2007. 国内功能派翻译理论研究述评.《上海翻译》第 4 期.
赫曼斯(Hermans，T.)，2007. 跨文化侵越——翻译学研究模式(II)：历史与意识形态问题(Crosscultural Transgressions — Research Models in Translation Studies II: Historical and Ideological Issues). 北京：外语教学与研究出版社.
洪明，2006. 企业外宣广告翻译的目的论维度.《外语学刊》第 5 期.
侯向群，2003. 主干清晰　多元丰富——论翻译学的理论框架模式.《外语与外语教学》第 4 期.
黄德先，2004. 民航陆空通话英语的特点与翻译.《中国科技翻译》第 4 期.
黄鸣奋，1997. 英语世界中国古典文学之传播. 上海：学林出版社.
霍姆斯(Holmes，J. S.)，2007. 译稿杀青！文学翻译与翻译研究文集(Translated! Papers on Literary Translation and Translation Studies). 北京：外语教学与研究出版社.
贾文波，2004. 应用翻译功能论. 北京：中国对外翻译出版公司.
蒋洪新，2001. 英诗新方向——庞德·艾略特诗学理论与文化批评研究. 武汉：湖北教育出版社.
拉斯顿(Ruston，S.)，2009. 浪漫主义. 上海：上海外语教育出版社.
乐黛云，王向远，2006. 比较文学研究. 福州：福建人民出版社.
勒菲弗尔(Lefevere，A.)，2004. 翻译、改写以及对文学名声的制控(Translation, Rewriting and the Manipulation of Literary Fame). 上海：上海外语教育出版社.
勒菲弗尔(Lefevere，A.)，2004. 翻译、历史与文化论集(Translation/History/Culture: A Sourcebook). 上海：上海外语教育出版社.
勒菲弗尔(Lefevere，A.)，2006. 文学翻译：比较文学背景下的理论与实践(Translating Literature: Practice and Theory in a Comparative Literature

Context). 北京:外语教学与研究出版社.
黎志敏,2008. 诗学构建:形式与意象. 北京:人民出版社.
李红霞,2010. 目的论视域下的政论文英译策略研究——以2010《政府工作报告》为例.《外国语文》第5期.
李玉良,2007.《诗经》英译研究. 济南:齐鲁书社.
理雅各,1992.《汉英四书》. 长沙:湖南出版社.
理雅各,2011.《诗经》. 北京:外语教学与研究出版社.
廖晟,2006. 从目的论视角解析吉祥物"福娃"的英译.《上海翻译》第2期.
刘象愚,2002. 从现代主义到后现代主义. 北京:高等教育出版社.
刘晓梅,2007. 目的论与汉英广告翻译.《西安外国语大学学报》第2期.
刘心莲,2001. 理解抑或误解? ——美国诗人庞德与中国之关系的重新思考.《外国语文》第6期.
刘岩,1999. 中国文化对美国文学的影响. 石家庄:河北人民出版社.
鲁宾逊(Robinson, D.),2006. 译者登场(The Translator's Turn). 北京:外语教学与研究出版社.
鲁宾逊(Robinson, D.),2007. 什么是翻译? 离心式理论,评判式介入(What is Translation? Centrifugal Theories, Critical Interventions). 北京:外语教学与研究出版社.
陆国飞,2006. 旅游景点汉语介绍英译的功能观.《外语教学》第5期.
潞潞,2003. 准则与尺度:外国著名诗人文论. 北京:北京出版社.
罗斯(Rose, M. G.),2007. 翻译与文学批评:翻译作为分析手段(Translation and Literary Criticism: Translation as Analysis). 北京:外语教学与研究出版社.
吕叔湘,2002. 中诗英译比录. 北京:中华书局.
马红,林建强,2007. 功能翻译理论与其翻译原则和方法.《外语学刊》第5期.
梅晓娟,2008. 翻译目的与翻译策略的选择——论《况义》中的天主教化和中国化改写.《外语学刊》第2期.
纳代尔(Nadel, I. B.),2001. 埃兹拉·庞德(The Cambridge Companion to Ezra Pound). 上海:上海外语教育出版社.
纳代尔(Nadel, I. B.),2008. 埃兹拉·庞德(The Cambridge Introduction to Ezra Pound). 上海:上海外语教育出版社.
纽马克(Newmark, P.),2006. 论翻译(About Translation). 北京:外语教学与研究出版社.
诺德(Nord, C.),2001. 目的性行为:释功能翻译理论(Translating as a Purposeful Activity: Functionalist Approaches Explained). 上海:上海外语教育出版社.
潘洞庭,2010. 目的论对商务翻译的启示.《外语学刊》第5期.
潘平亮,2006. 翻译目的论及其文本意识的弱化倾向.《上海翻译》第1期.

彭长江，2000. 翻译标准多，何以断是非.《外国语》第 5 期.
平洪，2002. 文本功能与翻译策略.《中国翻译》第 5 期.
申奥译，1985. 美国现代六诗人选集. 长沙：湖南人民出版社，
孙昌坤，2008. 目的文本取向的翻译研究——G. Toury 与 H. Vermeer 的研究模式比较分析.《外语与外语教学》第 9 期.
索金梅，2003. 庞德《诗章》中的儒学. 天津：南开大学出版社.
陶乃侃，2006. 庞德与中国文化. 北京：首都师范大学出版社.
陶友兰，2006. 翻译目的论观照下的英汉汉英翻译教材建设.《外语界》第 5 期.
汪榕培，任秀桦，1995.《诗经》中英文版. 沈阳：辽宁教育出版社.
王惠，匡芳涛，2008. 目的论与商业效应的契合——英汉电影名翻译的"源流汇"观.《西安外国语大学学报》第 2 期.
王建斌，2010. 泰山北斗 一代通儒——缅怀德国功能派翻译理论创始人汉斯·费梅尔教授.《中国翻译》第 3 期.
王建国，2004. 功能翻译理论与我国的翻译教材建设.《语言与翻译》第 2 期.
王小凤，2004. 文化语境顺应与文学翻译批评.《外语与外语教学》第 8 期.
王振平，任东升，2006. 目的与方法——对《尤利西斯》两个中译本的再思考.《外语研究》第 1 期.
王佐良，1997. 英国诗史. 南京：译林出版社.
威利，1997. 论语：汉英对照. 北京：外语教学与研究出版社.
位方芳，2007. 借鉴与挪用：德国功能主义翻译理论在中国.《解放军外国语学院学报》第 2 期.
温儒敏，李细尧，1986. 寻求跨中西文化的共同文学规律——叶维廉比较文学论文选. 北京：北京大学出版社.
文军，高晓鹰，2003. 功能翻译理论在文学翻译批评中的应用.《外语与外语教学》第 11 期.
文军，高晓鹰，2003. 归化异化，各具一格——从功能翻译理论角度评价《飘》的两种译本.《中国翻译》第 5 期.
吴南松，2003. 功能翻译理论及其在文学翻译批评中的适用性.《解放军外国语学院学报》第 3 期.
吴其尧，2006. 庞德与中国文化——兼论外国文学在中国文化现代化中的作用. 上海：上海外语教育出版社.
吴自选，2005. 德国功能派翻译理论与 CNN 新闻短片英译.《中国科技翻译》第 1 期.
许渊冲，2006. 翻译的艺术. 北京：五洲传播出版社.
杨建华，2009. 西方译学理论辑要. 天津：天津大学出版社.
杨琪，包通法，2006. "以文谋钱"的翻译目的论——广告文体翻译的理论思辨与实践.《上海翻译》第 3 期.

杨晓荣，2001. 翻译批评标准的传统思路和现代视野.《中国翻译》第 6 期.

叶维廉，2002. 叶维廉文集第 1 卷. 合肥：安徽教育出版社.

叶维廉，2002. 叶维廉文集第 2 卷. 合肥：安徽教育出版社.

叶维廉，2002. 叶维廉文集第 3 卷. 合肥：安徽教育出版社.

叶维廉，2006. 中国诗学. 北京：人民文学出版社.

叶维廉，2008. 庞德与潇湘八景. 台北市：台大出版中心.

伊兹拉·庞德，1998. 比萨诗章. 桂林：漓江出版社.

张锦兰，2004. 目的论与翻译方法.《中国科技翻译》第 1 期.

张美芳，2005. 翻译研究的功能途径. 上海：上海外语教育出版社.

张美芳，2005. 功能加忠诚——介评克里丝汀·诺德的功能翻译理论.《外国语》第 1 期.

张南峰，1995. 走出死胡同，建立翻译学.《外国语》第 3 期.

张南峰，2004. 中西译学批评. 北京：清华大学出版社.

张曙光，2007. 从现代主义到后现代主义：二十世纪美国诗歌. 哈尔滨：黑龙江大学出版社.

张长明，仲伟合，2005. 论功能翻译理论在法律翻译中的适用性.《语言与翻译》第 3 期.

赵毅衡，2003. 诗神远游：中国如何改变了美国现代诗. 上海：上海译文出版社.

赵毅衡，2007. 对岸的诱惑：中西文化交流记. 上海：上海人民出版社.

钟玲，2003. 美国诗与中国梦：美国现代诗里的中国文化模式. 桂林：广西师范大学出版社.

朱光潜，2005. 无言之美. 北京：北京大学出版社.

朱志瑜，2004. 类型与策略：功能主义的翻译类型学.《中国翻译》第 3 期.

祝朝伟，2005. 构建与反思. 上海：上海译文出版社.

邹振环，1996. 影响中国近代社会的一百种译作. 北京：中国对外翻译出版公司.

Appendix Cathay

SONG OF THE BOWMEN OF SHU

Here we are, picking the first fern-shoots
And saying: When shall we get back to our country?
Here we are because we have the Ken-nin for our foemen,
We have no comfort because of these Mongols.
We grub the soft fern-shoots,
When anyone says "Return," the others are full of sorrow.
Sorrowful minds, sorrow is strong, we are hungry and thirsty.
Our defense is not yet made sure, no one can let his friend return.
We grub the old fern-stalks.
We say: Will we be let to go back in October?
There is no ease in royal affairs, we have no comfort.
Our sorrow is bitter, but we would not return to our country.
What flower has come into blossom?
Whose chariot? The General's.
Horses, his horses even, are tired. They were strong.
We have no rest, three battles a month.
By heaven, his horses are tired.
The generals are on them, the soldiers are by them.
The horses are well trained, the generals have ivory arrows and quivers ornamented with fish-skin.
The enemy is swift, we must be careful.
When we set out, the willows were drooping with spring,
We come back in the snow,
We go slowly, we are hungry and thirsty,
Our mind is full of sorrow, who will know of our grief?
By Bunno, Reputedly 1100 B. C

THE BEAUTIFUL TOILET

Blue, blue is the grass about the river
And the willows have overfilled the close garden.

And within, the mistress, in the midmost of her youth,
White, white of face, hesitates, passing the door.
Slender, she puts forth a slender hand.

And she was a courtezan in the old days,
And she has married a sot,
Who now goes drunkenly out
And leaves her too much alone.
By Mei Sheng B. C. 140

THE RIVER SONG

This boat is of shato-wood, and its gunwales are cut magnolia,
Musicians with jeweled flutes and with pipes of gold
Fill full the sides in rows, and our wine
Is rich for a thousand cups.
We carry singing girls, drift with the drifting water,
Yet Sennin needs
A yellow stork for a charger, and all our seamen
Would follow the white gulls or ride them.
Kutsu's prose song
Hangs with the sun and moon.

King So's terraced palace
is now but barren hill,
But I draw pen on this barge
Causing the five peaks to tremble,
And I have joy in these words like the joy of blue islands.
(If glory could last forever
Then the waters of Han would flow northward.)

And I have moped in the Emperor's garden, awaiting an order-to-write!
I looked at the dragon-pond, with its willow-colored water
Just reflecting in the sky's tinge,
And heard the five-score nightingales aimlessly singing.

The eastern wind brings the green color into the island grasses at Yei-shu,
The purple house and the crimson are full of Spring softness.

South of the pond the willow-tips are half-blue and bluer,
Their cords tangle in mist, against the brocade-like palace.
Vine strings a hundred feet long hang down from carved railings,
And high over the willows, the find birds sing to each other, and listen,
Crying —'Kwan, Kuan,' for the early wind, and the feel of it.
The wind bundles itself into a bluish cloud and wanders off.
Over a thousand gates. over a thousand doors are the sounds of spring singing,
And the Emperor is at Ko.
Five clouds hang aloft, bright on the purple sky,
The imperial guards come forth from the golden house with their armor a-gleaming.
The Emperor in his jeweled car goes out to inspect his flowers,
He goes out to Hori, to look at the wing-flapping storks,
He returns by way of Sei rock, to hear the new nightingales,
For the gardens at Jo-run are full of new nightingales,
Their sound is mixed in this flute,
Their voice is in the twelve pipes here
By Rihaku, 8th Century A. D.

THE RIVER MERCHANT'S WIFE: A LETTER

WHILE my hair was still cut straight across my forehead
Played I about the front gate, pulling flowers.
You came by on bamboo stilts, playing horse,
You walked about my seat, playing with blue plums.
And we went on living in the village of Chokan:
Two small people, without dislike or suspicion.

At fourteen I married My Lord you,
I never laughed, being bashful.
Lowering my head, I looked at the wall.
Called to, a thousand times, I never looked back.

At fifteen I stopped scowling,
I desired my dust to be mingled with yours
Forever and forever and forever.
Why should I climb the look out?

At sixteen you departed,
You went into fat Ku-to-yen, by the river of swirling eddies,
And you have been gone five months.
The monkeys make sorrowful noise overhead.
You dragged your feet when you went out.
By the gate now, the moss is grown, the different mosses,
Too deep to clear them away!
The leaves fall early in autumn, in wind.
The paired butterflies are already yellow with August
Over the grass in the West garden;
They hurt me. I grow older.
If you are coming down through the narrows of the river Kiang,
Please let me know beforehand,
And I will come out to meet you
    As far as Cho-fu-Sa.
By Rihaku

POEM BY THE BRIDGE AT TEN-SHIN

March has come to the bridge head,
Peach boughs and apricot boughs hang over a thousand gates,
At morning there are flowers to cut the heart,
And evening drives them on the eastward-flowing waters.
Petals are on the gone waters and on the going,
    And on the back-swirling eddies,
But to-day's men are not the men of the old days,
Though they hang in the same way over the bridge-rail.

The sea's color moves at the dawn
And the princes still stand in rows, about the throne,
And the moon falls over the portals of Sei-go-yo,
And clings to the walls and the gate-top.
With head gear glittering against the cloud and sun,
The lords go forth from the court, and into far borders.
They ride upon dragon-like horses,
Upon horses with head-trappings of yellow metal,
And the streets make way for their passage.
    Haughty their passing,

Haughty their steps as they go into great banquets,
To high halls and curious food,
To the perfumed air and girls dancing,
To clear flutes and clear singing;
To the dance of the seventy couples;
To the mad chase through the gardens.
Night and day are given over to pleasure
And they think it will last a thousand autumns.
    Unwearying autumns.
For them the yellow dogs howl portents in vain,
And what are they compared to the lady Riokushu,
    That was cause of hate!
Who among them is a man like Han-rei
    Who departed alone with his mistress,
With her hair unbound, and he his own skiffsman!
By Rihaku

THE JEWEL STAIRS' GRIEVANCE

The jeweled steps are already quite white with dew,
It is so late the dew soaks my gauze stockings,
And I let down the crystal curtain
And watch the moon through the clear autumn
By Rihaku

Note. — Jewel stairs, therefore a palace. Grievance, therefore there is something to complain of. Gauze stockings, therefore a court lady, not a servant who complains. Clear autumn, therefore he has no excuse on account of the weather. Also she has come early, for the dew has not merely whitened the stairs, but soaks her stockings. The poem is especially prized because she utters no direct reproach.

LAMENT OF THE FRONTIER GUARD

By the north gate, the wind blows full of sand,
Lonely from the beginning of time until now!
Trees fall, the grass goes yellow with autumn,
I climb the towers and towers
    to watch out the barbarous land:
Desolate castle, the sky, the wide desert.

There is no wall left to this village.
Bones white with a thousand frosts,
High heaps, covered with trees and grass;
Who brought this to pass?
Who has brought the flaming imperial anger?
Who has brought the army with drums and with kettle-drums?
Barbarous kings.
A gracious spring, turned to blood-ravenous autumn,
A turmoil of wars-men, spread over the middle kingdom,
Three hundred and sixty thousand,
And sorrow, sorrow like rain.
Sorrow to go, and sorrow, sorrow returning.
Desolate, desolate fields,
And no children of warfare upon them,
    No longer the men for offence and defense.
Ah, how shall you know the dreary sorrow at the North Gate,
With Rihoku's name forgotten
And we guardsmen fed to the tigers
By Rihaku

EXILE'S LETTER

To So-Kin of Rakuyo, ancient friend, Chancellor of Gen.
Now I remember that you built me a special tavern
By the south side of the bridge at Ten-Shin.
With yellow gold and white jewels we paid for the songs and laughter,
And we were drunk for month on month, forgetting the kings and princes.
Intelligent men came drifting in, from the sea and from the west border
And with them, and with you especially,
There was nothing at cross purpose,
And they made nothing of sea-crossing or of mountain-crossing,
If only they could be of that fellowship,
And we all spoke out our hearts and minds, and without regret.
And then I was sent off to South Wei,
    smothered in laurel groves,
And you to the north of Raku-hoku,
Till we had nothing but thoughts and memories in common.
And then, when separation had come to its worst

We met, and travelled into Sen-Go
Through all the thirty-six folds of the turning and twisting waters,
Into a valley of the thousand bright flowers,
That was the first valley;
And into ten thousand valleys full of voices and pine-winds.
And with silver harness and reins of gold,
prostrating themselves on the ground,
Out came the East of Kan foreman and his company.
And there came also the 'True-man' of Shi-yo to meet me,
Playing on a jeweled mouth-organ.
In the storied houses of San-Ko they gave us more Sennin music,
Many instruments, like the sound of young phoenix broods.
The foreman of Kan-Chu, drunk, danced
　　because his long sleeves wouldn't keep still
With that music playing.
And I, wrapped in brocade, went to sleep with my head on his lap,
And my spirit so high it was all over the heavens.
And before the end of the day we were scattered like stars or rain.
I had to be off to So, far away over the waters,
You back to your river-bridge.

And your father, who was brave as a leopard,
Was governor in Hei-Shu and put down the barbarian rabble.
And one May he had you send for me,
　　despite the long distance;
And what with broken wheels and so on, I won't say it wasn't hard going,
Over roads twisted like sheep's guts.
And I was still going, late in the year,
　　in the cutting wind from the North,
And thinking how little you cared for the cost,
　　and you caring enough to pay it.
Then what a reception:
Red jade cups, food well set on a blue jeweled table,
And I was drunk, and had no thought of returning.
And you would walk out with me to the western corner of the castle,
To the dynastic temple, with water about it clear as blue jade,
With boats floating, and the sound of mouth-organs and drums,

With ripples like dragon-scales, going grass green on the water,
Pleasure lasting, with courtesans going and coming without hindrance,
With the willow flakes falling like snow,
And the vermilioned girls getting drunk about sunset,
And the waters a hundred feet deep reflecting green eyebrows
— Eyebrows painted green are a fine sight in young moonlight,
Gracefully painted —
And the girls singing back at each other,
Dancing in transparent brocade,
And the wind lifting the song, and interrupting it,
Tossing it up under the clouds.
    And all this comes to an end.
    And is not again to be met with.
I went up to the court for examination,
Tried Layu's luck, offered the Choyo song,
And got no promotion,
    and went back to the East Mountains
    White-headed.
And once again, later, we met at the South bridgehead.
And then the crowd broke up, you went north to San palace,
And if you ask how I regret that parting:
It is like the flowers falling at Spring's end,
    Confused, whirled in a tangle.
What is the use of talking, and there is no end of talking,
There is no end of things in the heart.
I call in the boy,
Have him sit on his knees here
    To seal this,
And I send it a thousand miles, thinking.
By Rihaku

FOUR POEMS OF DEPARTURE

Light rain is on the light dust
The willows of the inn-yard
Will be going greener and greener,
But you, Sir, had better take wine ere
    your departure,

For you will have no friends about
　　you
When you come to the gates of Go.
(Rihaku or Omakittsu)

SEPARATION ON THE RIVER KIANG

Ko-jin goes west from Ko-kaku-ro,
The smoke flowers are blurred over the river.
His lone sail blots the far sky.
And now I see only the river,
　　The long Kiang, reaching heaven.
　　Rihaku

TAKING LEAVE OF A FRIEND

Blue mountains to the north of the walls,
White river winding about them;
Here we must make separation
And go out through a thousand miles of dead grass.

Mind like a floating white cloud,
Sunset like the parting of old aquaintances
Who bow over their clasped hands at a distance.
Our horses neigh to each other
　　as we are departing
Rihaku

LEAVING -TAKING NEAR SHOKU

They say the roads of Sanso are steep,
Sheer as the mountains.
The walls rise in a man's face,
Clouds grow out of the hill
　　at his horse's bridle.
Sweet trees are on the paved way of the Shin,
Their trunks burst through the paving,
And freshets are bursting their ice
　　in the midst of Shoku, a proud city.

Men's fates are already set,
There is no need of asking diviners
Rihaku

THE CITY OF CHOAN

The phoenix are at play on their terrace.
The phoenix are gone, the river flows on alone.
Flowers and grass
Cover over the dark path
    where lay the dynastic house of the Go.
The bright cloths and bright caps of Shin
Are now the base of old hills.

The Three Mountains fall through the far heaven,
The isle of White Heron
    splits the two streams apart.
Now the high clouds cover the sun
And I can not see Choan afar
And I am sad.
Rihaku

SOUTH-FOLK IN COLD COUNTRY

The Dai horse neighs against the bleak wind of Etsu,.
The birds of Etsu have no love for En, in the north,
Emotion is born out of habit,
Yesterday we went out of the Wild-Goose gate,
Today from the Dragon-Pen.
Surprised. Desert turmoil. Sea sun.
Flying snow bewilders the barbarian heaven.

Lice swarm like ants over our accoutrements.
Mind and spirit drive on the feathery banners.
Hard fight gets no reward.
Loyalty is hard to explain.
Who will be sorry for General Rishogu,
    the swift moving,
Whose white head is lost for this province?

SENNIN POEM BY KAKUHAKU

The red and green kingfishers
　　flash between the orchids and clover,
One bird casts its gleam on another.

Green vines hang through the high forest,
They weave a whole roof to the mountain,
The lone man sits with shut speech,
He purrs and pats the clear strings.
He throws his heart up through the sky,
He bights through the flower pistil
　　and brings up a fine fountain.
The red-pine-tree god looks at him and wonders.
He rides through the purple smoke to visit the sennin,
He takes 'Floating Hill'* by the sleeve,
He claps his hand on the back of the great white sennin.

But you, you dam'd crowd of gnats,
Can you even tell the age of a turtle?

* Name of sennin (spirit.)

A BALLAD OF THE MULBERRY ROAD

The sun rises in south east cirner of things
To look on the tall house of the Shin
For they have a daughter names Rafu,
(pretty girl)
She made the name for herself: 'Gauze Veil,'
For she feeds mulberries to silkworms.
She gets them by the south wall of the town.
With green strings she makes the warp of her basket
She makes the shoulder-straps of her basket
　　from the boughs of Ketsura,
And she piles her hair up on the left side of her head-piece.

Her earring are made of pearl,

Her underskirt is of green pattern-silk,
Her overskirt is the same silk dyed in purple,
And when men going by look at Rafu
　　They set down their burdens,
They stand and twirl their moustaches.
(Fenolloso Mss. , very early)

OLD IDEA OF CHOAN BY ROSORIU

I

The narrow streets cut into the wide highway at Choan,
Dark oxen, white horses,
　　drag on the seven coaches with outriders
The coaches are perfumed wood,
The jeweled chair is held up at the crossway,
Before the royal lodge:
A glitter of golden saddles, awaiting the princes;
They eddy before the gate of the barons.
The canopy embroidered with dragons
　　drinks in and casts back the sun.
Evening comes.
　　The trappings are bordered with mist.
The hundred cords of mist are spread through
　　and double the trees,
Night birds, and night women,
Spread out their sounds through the gardens.

II

Birds with flowery wing, hovering butterflies
　　crowd over the thousand gates,
Trees that glitter like jade,
　　terraces tinged with silver,
The seed of a myriad hues,
A net-work of arbors and passages and covered ways,
Double towers, winged roofs,
　　border the network of ways:
A place of felicitous meeting.
Riu's house stands out on the sky,
　　with glitter of color

As Butei of Kan made the high golden lotus
　　to gather his dews,
Before it another house which I do not know:
How shall we know all the friends
　　whom we meet on strange roadways?

TO-EM-MEI'S "THE UNMOVING CLOUD"

' Wet springtime. ' says To-em-mei,
　　' Wet spring in the garden. '

I

The clouds have gathered, and gathered,
　　and the rain falls and falls,
The eight ply of the heavens
　　are all folded into one darkness,
And the wide, flat road stretches out.
I stop in my room towards the East, quiet, quiet,
I pat my new cask of wine.
My friends are estranged, or far distant,
I bow my head and stand still.

II

Rain, rain, and the clouds have gathered,
The eight ply of the heavens are darkness,
The flat land is turned into river.
　　'Wine, wine. here is wine!'
I drink by my eastern window
I think of talking and man,
And no boat, no carriage, approaches.

III

The trees in my east-looking garden
　　are bursting out with new twigs,
They try to stir new affection
And men say the sun and moon keep on movin
　　because they can't find a soft seat.
The birds flutter to rest in my tree,
　　and I think I have heard them saying,
'It is not that there are no other men
But we like this fellow the best,

But however we long to speak
He cannot know of our sorrow.'
T'ao Yuan Ming, A.D. 365-427

THE SEAFARER

From the Anglo-Saxon

May I for my own self song's truth reckon,
Journey's jargon, how I in harsh days
Hardship endured oft.
Bitter breast-cares have I abided,
Known on my keel many a care's hold,
And dire sea-surge, and there I oft spent
Narrow nightwatch nigh the ship's head
While she tossed close to cliffs. Coldly afflicted,
My feet were by frost benumbed.
Chill its chains are; chafing sighs
Hew my heart round and hunger begot
Mere-weary mood. Lest man know not
That he on dry land loveliest liveth,
List how I, care-wretched, on ice-cold sea,
Weathered the winter, wretched outcast
Deprived of my kinsmen;
Hung with hard ice-flakes, where hail-scur flew,
There I heard naught save the harsh sea
And ice-cold wave, at whiles the swan cries,
Did for my games the gannet's clamour,
Sea-fowls, loudness was for me laughter,
The mews' singing all my mead-drink.
Storms, on the stone-cliffs beaten, fell on the stern
In icy feathers; full oft the eagle screamed
With spray on his pinion.
Not any protector
May make merry man faring needy.
This he little believes, who aye in winsome life
Abides 'mid burghers some heavy business,
Wealthy and wine-flushed, how I weary oft

Must bide above brine.
Neareth nightshade, snoweth from north,
Frost froze the land, hail fell on earth then
Corn of the coldest. Nathless there knocketh now
The heart's thought that I on high streams
The salt-wavy tumult traverse alone.
Moaneth alway my mind's lust
That I fare forth, that I afar hence
Seek out a foreign fastness.
For this there's no mood-lofty man over earth's midst,
Not though he be given his good, but will have in his youth greed;
Nor his deed to the daring, nor his king to the faithful
But shall have his sorrow for sea-fare
Whatever his lord will.
He hath not heart for harping, nor in ring-having
Nor winsomeness to wife, nor world's delight
Nor any whit else save the wave's slash,
Yet longing comes upon him to fare forth on the water.
Bosque taketh blossom, cometh beauty of berries,
Fields to fairness, land fares brisker,
All this admonisheth man eager of mood,
The heart turns to travel so that he then thinks
On flood-ways to be far departing.
Cuckoo calleth with gloomy crying,
He singeth summerward, bodeth sorrow,
The bitter heart's blood. Burgher knows not —
He the prosperous man — what some perform
Where wandering them widest draweth.
So that but now my heart burst from my breast-lock,
My mood 'mid the mere-flood,
Over the whale's acre, would wander wide.
On earth's shelter cometh oft to me,
Eager and ready, the crying lone-flyer,
Whets for the whale-path the heart irresistibly,
O'er tracks of ocean; seeing that anyhow
My lord deems to me this dead life
On loan and on land, I believe not

That any earth-weal eternal standeth
Save there be somewhat calamitous
That, ere a man's tide go, turn it to twain.
Disease or oldness or sword-hate
Beats out the breath from doom-gripped body.
And for this, every earl whatever, for those speaking after —
Laud of the living, boasteth some last word,
That he will work ere he pass onward,
Frame on the fair earth 'gainst foes his malice,
Daring ado...
So that all men shall honour him after
And his laud beyond them remain 'mid the English,
Aye, for ever, a lasting life's-blast,
Delight mid the doughty.
Days little durable,
And all arrogance of earthen riches,
There come now no kings nor Caesars
Nor gold-giving lords like those gone.
Howe'er in mirth most magnified,
Whoe'er lived in life most lordliest,
Drear all this excellence, delights undurable!
Waneth the watch, but the world holdeth.
Tomb hideth trouble. The blade is layed low.
Earthly glory ageth and seareth.
No man at all going the earth's gait,
But age fares against him, his face paleth,
Grey-haired he groaneth, knows gone companions,
Lordly men are to earth o'ergiven,
Nor may he then the flesh-cover, whose life ceaseth,
Nor eat the sweet nor feel the sorry,
Nor stir hand nor think in mid heart,
And though he strew the grave with gold,
His born brothers, their buried bodies
Be an unlikely treasure hoard.
"Seafarer" appeared in
Ripostes (1912) and then
again in Cathay (1915)

The Alchemist
Chant for the Transmutation of Metals
SA? L of Claustra, Aelis, Azalais,
As you move among the bright trees;
As your voices, under the larches of Paradise
Make a clear sound,
Sa? l of Claustra, Aelis, Azalais,
Raimona, Tibors, Berangèr?,
'Neath the dark gleam of the sky;
Under night, the peacock-throated,
Bring the saffron-coloured shell,
Bring the red gold of the maple,
Bring the light of the birch tree in autumn
Mirals, Cembelins, Audiarda,
　　　　　　Remember this fire.
Elain, Tireis, Alcmena
'Mid the silver rustling of wheat,
Agradiva, Anhes, Ardenca,
From the plum-coloured lake, in stillness,
From the molten dyes of the water
Bring the burnished nature of fire;
Briseis, Lianor, Loica,
From the wide earth and the olive,
From the poplars weeping their amber,
By the bright flame of the fishing torch
　　　　　　Remember this fire.
Midonz, with the gold of the sun, the leaf of the poplar,
by the light of the amber,
Midonz, daughter of the sun, shaft of the tree,
silver of the leaf, light of the yellow of the amber,
Midonz, gift of the God, gift of the light,
gift of the amber of the sun,
　　　　　　Give light to the metal.
Anhes of Rocacoart, Ardenca, Aemelis,
From the power of grass,
From the white, alive in the seed,

From the heat of the bud,
From the copper of the leaf in autumn,
From the bronze of the maple, from the sap in the bough;
Lianor, Ioanna, Loica,
By the stir of the fin,
By the trout asleep in the grey green of water;
Vanna, Mandetta, Viera, Alodetta, Picarda, Manuela
From the red gleam of copper,
Ysaut, Ydone, slight rustling of leaves,
Vierna, Jocelynn, daring of spirits,
By the mirror of burnished copper,
O Queen of Cypress,
Out of Erebus, the flat-lying breadth,
Breath that is stretched out beneath the world:
Out of Erebus, out of the flat waste of air, lying beneath the world;
Out of the brown leaf-brown colourless
Bring the imperceptible cool.
Elain, Tireis, Alcmena,
Quiet this metal!
Let the manes put off their terror, let them put off their aqueous bodies with fire.
Let them assume the milk-white bodies of agate.
Let them draw together the bones of the metal.

Selvaggia, Guiscarda, Mandetta,
Rain flakes of gold on the water,
Azure and flaking silver of water,
Alcyon, Phaetona, Alcmena,
Pallor of silver, pale lustre of Latona,
By these, from the malevolence of the dew
Guard this alembic.
Elain, Tireis, Alodetta
Quiet this metal